Methods
for Political Inquiry

Methods for Political Inquiry

The Discipline, Philosophy, and Analysis of Politics

Edited by

Stella Z. Theodoulou

Rory O'Brien

California State University, Northridge

Prentice Hall
Upper Saddle River, New Jersey 07458

Library of Congress Cataloging-in-Publication Data

Methods for political inquiry : the discipline, philosophy, and
  analysis of politics / [edited by] Stella Z. Theodoulou, Rory
  O'Brien
     p.   cm.
  Includes bibliographical references.
  ISBN 0-13-675562-3 (paper)
  1. Political science. 2. Political science—Methodology.
I. Theodoulou, Stella Z. II. O'Brien, Rory.
JA66.U54 1999
320'.01—dc21
                                        98-3319
                                          CIP

Editorial director: Charlyce Jones Owen
Editor in chief: Nancy Roberts
Acquisitions editor: Beth Gillett
Editorial/production supervision
  and interior design: Mary Araneo
Buyer: Bob Anderson
Art director: Jayne Conte
Cover designer: Bruce Kenselaar
Marketing Manager: Christopher DeJohn

This book was set in 10/12 Palatino by A & A Publishing Services,
Inc., and was printed and bound by Courier Companies, Inc.
The cover was printed by Phoenix Color Corp.

 © 1999 by Prentice-Hall, Inc.
Simon & Schuster/A Viacom Company
Upper Saddle River, New Jersey 07458

Printed in the United States of America

10 9 8 7 6 5 4 3 2 1

ISBN 0-13-675562-3

Prentice-Hall International (UK) Limited, *London*
Prentice-Hall of Australia Pty. Limited, *Sydney*
Prentice-Hall Canada Inc., *Toronto*
Prentice-Hall Hispanoamericana, S.A., *Mexico*
Prentice-Hall of India Private Limited, *New Delhi*
Prentice-Hall of Japan, Inc., *Tokyo*
Simon & Schuster Asia Pte. Ltd., *Singapore*
Editora Prentice-Hall do Brasil, Ltda., *Rio de Janeiro*

To those who make us whole
for
Marti, Alexandra, and Andrea

Contents

Part Two
The Philosophical Debate: Theories and Paradigms

Part Three
The Analysis of Politics

Preface

Everyone has heard the phrase *user friendly* as it is employed to sell hardware and software. And yet, in the computer age, it is still a term that cannot be applied to the vast majority of texts that deal with political science research methodology or inquiry. Many political science students feel lost or bored by the sorts of things instructors assign as reading in their research methods courses. The significance of this, for both the students and the instructor, is that students fail to truly comprehend how and why we study politics in the ways that we do. With the increase in the desire for quantification and the use of sophisticated computer software, many political science students learn research methodology in a vacuum. Thus, many students do not see how our discipline has evolved to its present state, ignoring the philosophy behind political inquiry.

Instructors often try to rectify this situation by discussing the development of the scientific approach but without truly acknowledging the evolution of the discipline. As a result, students do not truly understand methodology because they are not taught that the quantitative study of politics is only a means to an end, not the end itself. To get a correct understanding of political science research methodology, students should (1) learn about the evolution of political science as a discipline, (2) understand the philosophy behind the analysis of politics, and (3) master the methods for studying political phenomena. Only when this is achieved can the student comprehend and analyze much of what is written in the field of political science. The purpose of this text is to provide students with such an overview of the discipline.

Methods for Political Inquiry emerges from courses that we have developed and taught over the years and from our many discussions with colleagues and students about the problems of teaching research methodology.

Based on our experiences, we have chosen to include a variety of perspectives that all communicate the common theme that research methodology is challenging and exciting. These readings help explain to students what political science research is— how you do it, when to do it, and what pitfalls might lie ahead.

The text provides the tools necessary for the student to conduct research properly in the field of political science. *Methods for Political Inquiry* is designed to help students develop a working knowledge of how we have come to think about politics and the research skills that are necessary to handle the information that we collect about political phenomena. *Methods for Political Inquiry* will provide students with a systematic approach to the discipline and to the principles around which political inquiry should be organized. Thus, students will be exposed to materials on the fundamental assumptions of political inquiry in addition to the specific devices necessary for gathering and collecting data about political phenomena.

Within the selected readings, we (1) explore what political scientists do today as opposed to what they did in the past, (2) identify what the current concerns and issues are, (3) provide a methodological foundation for reading, understanding, and criticizing the existing literature, and, finally, (4) discuss the qualitative and quantitative techniques available to researchers.

We want readers of this book to take away an understanding of two basic concepts. The first is the idea that political science has evolved as a discipline. Although the questions that interest political scientists remain essentially the same over time, the way in which we attempt to answer those questions has changed. The second is that quantitative techniques contribute to a clearer understanding of political and policy problems.

In sum, we have designed *Methods for Political Inquiry* to not only fill a gap in the marketplace, but also to advance the ways in which we analyze politics. By making the process of research more "user friendly," we seek to encourage greater application of the methods available to future practitioners of our craft. *Methods for Political Inquiry* will contribute to the discipline by providing a balanced overview of both theory and applications of critical ideas in political science. By presenting the diversity of ideas that makes political science what it has evolved into over time, we hope to engage both instructors and students in the discourse on political inquiry.

ACKNOWLEDGMENTS

As authors we wish to acknowledge those individuals who have helped to make this endeavor a reality. First, to our editors and representatives at Prentice Hall, many thanks for your continued support. Thanks also to the following reviewers for their comments: JoAnne Myers of Marist College, Pamela

1

Where We Stand Today: The State of Modern Political Science

Stella Z. Theodoulou and Rory O'Brien

In this chapter, we will look at how political science developed as a discipline. Most people use the word *politics* without fully defining what it is they are interested in. However, it is easy to know when you are involved in a political discussion. In this sense, there seems to be a shared definition we all seem to work with in society to understand one another when we are talking about politics. The study of political phenomenon by applying scientific techniques involves multiple steps, including theory development, hypothesis building and testing, the drawing of conclusions that are based on the strengths or weaknesses of those hypotheses, and, ultimately, the proving of the theories themselves. In this way, political science operates in a circle, with empirical research being fueled by theory development, and theory, in turn, being the outcome of research findings.

We begin with an assessment of where our discipline is today and where it has come from. Political science, especially in terms of research methodology, has come into its own during the latter half of the twentieth century. As we step into the next millennium, we need to create a map for practitioners of our trade to follow. Before we can do that, we must first establish the groundwork in which the discipline finds its genesis.

TRACING THE DEVELOPMENT OF THE DISCIPLINE

Since the beginning of time, people have observed, thought about, evaluated, and analyzed politics. Thus, the study of politics is not a new phenomenon, and the broad questions and interests of political scientists remain in many ways the same over time. However, what has changed is the way in which political scientists have tried to find the answers to the questions. There is a growing

1

body of literature that identifies and disusses the evolution of the discipline.[1] Within such a discussion, it is clear to see that political scientists over time have taken different paths in their study of politics. Authors might disagree on whether to label these paths eras, approaches, orientations, models, or methods, but at least there is general consensus that at different times different directions have been taken and are still being taken by political scientists in their quest for political knowledge.

In the following discussion, we will identify four general paths that political scientists have taken over the years. Some may be surprised at the ommission of what they consider to be other paths, such as feminism, discourse analysis, rational choice theory, and Marxism. However, it is our opinion that all of these are approaches that fall within our four general paths rather than being distinctive paths themselves.

Many would argue that we can trace the development of the discipline directly to the social disorder of the Athenian city-state and the response to it by Socrates, Plato, and Aristotle. These first political philosophers and those that follow them take a theoretical path in their study of politics.

THE THEORECTICAL PATH (FROM 600 B.C.)

Perhaps the most audacious statement we can make from an epistemological point of view is embodied in our fundamental assumption that it is even possible for us to possess knowledge about human social interaction. Observation might easily lead us to conclude that human behavior is too erratic to ever be understood fully, and, if understood, is difficult to predict. And yet, these are the foundational aspects of how we go about studying society. Since the early nineteenth century, our study of society has been based on the positivism of Compte. This french *philosophe* advanced the theory that the social order could be studied in a logical fashion. In contrast to the metaphysical reasoning of the Age of Enlightenment preceding him, and in a continued reaction to the earlier Christian era in Europe, Compte sought to ground a view of society in the sober logic of empirical investigation and analysis.

Thus, in the modern age, many have fallen victim to merely focusing on the empirical, and in the process an important aspect of what gives motivation to the research process itself has been missed. Research gives expression to theories, or ideas. Without those ideas, the research project would be meaningless. If we think of political ideas as a series of questions that are posed to humankind across a tradition, and political phenomena as the tangible (and testable) manifestations of possible answers to those questions, we see the relationship between theory and scientific research more clearly. Throughout our history, each age has presented us with both questions and answers. What we think of as *political theory* is a coherent body of work that has, in some sense, transcended time to provide us with enduring questions that continue to help us to evaluate current circumstances, as well as create solutions as we look towards the future.

Theory provides the context for the study of political science through the development of models and through the development of normative conclusions or prescriptions. Whereas empirical research yields empirical conclusions, normative pursuits involve questions about "what ought to be" or what "should be." Normative prescriptions are, thus, suggestions or recommendations concerning how society might best be configured.

Normative theory leads to empirical research in two ways. First, normative questions can drive empirical projects. In order to conduct research of any kind one must begin with a question, the answer to which may be elusive. The research questions that lead to fruitful hypotheses are grounded in a theoretical foundation. Moving in this way, from theory to practice, scientific research gives practical application to the solely theoretical.

Second, theory can, and regularly does, arise from the practice of normal scientific enquiry. As social scientists realize how and in what ways their theoretical foundations differ from reality they are able to adjust their theories so as to better describe and predict the political world. Very few political theorists think like Plato did that the abstract forms of physical things are distinct from those things themselves. Instead, political theorists are involved in a journey of discovery that allows them to constantly update and refine theoretical perspectives so as to more effectively represent testable circumstances. Ultimately, these adjustments to theory lead to further scientific investigation, beginning the process anew.

Finally, political theory creates models that political scientists can utilize to gain a broader understanding of their concepts and hypotheses. Models are artificial structures constructed by political scientists. They are human artifacts, made with the express purpose of developing ways in which students of society can more easily view the political order. Models are merely ways for us to get our minds around a concept as big as society itself. In essence, models provide the testing ground for hypotheses. But in a deeper context, the logical tests performed by our own intellects provide the most fertile ground for the creation of new political ideas and insights.

What Are We Looking For?

For the purpose of better understanding society in general and the political order in particular, political theorists have traditionally looked at various fundamental aspects of both social ideas and social organizations. Among these are our notions of what human nature is, what constitutes the "good life," and what terms such as *justice* and *equality* really mean to us. Additionally, the way we conceptualize freedom, democracy, power, and social cohesion all say something about our views of politics. Human society is dynamic and rarely, if ever, static. As the social and political order of societies' change it is crucial to have some enduring ideas about how to assess that change. This is precisely what political theory provides in the form of a conceptual framework. Political philosophy is about developing ways and means for not only thinking about such things, but for using our ideas constructively to better understand society.

Human Nature

We'll begin by considering our motivations and activities in society based on who we are. This is what philosophers refer to as *human nature*. We often take for granted the composition of psychological elements that we refer to as our nature. Generally, we do not have to think about such things. But at the heart of any political theory is a conception of human nature. This is because society, which is made up of many individuals, is but a reflection of our nature, or our essential characteristics, on a large scale. When we view society as the reflection of many individuals, we can ask questions such as "Why are certain policies popular, or unpopular?" and "Why do some forms of government work better than others?"

Some political theorists take a dim view of human nature, pronouncing us to be wild beasts if not constrained by the forces of a strong and powerful government.[2] Other theorists speak to the human spirit, and seek ways to aid in its liberation and fulfillment.[3] Some thinkers find us to be hard-working and generous, while others see us as lazy and mean-spirited. But in every case, political theorists utilize their view of human nature to help them in the construction of their model of the social order.

The Good and the Just

In everyday language we talk about what is right and wrong, just or unjust, without taking the time to really formulate a position on these matters. In posing questions about what is *good* and what is *just*, the theorist develops ideas that help us to consider social successes (as well as failures) in order to further our general knowledge about the social world. At the same time we create categories through which we interpret our world.

When we talk about *the good* we are referring to our highest ideals. The best, finest, mostly highly valued are all captured by our notion of the good. When political theorists refer to the good they do not mean merely what we as individuals think is good. This *good* is not simply the opposite of *bad*. Humans often find that which is expedient to be the good. In other words, we may casually think of what we like as being good, or what is easiest as being the best. In many instances, modern society emphasizes that which is expedient over that which we know is truly good. Through the process of focusing on what is expedient we lose sight of any deeper value that the good may represent.

Methods
for Political Inquiry

Rodgers of the University of Wisconsin at La Crosse, and William Kelly of Auburn University. Thanks to Marcy Pearlman, wherever you are! To our research assistant, Shelia Onnen, our gratitude for your tireless efforts. And, finally, to our respective families, thank you for your patience, love, and humor.

Stella Z. Theodoulou
Rory O'Brien
Northridge, California

The notion of "the good life" makes reference to how each member of society might live so as to work toward developing his or her individual potential, and help to create a stronger community. The good life leads to happiness, in that excellence is its own reward.[4] When philosophers talk about happiness, they mean something that goes beyond material possessions.

By the same measure, *justice,* as well as our notions of the just, have at their roots the way we conceive of community. Every aspect of how a society is oriented tells us about that society's notions of justice. From distribution of wealth to welfare policy, from tax codes to educational requirements, all of these things refer us back to a concept of justice. And, if the members of society believe that in order to live together there must be a commonly agreed upon set of ideas about what is right and wrong (as every society does), the rules that are created on the basis of that contract will dictate the outlines of a theory of justice.[5]

Everything Put Together, Sooner or Later, Falls Apart

Politics is sometimes defined simply as power, and the ways in which power is distributed in society. All of the important structures and benefits of a society are arranged on the basis of the distribution of power. In most cases, the extent to which justice is dispersed in society also has to do with the distribution of power. And the actual foundations of justice are often created as a form of compromise between competing interests. In fact, virtually all aspects of the political realm are influenced by how we construe power. But regardless of the ways in which power has been configured in various societies, across many cultures and throughout time (what we refer to as *transculturally* and *transhistorically)* power alone has never held a social group together. This leads us to ask, "Why do humans stay together in social groups?" And, it further begs the question, "Why do those groups sometimes disintegrate?" We'll take this up when we discuss *social contract* and *alienation.*

Social Contract

A *contractarian* view of society is based on the notion that in order to stay together, a group of people must have some common purposes.[6] Furthermore, the political order must be based on ideas that are agreeable to a sizable portion of the population. Contractarian perspective says that these political ideas form a *contract,* or agreement, between the people and the government. Here we are using the idea of a social contract to help us understand a larger concept, social cohesion. For instance, Aristotle thinks that part of what keeps human societies together is the fact that we are "social animals" in the sense that we only function well in the social milieu. Without others to live with in society, Aristotle notes, we would never be able to do our "civic duty," which, in part, involves our virtuously following common moral and ethical rules.

In his view, the pleasure derived from the experience of excellence as a social being far outstrips that enjoyed as a consequence of one of our generally hedonistic pursuits. Furthermore, according to Aristotle, we are in essence social animals. Much of Aristotle's view of the world is based on the notion that everything is made up of essential qualities that make particular things what they are.[7] Said differently, we can only reach our own individual potential if we exist in a social world.

Taking another political thinker, John Locke, we get a further elaboration of how a society is held together. In Locke's view, the power of government is controlled only through a formal procedural development like a constitution. In fact, we can view a constitution as the physical manifestation of a social contract. Although the contract itself goes far beyond the structure of any document, the reality is that the constitution (and the laws that are generated from it) are the embodiment of the broader contract. The point here is that citizens, in a sense, own the document itself. That they not only agree to its tenets, but, on a deeper level, are the source of the contents of the constitution. In this way, a temporal, material document has the ability to truly represent the wishes and finer aspirations of a social group.

People form together in social groups primarily because the alternative is relatively distasteful. In the main, human beings have found it far easier to agree to some set of rules, or compact, than they have found it to live together each with his or her own total license. Locke articulated this clearly, fully realizing that the better instincts in humankind would almost always prove to be subordinate to our baser motives. However, the point for those of us who are students of politics is that there appears to be a human striving for the safety and security of an organized social order. This observation alone may give us hope to move forward into the future armed with the sense that regardless of the countless examples of ruined societies, we may, in time, find ways to live with one another while reducing friction.

At the same time, Locke's entire project is held together on the basis of another tenet. According to Locke, the *legitimacy* of government rests in the consent of those who are governed. Said differently, the true power of government ought to lie in the fact that the people of a nation accept, or consent to that government, not merely in the government's ability to coerce the citizenry. A liberal government, founded on the consent of those governed, allows for the development of some of our most cherished political ideas. Equality, freedom, and democracy are nurtured in the Lockean-liberal schema, and representation in government is a natural outcome of legitimacy based on consent.

Alienation

Why don't societies stay together? A quick review of human history shows us that, in general, we seem to like changing social orders on a regular basis. There have been few governments throughout time that have been able to hold societies together for more than a few generations. Often governments are overthrown through revolutions. The revolutionary change of existing social orders has been a common thread around the world during the past three hundred years, and yet we have not learned much that helps us predict exactly where or when a revolution might next take place. Although we understand the larger social forces that *may* lead down the revolutionary road, when a revolution *will* take place is most often a function how long the human spirit will endure before demanding liberating change.[8] In some societies (such as Europe during the Middle Ages), it has taken centuries to bring about change. In other situations (China during this century), change has come about quite rapidly.

We may be able to better understand more readily yet a different aspect of social cohesion, or the lack thereof. Social scientists use the term *alienation* to refer to a sense of being disconnected or separated from other people, things, experiences, and even ourselves. For instance, in the Marxist model of society, alienation is utilized to help explain why people feel a lack of connection with the work they are doing. In essence, when we are alienated from our work we are alienated from our own lives. If the level of this alienation is high enough, or if it goes on for too long a period of time, Marxist theory suggests that the social order may break down, leading to revolution.[9]

Although Marx's concern with alienation is focused in the economic sphere, this concept is also helpful in describing other ways in which people become disengaged from society. When a government is repressive, its citizens become alienated from the political order itself. The most effective way to overcome this disconnectedness between the people and the distribution of power in a society is through radical change. Whether one advocates Lockean liberalism or Marxist economics makes little difference. The reality is that the lack of efficacy (or feeling of possessing political power), that groups of citizens, or entire populations often experience leads to a form of alienation which is remedied through the overthrow of an existent government.

In summary, political theory functions to provide a groundwork, or foundation for our continued research and observation of social phenomena. By probing some of our deeper questions about society and our own nature, theory gives us the ability to logically arrange our knowledge about the political order. By gaining a greater understanding of both those things that we can empirically measure and those that we only draw normative conclusions about, we learn about all aspects of the social world.

THE TRADITIONALIST PATH (FROM THE 1850s)

This is essentially a collection of different emphasises brought together under the generic heading of *traditionalism*. However, within the tradition we can identify three dominant thrusts. The first is the *historical* thrust, which argues that the primary method of understanding politics is to draw lessons from history and apply them to politics. Much of the work undertaken in this area results in what we call *case studies*. Extensive use of generalizations are made in this type of research as the case study is used to test the assumptions of the researcher. The main problem with such research is that it is hard to apply findings beyond the case under study.

The second major thrust within traditionalism is the *legalistic* perspective, which views political science as mainly the study of laws, structures, institutions, and constitutions founded upon law. The last major thrust is the *institutional* view, which came about as a reaction to the historical and legalistic directions that the study of politics was undertaking. The emphasis is on the description of political institutions and structures. Thus, institutionalists would argue that political institutions should be researchers' primary focus, and that when we discuss them we should do so by looking at their powers, roles, and functions. The vast majority of introductory American government textbooks are written from this perspective. The weakness with the institutional emphasis is it goes little beyond description and thus there is little explanation as to the why or how of events or trends.

THE BEHAVIORALIST PATH (FROM THE 1950s)

Behavioralism came about as a protest to traditionalism, in particular to the institutionalist emphasis. The behavioralist path was advocated by a group of political scientists who claimed that traditionalism was not producing truly reliable political knowledge, and that rather than study structures and how they are supposed to function, we should be concerned with what is actually happening within the polity. The behavioralist path concentrates on the behavior of political actors and stresses the use of scientific method to study politics. Thus behavioralists argue that, although we cannot ignore institutions and their structural components, it is the activity within and the behavior around an institution that is of more concern. Yes, it is important to know the structure of the executive office, but it is more crucial to know why one president has more power than another, or why one bill gets passed by Congress and another does not. In their study of politics, behavioralists use scientific methodology and thus stress the empirical. They argue we should adopt natural science as a model for social inquiry. Thus, all political research should display scientific principles and characteristics as determinism, observation, objectivity, verification, explanation, classification, and prediction. In their quest for scientific method and the need for rigorous and systematic research, behavioralists introduce statistical, mathematical, and other quantitative analyses of data to the discipline.

Behavioralism has by no means been universally accepted by political scientists. In fact, it has been criticized on many fronts. Critics are both political scientists who adhere to the traditionalist and theoretical paths as well as those who have attempted to push the boundaries of what we study and how we study politics into new applied settings. Such political scientists we will label as *neoeclectics*. They have most commonly been referred to as *post-behavioralists*.[10] The logic behind this is that they came just after behavioralism. However, this hides the diffuse and varied interests and activities of such political scientists. They have, in fact, formulated the latest path in studying politics. However, before we look at what they do we should consider two main criticisms of behavioralism, for that will explain neoeclecticism to a great degree.

The first criticism of behavioralism is that in their desire to follow the scientific method and their obsession with quantification, behavioralists have not always studied the most important political questions. A second criticism of behavioralists is that they have avoided normative issues and a discussion of values and thus there is no discussion of what should be. In short, the critique of behavioralism is that there is an obsession with methodology at the expense of what we study as political scientists.

THE NEOECLECTIC PATH (FROM THE 1970s)

The neoeclectic view has been taken by a group of political scientists who argue political science has to become relevant once again. They argue that attention should be focused beyond the empirical and that value judgements about government and politics must be considered. Neoeclectics are interested in describing both the goals of political acitivity as well as how to achieve those goals. Thus, there is an explicit place for normative considerations alongside empirical applications in the study of politics. Neoeclectics are not advocating an end to the scientific study of politics; rather, they argue such skills should be applied to the solution of crucial social and political problems. Neoeclectics use quantification to aid them in this quest and attempt to show the utility of quantification in the study of politics. Thus, we can term the neoeclectic path as the applied study of politics. Neoeclectics do not have a single method or focus; rather, they try to push the boundaries of how and what we study. They often consider problems that traditionalists and behavioralists would consider outside of the realm of political science. Many neoeclectics study public policy.

WHERE WE STAND TODAY AND WHAT WE HAVE BECOME

In recent years, it seems as if we have gotten lost in *how* we study politics, rather than in *what* we study about the world of politics. Said differently, we have allowed our attention to focus on our methods instead of our actual areas of concern. We have become adept at the manipulation of empirical data while leaving behind the very reasons that we seek knowledge about politics in the first place. Through our interest in quantifiable bits of information we have taken the *politics* out of political science. This obsession with quantification, we will argue, has come at the expense of our understanding of society and the polity.

We have left behind the larger questions about social and political life in our rush towards neutrality. For decades, political scientists have struggled to be perceived as "value free" when in reality we have needed the opposite, to return what value sensitivity we have lost and develop an even greater ability to infuse value into our discussion of politics in the future. Political scientists need to be intersubjective rather than value free; that is, to acknowlege our values and how they frame our inquiry. To a great degree, we have learned that neutrality extinguishes debate. It is precisely to the degree that political science is capable of bringing a deeper level of value into our discourse on the political order that we will be successful in appropriately responding to a diversity of ideas.

As a discipline, the challenge to political science is to move forward in meaningful ways. It is not enough to trace where we have come from or merely to establish where we stand today. As previously discussed, the empirical is crucial in terms of our understanding of political and social phenomena. But, the key element here is to reintroduce the normative into our current discussion of the political world. Ultimately, the symbiotic relationship between empirical and normative theory construction allows the discipline to come full circle where scientific research is fueled by more profound considerations.

The important questions regarding politics have always been the same. In many ways, it seems as if political scientists are constantly trying to come up with a new list. Often, in our rush to find quantifiable answers we leave the dynamic qualities out of our study. Academics routinely write and lecture about the political realm as if it is some sort of fossil or specimen frozen in time. Those of us who have a passion for politics must return the zest to our pursuit of knowledge about the political world so that we can move together towards answering the enduring questions. The question before us concerns the nature of the discipline itself. Are we history, law, or philosophy? Or, are we the behaviorists and postbehaviorists, and all those "post-posts" who have come since? Indeed, political science is all of these disparate things, having its roots in the study of philosophy and its future in sophisticated, computerized statistical analysis. But the true science of politics is an *ideal* that combines all of these areas.

In other words, it is possible to construe political science as a sort of ideal type that integrates a diversity of intellectual categories, each of which has something to offer the other. If we view our discipline in this manner, it is possible to imagine political scientists creating the context for our continued study and greater understanding of the political world.

The context of our discipline is similar to a large jigsaw puzzle, and each subdiscipline is another piece of the puzzle. While we can understand separately the different elements of political science, the whole thing lacks a clarity of perspective until all of the pieces are in place. Essentially, the pieces themselves are no more, or less, than separate paradigms, in the sense that each subdivision of the discipline tends to see the world through its own lens. These paradigmatic lenses, or mental templates, that drive our study of the political world each reflect a different interpretation of reality. Collectively, the mosaic of these subdisciplines in political science gives a richness to the whole that is not at all diminished by their number.

As the various component elements of political science represent different viewpoints we must have some sense of the entire discipline as a project in order to understand it. We need to know where the discipline is at today, and indeed where it is headed in the future. By thinking about political science as a *project* (rather than as *merely* an academic area of interest, for instance), we remind ourselves that our discipline is constantly changing and evolving. It is also necessary to gain a general understanding of what the discipline is all about before it is truly possible to analyze the conclusions of political science appropriately. It is only by assessing the tapestry made up of the many subfields that we bring sharply into focus the *teleology*, or final cause, in Aristotle's words, of political science. In the following chapters, we will present (1) how political science can be understood as a discipline, (2) the philosophy behind much of what is written about politics, and (3) how the analysis of political inquiry is conducted.

As you proceed through each chapter, answer the following questions. The first question to ask yourself is, "Has political science forgotten the linkages between the various subfields within the discipline?" In other words, do the pieces of the larger jigsaw puzzle, known as politics, lack connection with each other? Without communication between the subfields, the discipline lacks coherence. How can we bring a greater coherence to the study of politics through the integration of the various subfields?

Our second question is, "Why do we want to know what it is we want to know?" As we have become sure of the hows and whats of the research process, we need to recapture our sense of *why* we pursue knowledge about politics and political life. What does it take for dedicated political scientists to return this intellectual curiosity to our pursuit? Finally, in order to return politics to the intersubjective study of the dynamic between people and institutions in society we must allow ourselves to consider the normative as well as the empirical. The question is, how can researchers accomplish this, thus allowing empirical investigation to be informed by normative considerations?

NOTES

1. See Gabriel Almond, *A Discipline Divided, Schools and Sects in Political Science* (Newbury Park: Sage Publishing, 1990); David Easton, *Political Science in the United States: Past and Present* (London & New York: Routledge, 1991);

David Easton, John G. Gunell, and Luigi Graziano (eds.), *The Development of Political Science: A Comparative Study* (London & New York: Routledge, 1991); James Farr and Raymond Seidelman, *Discipline & History: Political Science in the United States* (Ann Arbor: University of Michigan Press, 1993).

2. See David Easton, John G. Gunnell, and Luigi Graziano (eds.) *The Development of Political Science: A Comparative Study* (London & New York: Routledge, 1991).

3. See St. Augustine; for instance, *City of God* (New York: Doubleday & Company, Inc.,1958); or Thomas Hobbes, *Leviathan* (New York: Penguin Books, 1968). See Karl Marx and Friedrich Engels, *The Communist Manifesto* (New York: Bantam Books, 1992).

4. We refer here to the way Aristotle in the *Nichomachean Ethics* (Indianapolis:Bobbs-Merrill Educational Publishing, 1962), characterizes the good life.

5. See chapter one of John Rawls, *A Theory of Justice* (Cambridge, Massachusetts:The Belknap Press, 1971).

6. This notion is fully discussed in the second of John Locke's *Two Treatises of Government* (New York: New American Library, 1963).

7. The best discussion of this idea is found in Section X of Aristotle, *Nichomachean Ethics*.

8. See Barrington Moore, Jr., *Social Origins of Dictatorship and Democracy* (Boston: Beacon Press, 1967).

9. See Isaac D. Balbus, *Marxism and Domination* (Princeton, New Jersey: Princeton University Press, 1982).

10. See David Easton, "Political Science in the United States: Past and Present," in *Discipline and History: Political Science in the U.S.: Part 4.* (ed.) James Farr and Raymond Seidelman (Ann Arbor: University of Michigan Press, 1993).

2

What Is Politics?

Robert Dahl

NATURE OF THE POLITICAL ASPECT

What distinguishes the political aspect of human society from other aspects? What are the characteristics of a political system as distinct, say, from an economic system? Although students of politics have never entirely agreed on answers to these questions, they tend to agree on certain key points. Probably no one would quarrel with the notion that a political system is a pattern of political relationships. But what is a political relationship?[1]

On this question, as on many others, an important (though not always entirely clear) place to start is Aristotle's *Politics* (written ca. 335–332 B.C.). In the first book of the *Politics,* Aristotle argues against those who say that all kinds of authority are identical and seeks to distinguish the authority of the political leader in a political association (or polis) from other forms of authority, such as the master over the slave, the husband over the wife, and the parents over the children.

Aristotle takes for granted, however, that at least one aspect of a political association is the existence of *authority* or *rule.* Indeed, Aristotle defines the polis, or political association, as the "most sovereign and inclusive association," and a constitution (or polity) as "the organization of a polis, in respect of its offices generally, but especially in respect of that particular office which is sovereign in all issues."[2] One of Aristotle's criteria for classifying constitutions is the portion of the citizen body in which final *authority* or *rule* is located.

Ever since Aristotle's time, the notion has been widely shared that a political relationship in some way involves authority, ruling, or power. For

Dahl, Robert. 1984. *Modern Political Analysis,* 4th ed. Upper Saddle River, New Jersey: Prentice Hall, pp. 8–18.

example, one of the most influential modern social scientists, the German scholar Max Weber (1864–1920), postulated that an association should be called political "if and in so far as the enforcement of its order is carried out continually within a given territorial area by the application and threat of physical force on the part of the administrative staff." Thus, although Weber emphasized the territorial aspect of a political association, like Aristotle he specified that a relationship of authority or rule was one of its essential characteristics.[3]

To take a final example, a leading contemporary political scientist, Harold Lasswell, defines "political science, as an empirical discipline, [as] the study of the shaping and sharing of power" and "a political act [as] one performed in power perspectives."[4]

The areas of agreement and disagreement in the positions held by Aristotle, Weber, and Lasswell on the nature of politics are ilustrated by Figure 2–1. Aristotle, Weber, and Lasswell, and almost all other political scientists, agree that political relationships are to be found somewhere within circle A, the set of relationships involving power, rule, or authority. Lasswell calls *everything* in A political, by definition. Aristotle and Weber, on the other hand, define the term "political" so as to require one or more additional characteristics, indicated by circles B and C. For example, to Weber the domain of the political would not be everything inside A or everything inside B (territoriality) but everything in the area of overlap, AB, involving both rule *and* terri-

FIGURE 2–1

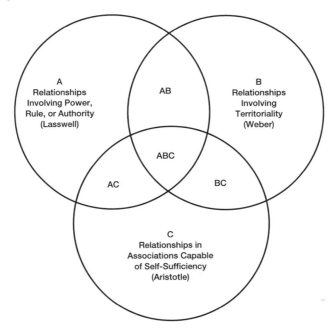

toriality. Although Aristotle is less clear than either Weber or Lasswell on the point, doubtless he would limit the domain of the political even further—e.g., to relationships in associations capable of self-sufficiency (C); hence to Aristotle "politics" would be found only in the area ABC.

Clearly, everything that Aristotle and Weber would call political, Lasswell would too. But Lasswell would consider as political some things that Weber and Aristotle might not; a business firm or a trade union, for example, would have "political" aspects. Contemporary students of politics do in fact study the political aspects of business firms, labor unions, and other "private" associations,[5] and contemporary political analysis tends to accept a broader definition of what is political than that of Aristotle. Let us therefore boldly define a political system as follows:

> A political system is any persistent pattern of human relationships that involves, to a significant extent, power, rule, or authority.

THE UBIQUITY OF POLITICS

Admittedly, this definition is very broad. Indeed, it means that many associations that most people do not ordinarily regard as "political" possess political systems: private clubs, business firms, labor unions, religious organizations, civic groups, primitive tribes, clans, perhaps even families. Three considerations may help clarify the unfamiliar notion that almost every human association has a political aspect:

(1) In common parlance we speak of the "government" of a club, a firm, and so on. In fact, we may even describe such a government as dictatorial, democratic, representative, or authoritarian; and we often hear about "politics" and "politicking" going on in these associations.

(2) A political system is only *one* aspect of an association. When we say that a person is a doctor, or a teacher, or a farmer, we do not assume that he is *only* a doctor, *only* a teacher, *only* a farmer. Probably no human association is exclusively political in all its aspects. People experience many other relationships than power and authority: love, respect, dedication, shared beliefs, and so on.

(3) Our definition says virtually nothing about human *motives*. It definitely does not imply that in every political system people are driven by powerful inner needs to rule over others, that leaders passionately want authority, or that politics is inherently a fierce struggle for power. Conceivably, relationships of authority could exist even among people none of whom had a passion for power, or in situations where poeple who most ardently thirsted for authority had the least chance of acquiring it. Thus the Zuni Indians of the American

Southwest are reported to have had a very strong sense that power-seeking was illicit and power-seekers must not be given power.[6] Closer to our own experience is the not uncommon view among members of American private organizations of various kinds that those who want most intensely to head the organization are least suited to do so, while the most suitable are among those who least want the job. But whatever the evidence from anthropology or folklore may be the central point is this: our highly general definition of a political system makes practically no assumptions as to the nature of human motives. Despite its breadth, the definition helps us make some critical distinctions that are often blurred in ordinary discussions.

Politics and Economics.   Political analysis deals with power, rule, or authority. Economics concerns itself with scarce resources or the production and distribution of goods and services. Politics is one aspect of a great variety of human institutions: economics is another aspect. Hence an economist and a political scientist might both study the same concrete institution—the Federal Reserve system, for example, or the budget; but where the economist would concern himself primarily with problems involving scarcity and the use of scarce resources, the political scientist would deal primarily with problems involving relationships of power, rule, or authority. Like most distinctions between subjects of intellectual inquiry, however, that between politics and economics is not perfectly sharp.

Political Systems and Economic Systems.   Many people indiscriminately apply terms like "democracy," "dictatorship," "capitalism," and "socialism" to both political and economic systems. This tendency to confuse political with economic systems stems from the lack of a standardized set of definitions, from ignorance of the historical origins of these terms, and probably in some cases from a desire to exploit a highly favorable or unfavorable political term like "democracy" or "dictatorship" in order to influence attitudes toward economic systems.

It follows from what has just been said, however, that the political aspects of an institution are not the same as its economic aspects. Historically, the terms "democracy" and "dictatorship" have usually referred to political systems, whereas "capitalism" and "socialism" have referred to economic institutions. From the way the terms have been used historically, the following definitions might be appropriate: (1) A democracy is a political system in which the opportunity to participate in decisions is widely shared among all adult citizens. (2) A dictatorship is a political system in which the opportunity to participate in decisions is restricted to a few. (3) Capitalism is an economic system in which most major economic activities are performed by privately owned and controlled firms. (4) Socialism is an economic system in which most major activities are performed by agencies owned and controlled by the government.

Each pair of terms implies a dichotomy, and dichotomies are often unsatisfactory. In fact, many political systems are neither wholly democratic nor wholly dictatorial; and in many countries private and governmental operations are mixed together in all sorts of complex ways.[7] These mixtures not only demonstrate the shortcomings of the dichotomy "capitalism—socialism" but also emphasize the fact that some institutions and processes can be viewed as part of the economic system for certain purposes and as part of the political system for others. The point to be kept in mind is that in spite of, or even because of, this intermixing it has proved to be intellectually fruitful to distinguish some aspects of life as "economic" and other aspects as "political."

DEFINITIONS AND EMPIRICAL PROPOSITIONS

A moment ago, I offered a definition of the term "political system," showed some of the things that the definition implies or does not imply, and, by way of further clarification, indicated how it differs from the definition of an economic system. According to a view widely held among philosophers of science, I was engaged in the process of stipulating a *nominal* definition of the term. According to this conception a definition is a proposed treaty, so to speak, governing the use of terms.[8]

To be clear-headed about terms often helps one to be clear-headed about politics, which happens to be an activity in which language is extraordinarily ambiguous and often used for perverse and propagandistic purposes. Yet one ought to be clear, too, about the limitations of definitions. Nominal definitions do not, by themselves, tell us anything about "fact," about what goes on in the "real" world. Nothing can be shown to be true or false about the real world of politics (or economics, or whatever) simply by defining a term. Definitions may help us to understand our language; they do not, unaided, help us to understand what is going on in the world. For that, we need *empirical propositions,* which assert something more than a definition, something that can, at least in principle, be confirmed or refuted by experience.

Here, for example, is an empirical statement: "In 1969, no country with a per capita GNP of less than $200 a year had a legal opposition party with more than 10 percent of the seats in Parliament." If we want to decide whether this statement is true, some of the terms will have to be carefully defined. What, for example, do we mean by "a legal opposition party"? But no matter how long we go on discussing definitions, in the end we shall not be able to decide whether the proposition is true or false unless we examine some "facts"—empirical data, evidence, experience, information about the "real" world, call it what you will. (Incidentally, the proposition is falsified by at least one case: India.) Once made, the point must seem perfectly obvious. Yet *the failure to distinguish between a definition and an empirical proposition is common in political analysis.*

Consider, for example, the much-debated question of the relationships between capitalism, socialism, and democracy. If one is willing to use these terms as they were defined a moment ago, four relationships would be logically possible:

	The Political System is:	The Economic System is:
I	A Democracy	Capitalism
II	A Democracy	Socialism
III	A Dictatorship	Capitalism
IV	A Dictatorship	Socialism

None of these combinations is excluded by definition. Whether each combination actually does exist, or how likely it may be, can only be determined by studying actual political and economic systems. Is it true, as advocates of capitalism sometimes argue, that in industrial nations democracy could not exist without a capitalist economy? Is it true, as Lenin and other communists have argued, that a capitalist economy can exist only under a political dictatorship? Although questions like these are never easy to answer, in principle we can do so only by examining all (or a fair sample) of past and present political and economic systems to see what combinations do or probably could exist. But we *cannot* answer these questions by debating definitions.

Systems and Subsystems.   Any collection of elements that interact in some way with one another can be considered a system: a galaxy, a football team, a legislature, a political party.[9] In thinking about political systems, it is helpful to keep in mind four points that apply to systems of any kind:

(1) To call something a system is an abstract way (or, as some scholars say, an analytic way) of looking at concrete things. One should therefore be careful not to confuse the concrete thing with the analytic "system." A "system" is an aspect of things in some degree abstracted from reality for purposes of analysis—the circulatory system of a mammal or the personality system of a human being are examples.

(2) In order to determine what lies within a particular system and what lies outside it, we need to specify the *boundaries* of that system. Sometimes this task is fairly easy, as in the case of the solar system or the United States Supreme Court, but often it requires a somewhat arbitrary decision. For example, what would we consider to be the boundaries of our two major parties? Would we include only party officials? Or would we also include all those who register as Democrats or Republicans? Or those who identify themselves as one or the other, even though they do not register? Or those who vote regularly for the one party or the other? Later on, I shall offer one definition of the "boundaries" of a political system.

(3) One system can be an element, a subsystem, of another. The earth is

a subsystem of our solar system, which is a subsystem of our galaxy, which is a subsystem of the universe. The Foreign Relations Committee is a subsystem of the United States Senate, which is a subsystem of the Congress, etc.

(4) Something may be a subsystem of two or more different systems that overlap only in part. A college professor might be an active member of the American Association of University Professors, the Democratic party, and the PTA.

It is useful to keep these observations in mind in considering the difference between a political system and a social system.

Political Systems and Social Systems.   What is a democratic society? a free society? a socialist society? an authoritarian society? an international society? In what way is a social system distinguished from a political system?

Questions like these are particularly difficult to answer because the terms "society" and "social system" are used loosely, even by social scientists. In general, however, the term "social" is intended to be inclusive; economic and political relations are specific kinds of social relations. Although "social system" is sometimes given a more specific meaning, it too is a broad concept. Thus, Talcott Parsons, a leading American sociologist, defines a social system by three characteristics: (1) two or more persons interact; (2) in their actions they take account of how the others are likely to act; and (3) sometimes they act together in pursuit of common goals.[10] Obviously, then, a social system is a very inclusive kind of order.

According to Parsons' usage, a political system or an economic system would be parts, aspects, or subsystems of a social system. This way of looking at the matter is illustrated in Figure 2–2, where AC represents the set of all political subsystems and ABC represents subsystems that can be considered as either political or economic, depending on which aspect we are concerned with. Examples of ABC would be General Motors, the United States Bureau of the Budget, or the Board of Governors of the Federal Reserve System.

Thus, a democratic *society* could be defined as a social system that has not only democratic political (sub)systems but also a number of other subsystems that operate so as to contribute directly or indirectly to the strength of the democratic political processes. Conversely, an authoritarian society would, by definition, contain many important subsystems, such as the family, the churches, and the schools, all acting to strengthen authoritarian political processes. Let us consider two examples.

In his famous *Democracy in America* (1835–40) the illustrious French writer Alexis de Tocqueville listed a number of "principal causes which tend to maintain the democratic republic in the United States." His list included not only the constitutional structure but the absence of a large military establishment, equality in social and economic conditions, a prosperous agricultural economy, and the mores, customs, and religious beliefs of Americans.[11] In

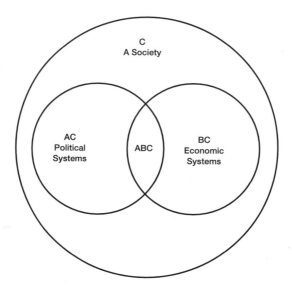

FIGURE 2–2

Tocqueville's view the prospects for a healthy democratic *political* system in the United States were enormously strengthened by the fact that a highly democratic Constitution was reinforced by many other aspects of the *society.* Hence American society could properly be called a democratic society.

By contrast, many observers were pessimistic about the prospects of democracy in Germany after World War II, because they believed that many aspects of German society were highly authoritarian and tended to undermine democratic political relations; they had chiefly in mind the wide tendency for social institutions of all kinds to take on a strong pattern of dominance and submission—the family, schools, churches, business, and all relations between government officials, whether policemen or civil servants, and ordinary citizens. The fact that political democracy had to be instituted in a predominantly authoritarian social environment was not particularly auspicious for the future of democracy in Germany. A number of recent observers, on the other hand, feel more optimistic about the future of political democracy in Germany precisely because they see evidence that the authoritarian character of other social institutions has been declining.

Government and State.   In every society, people tend to develop more or less standard expectations about how they and others will behave in various situations. One learns how to behave as a host or a guest, a parent or grandparent, a "good loser," a soldier, a bank clerk, a prosecutor, a judge, and so on. Patterns like these, where a number of people share roughly similar expectations about how to behave in particular situations, are sometimes called *roles.* We all play various roles, and frequently shift from one role to another very rapidly. The football player who attends classes before the big game, and then goes out with his girl afterwards, has to shift almost as rapidly as a good broken-field runner among his various roles as student, competitive athlete, and suitor.

Whenever a political system is complex and stable, political roles develop. Perhaps the most obvious political roles are played by persons who create, interpret, and enforce rules that are binding on members of the political system. These roles are *offices*, and the collection of offices in a political system is what constitutes the government of that system. At any given moment, of course, these offices, or roles, are (aside from vacancies) filled by particular individuals, concrete persons—Senator Foghorn, Judge Cranky, Major Twimbly. But in many systems the roles remain much the same even when they are played by a succession of individuals. To be sure, different actors may—and usually do—interpret the role of Hamlet or Othello in different ways, sometimes in radically different ways. So too with political roles. Jefferson, Jackson, Lincoln, Theodore Roosevelt, Wilson, and Franklin Roosevelt, for example, each enlarged the role of President beyond what he had inherited from his predecessors by building new expectations in people's minds about what a President should or legitimately could do in office. "There are as many different ways of being President," Nelson Polsby says, "as there are men willing to fill the office."[12] Yet expectations as to the proper role of the President also limit the extent to which he can make of it what he wishes—a fact dramatized by President Johnson's decision in 1968 not to seek re-election because, in effect, he could no longer play the presidential role in the way that he believed the office required.

But—a reader might ask—in defining "government" as we have just done, don't we create a new problem for ourselves? If there are a great variety of political systems—from trade unions and universities to countries and international organizations—what about *the* Government? After all, in the United States, as in most other countries, when you speak of *the* government everyone seems to know what you mean. Of all the governments in all the various associations of a particular territory, generally one is in some way recognized as *the* Government. How does the Government differ from other governments? Consider three possible answers.

(1) *The* Government pursues "higher" and "nobler" purposes than other governments. There are at elast three difficulties with this proposal. First, because people disagree about what the "higher" or "nobler" purposes are that the Government pursues, and even whether a given purpose is or is not being pursued at any given moment, this criterion might not be very helpful in trying to decide whether this or that government is *the* Government. Second, despite the fact that people often disagree over how to rank purposes or values and may even hold that *the* Government is pursuing evil ends, they still agree on what is and what is not *the* Government. An anarchist does not doubt

that he is being oppressed by *the* Government. Third, what about bad Governments? For example, do democratic and totalitarian Governments *both* pursue noble purposes? That point seems logically absurd.

Our first proposed answer, then, confuses the problem of defining Government with the more difficult and more important task of deciding on the criteria for a "good" or "just" Government. Before anyone can decide what the *best* Government is, he must know first what the Government is.

(2) Aristotle suggested another possibility: *the* Government is distinguished by the character of the association to which it pertains—namely, a political association that is self-sufficient, in the sense that it possesses all the qualities and resources necessary for a good life. This definition suffers from some of the same difficulties as the first. Moreover, if it were strictly applied we should have to conclude that no Governments exist! Aristotle's idealized interpretation of the city-state was very far from reality even in his day. Athens was not self-sufficient culturally, economically, or militarily. In fact she was quite unable to guarantee her own peace or independence; without allies, she could not even maintain the freedom of her own citizens. What was true of the Greek city-states is of course equally true today.

(3)*The Government is any government that successfully upholds a claim to the exclusive regulation of the legitimate use of physical force in enforcing its rules within a given territorial area.*[13] The political system made up of the residents of that territorial area and the Government of the area is a "State."[14]

This definition immediately suggests three questions:

(1) Can't individuals who aren't Government officials ever legitimately use force? What about parents spanking their children? The answer is, of course, that the Government of a State does not necessarily *monopolize* the use of force; but it has the exclusive authority to set the limits within which force may legitimately be used. The Governments of most States permit private individuals to use force in some circumstances. For example, although many Governments forbid cruel or excessive punishment of children, most permit parents to spank their own offspring. Boxing is permitted in many countries.

(2) What about criminals who go uncaught? After all, no country is free of assault, murder, rape, and other forms of violence, and criminals sometimes escape the law. The point is, however, that the claim of the Government of the State to regulate violence and force is successfully upheld, in the sense that few people would seriously contest the exclusive right of the State to punish criminals. Although criminal violence exists, it is not legitimate.

(3) What about circumstances of truly widespread violence and force, such as civil war or revolution? In this case no single answer will suffice. (Remember the disadvantages of dichotomous definitions.) For brief periods, no State may exist at all, since no government is capable of upholding its claim to the exclusive regulation of the legitimate use of physical force. Several gov-

ernments may contest for the privilege over the same territory. Or what was formerly a territory ruled by the Government of one State may now be divided and ruled by the Governments of two or more States, with gray Stateless areas where they meet.

We can be reasonably sure of one thing. When large numbers of people in a particular territory begin to doubt or deny the claim of the Government to regulate force, then the existing State is in peril of dissolution.

NOTES

1. For a brief discussion of recent views on the scope of political science, see Oran R. Young's companion volume in this series, *Systems of Political Science*, Chapter One.
2. Ernest Barker, ed., *The Politics of Aristotle* (New York: Oxford University Press, 1962), pp. 1, 110.
3. *The Theory of Social and Economic Organization*, trans. A. M. Henderson and Talcott Parsons (New York: Oxford University Press, 1947), pp. 154, 145–153.
4. Harold D. Lasswell and Abraham Kaplan, *Power and Society* (New Haven: Yale University Press, 1950), pp. xiv, 240.
5. On the Oregon Education Association, see Norman R. Luttberg and Harmon Zeigler, "Attitude Consensus and Conflict in an Interest Group: An Assessment of Cohesion," *American Political Science Review*, Vol. 60 (September, 1966), pp. 655–666. On a union, see the highly important work by S. M. Lipset, M. A. Trow, and J. S. Coleman, *Union Democracy: The Internal Politics of the International Typographical Union* (Glencoe, IL.: The Free Press, 1956). See also Robert A. Dahl, "Business and Politics," in R. A. Dahl, M. Haire, and P. F. Lazarsfeld, *Social Science Research on Business: Product and Potential* (New York: Columbia University Press, 1959), pp. 1–44. A study of the internal "politics" of a more obviously "political" but nonetheless private interest group is Harry M. Scoble's analysis of the National Committee for an Effective Congress: *Ideology and Electoral Action* (San Francisco: Chandler Publishing Co., 1967).
6. Ruth Benedict, *Patterns of Culture* (Boston: Houghton Mifflin Company, 1934).
7. See the descriptions of France, Britain, Italy, Austria, Sweden, the Netherlands, Germany, and the U.S. in A. Shonfield, *Modern Capitalism* (London: Oxford University Press, 1965).
8. There is a voluminous literature on definitions and their place in the empirical sciences. To explore further, the reader could start with the judicious discussion in Abraham Kaplan, *The Conduct of Inquiry* (San Francisco: Chandler Publishing Co., 1964), Chapter 2, and Vernon Van Dyke, *Political Science: A Philosophical Analysis* (Stanford: Stanford University Press, 1960), Chapter 6.
9. The reader should consult Oran R. Young, *Systems of Political Science*, Chapters Two and Three, for a discussion of definitions of the term "system," the nature of general systems theory, and the utility of the systems approach in political science. The most extensive attempt to apply systems theory to political science is in the work of David Easton: see *A Framework for Political Analysis* (Englewood

Cliffs, NJ: Prentice-Hall, Inc. 1965) and *A Systems Analysis of Political Life* (New York: John Wiley & Sons, Inc., 1965).

10. Talcott Parsons and Edward A. Shils, eds., *Toward a General Theory of Action* (Cambridge, MA: Harvard University Press, 1951), p. 55. For a discussion of the meaning and history of the concept "society," see "Society," *International Encyclopedia of the Social Sciences* (New York: Macmilland and Free Press, 1968), Vol. 14, pp. 577 ff.

11. Alexis de Tocqueville, *Democracy in America* (New York: Vintage Books, 1955), Vol. 1, p. xx.

12. See Polsby's *Congress and the Presidency,* a companion book in this series. Polsby compares the presidents from Franklin Roosevelt to Lyndon Johnson. For a comparison of how Coolidge and Hoover interpreted the presidential role, see James D. Barber, "Classifying and Predicting Presidential Styles: Two 'Weak' Presidents." *Journal of Social Issues,* Vol. 24 (July, 1968), pp. 51–80.

13. Adapted from Weber, *op. cit.,* p. 154, by substituting "exclusive regulation" for "monopoly" and "rules" for "its order."

14. Capitalized here to avoid confusion with constituent states in federal systems.

3

The State in Political Study:
How We Become What We Study

Theodore Lowi

This presidential pilgrimage is over, and I can report that the American Political Science Association is alive and well. But a pilgrimage is not a journey into happiness. A pilgrimage is a search, and no pilgrimage is fulfilled until the pilgrim returns and shares the pains of discovery.

From out of their early pilgrimage, the Quakers cried, "Speak truth to power. From out of my pilgrimage I responded, "Who's listening?" and "What truths do we have to impart?" On my pilgrimage I listened in on the conversation between political science and power, and it is my duty to report that the terms of discourse have been set by power. We are not the teachers we thought ourselves to be.

The insights of my pilgrimage began with my awakening to three facts: (1) U.S. political science is itself a political phenomenon and, as such, is a product of the state; (2) there is not one science of politics but several, each the outcome of a particular adaptation to what it studies; and (3) even assuming that we are all sincerely searching for the truth (and it is more interesting to assume that), there are reasons other than the search for truth why we do the kinds of political science we do and why particular subdisciplines become hegemonic. In sum, every regime tends to produce a politics consonant with itself; therefore every regime tends to produce a political science consonant with itself. Consonance between the state and political science is a problem worthy of the attention of every political scientist.

To explore the relation between the state and political science, I have chosen case studies of the three hegemonic subdisciplines of our time—pub-

Lowi, Theodore. 1992. "The State in Political Study: How We Become What We Study," *American Political Science Review* 86:1–7.

lic opinion, public policy, and public choice—preceded by an overview of the transformation from the old to the new state and the old to the new political science. I will conclude with a brief evaluation of the consequences for political science of being a "dependent variable."

There is no need to document for political scientists the contention that the American state until the 1930s was virtually an oxymoron. The level of national government activity was almost as low in 1932 as it had been in 1832. However, although a number of large social movements had failed to expand the national government after the Civil War, they had succeeded in nationalizing the focus of U.S. politics. The Civil War and industrialization made us one nation in fact. *Wabash, St. Louis,* and *Pacific Railway* v. *Illinois* of 1886 (118 U.S. 557) contributed with the doctrine that the state governments were constitutionally incompetent to confront the nationalizing economy. The media transferred their dependence from the highly localized political parties to the corporations seeking mass sales through advertising.

Political science as a profession was a product of this nationalization of political focus. Intellectual historians such as Somit and Tannenhaus (1967) and Seidelman (1985) report that the APSA was part of the progressive reform movement. Somit/Tannenhaus report that only 20% of the first decade's membership were "professors and teachers" (p.55). From out of the beginnings in the 1890s, where the writing was "legalistic, formalistic, conceptually barren and largely devoid of what would today be called empirical data" (p.69), the founders of the association were committed to political realism, which meant facts, the here and now, and the exposure of the gap between the formal institutions and the realities. James Bryce, in his address as the fourth association president in 1909, urged political scientists to "Keep close to the facts. Never lose yourself in abstractions. . . . The Fact is the first thing. Make sure of it. Get it perfectly clear. Polish it till it shines and sparkles like a gem" (quoted in Somit and Tannenhaus 1967, 70). The title of Woodrow Wilson's presidential address to the seventh annual meeting of the APSA was "The Law and the Facts." Early in his speech he said, "I take the science of politics to be the accurate and detailed observation of [the] processes by which the lessons of experience are brought into the field of consciousness, transmuted into active purposes, put under the scrutiny of discussion, sifted, and at last given determinate form in law" (1911, 2). But these were not facts for themselves alone. Some early political scientists were active reformers, others were radical muckrakers, and a few may have been completely aloof. But facts were to be put in the service of assessment: Did a given political institution meet its purpose? Accordingto Wilson, political scientists should serve as a kind of "self-constituted commission.. . to discover, amidst our present economic chaos, a common interest, so that we might legislate for the whole country instead of this, that, or the other interest, one by one" (pp. 6–7).

There is no evidence to suggest that the founding generation were trying to form an *intelligentsia,* defined as an organization of intellectuals in opposition to the state. There was, in fact, no state to organize against. If anything, there was a memory trace of the two states that conducted the most devastating total war in history up to 1865. But both states were dismantled quickly after the Civil War and were folded back into the "stateless polity" of the restored Union (Bensel 1990). One could say, however, that the early APSA was a kind of *counter*intelligentsia formed in defense of a state that did not yet exist. The political science of the entire first generation of the APSA was formed around politics—the observable, the immediate, and the short-run purpose to be served. But politics was not only a phenomenon, it was a problem. For example, to Goodnow, the purpose of the political science was to show "particularly from a consideration of political conditions as they now exist in the U.S., that the formal governmental system as set forth in the law is not always the same as the actual system" (quoted in Ross 1991, 274). And for most of them, there was a handy solution to the problem of politics—government, properly characterized as the "building of a new American state" (Skowronek 1982). This goal of a new American state can, in turn, be characterized as a stateless government, or an enlightened administration. Woodrow Wilson, while still an obscure professor of political science at Johns Hopkins, sounded the call for the study of administration in 1887. This should be understood, however, within the context of his still larger declaration that the era of constitution making was closed "so far as the establishment of essential principles is concerned" (quoted in Ross 1991, 275). Administration could be a solution to politics because, in Wilson's words, we could have the Prussian state breathe free American air (Wilson 1887). As Seidelman puts it, "the study of politics for Wilson thus had to evolve into a study of America's cultural uniqueness and European administration" (1985, 44). Wilson was confirming the unarticulated major premise of political science, namely, that the American system was permanent and that the science of politics involved the study and assessment of political things within a permanent and unique context. We were one republic, then and forever. Political scientists could remain a counterintelligentsia not because all members shared the Lockean liberal consensus but because they were scientists in the state-building business even while, as with Bentley, they were attacking the very concept of the state as "soul stuff" (ibid., 70–71). For the same reason, political science was atheoretical. Works produced by the founding generation stand up well even by today's standards of science and are superior to most of ours in the quality of the knowledge they brought to bear and in their use of the English language. But the work remained essentially empirical and became almost technocratic in its participation in the reform movement, primarily because it had no concept of an alternative regime in the United States.

It should have been unmistakably clear to any political scientist of 1887 or later that the American system after the Civil War was a new regime, deserving a new name. Why not the Second Republic? The answer is that that would have suggested an impermanence to the American regime. if a Second Republic, why not a Third and Fourth? My wife sometimes introduces me to her friends as her first husband. That is a sobering sobriquet. Political science was atheoretical because it had no concept of a Second Republic or of any other alternative regime. Eventually, political scientists would virtually rewrite democratic theory to accommodate political parties and would rewrite republican theory to accommodate the devolution of constitutional powers from Congress to the presidency. But this was not a self-conscious act of political theory; it was part of "the study of political conditions as they exist." In the stateless polity of the founding epoch, the science of politics was the study of politics and of political institutions within a timeless, as well as a uniquely American, framework.

In my opinion, the golden age of U.S. political science came toward the end of this founding epoch, which corresponds, of course, with the end of the stateless polity. Works of political science of the 1930s and 1940s were magnificent in their ability to describe a complex political whole; thorough, honest, and imaginative in their use of statistics to describe a dynamic reality; and powerful and cogent in pointing out flaws and departures from U.S. ideals. But this was the sentimental part of my journey. To yearn for those particular studies of elections, case studies of interest groups and policymaking, histories of party systems and representation in Congress is to yearn also for the luxury of the First Republic, now that we are irreversibly in the Second and possess at least the bare beginnings of an awareness of the possibility of regime change in the United States.

Surely by now there has been, in fact, a change of regime, which I call the Second Republic, for lack of an established enumeration. It is not the French state or the Prussian state; but at least, we can say that the American state is no longer an oxymoron. Here, all too briefly, are its relevant high spots: (1) it is a positive, not a reactive, state, from the start centered on the executive branch; (2) constitutional limits on the powers of the national government over the economy and on the distribution of power among the branches within the national government were very quickly laid to rest; (3) many aspects of politics that had traditionally been private (e.g., registration, ballots, election administration, nomination, job patronage, polling, and campaign finance) have been governmentalized—that is, modern government has assumed responsibility for its own politics; (4) political parties, like nuclear families, have declined for lack of enough to do; (5) bureaucracy, independent of party and Congress, has expanded in size and scale approaching autonomy as a social force; and, (6) intimately connected with (5), government has become intensely committed to science. This was no accident, and it is no mere policy. Science is an inherent part of the new, bureaucratized state, in at least two dimensions: First, it involves a commitment to building science as an institution, that is, a commitment to government *for* science; and second, it involves a commitment to government *by* science—that is to say, it involves scientific decision making. This has been properly characterized as *technocratization*, which I take to mean "to predict in order to control" (compare Mills 1959, 113). But another to-me-more-interesting but less appreciated part of this aspect of the expansion of science is that *economics has replaced law as the language of the state.*

What Tocqueville said of the First Republic we may say of the Second: "A new science of politics is needed for a new world" (quoted in Wood 1969, v). But life is not quite so simple. If modern states are differentiated, there are almost certain to be several sciences of politics, rather than just one. We tend to call these subdisciplines; but despite continuities and overlaps, they are quite distinct. Each can be understood as a product of the phenomena it studies; but I am concerned here not to explain or place them all but only to understand the "hegemonics" of disciplines—why public opinion, public policy, and public choice became hot topics and when.

Some call public opinion behavioral science. I think I am more accurate calling it public opinion. Observers from an alien intellectual planet would find it most peculiar that the study of individual opinions and attitudes could be called behavioral—until they deconstructed the discourse between the new bureaucratized state and the new political science. Here is my deconstruction:

1. If science is to be public, it must be neutral.

2. It must also be rational and therefore concern itself with rational phenomena, that is, orderly, repeatable, predictable phenomena. This is precisely what makes science and bureaucracy so compatible. Karl Mannheim, in 1929, over 20 years before the behavioral revolution, wrote, "Bureaucratic thought is permeated by measurement, formalization, and systematization on the basis of fixed axioms . . . [such that] only those forms of knowledge were legitimate which touched and appealed to what is common to all human beings" (1936, 167).

3. Science also has to be microscopic, down to the irreducibly smallest unit. It is no paradox that as our state grew larger, the units of analysis in our social science became smaller. This is a profoundly important aspect of rationality: out of small units, large numbers grow; and large numbers behave according to the regularities of mathematical probability. (In this context it is easy to understand why Arthur Bentley's appeal "to fashion a tool" with the group as the smallest unit of analysis was first uttered in 1907 and not really heard, or responded to, until over 40 years later [see Seidelman 1985, 72–74].)

4. Science, like administration, has to follow a prescribed method. As Robert Wiebe put it, "Bureaucratic thought . . . made 'science' practically synonymous with 'scientific method'. Science had become a procedure . . . rather than a body of results" (1967, 147).

5. The language itself has to be microscopic; that is, science has to be translated into the language of variables.

The phenomena and methodology of public opinion obviously meet all the requirements of a science that would be consonant with bureaucratic thinking. And now consider the units of analysis within the sample surveys that give public opinion its link to political behavior: voting and participation. These display an even stronger consonance with the state, in that these are approved political behavior (i.e., political behavior sponsored by the state and needed by regimes and elites to maintain their legitimacy).

Some see behavioral science as a large step toward hard science and, through that, an advancement toward greater enlightenment about society and politics. I do not disagree. But my political analysis tells me also that the hegemony of the subdiscipline of behavioral science or public opinion was to a large extent a product of its compatibility with bureaucratic thoughtways, rather than the result of successful discourse within political science.

It is important to emphasize, however, that the hegemony of the subdiscipline of public opinion is a case of natural selection, not one of political maneuvering or intellectual opportunism. Anyone personally acquainted with the people who made the behavioral revolution in political science would agree that if political skill were required to succeed, there would be no survey research centers—probably no behavioral science at all. It is their very lack of attention to playing the political game that makes the success of their field so interesting. The explanation is to be found not in politics in the vulgar sense but politics in the higher sense—the politics of state building.

The Second Republic, having put a new emphasis on science, also determined what that science would be. The capacity to engage in public opinion research in political science had been in existence since at least the late nineteenth century. Statistics, which takes its name from *state* and *statist*, reached maturity still earlier in the nineteenth century and grew in importance as states democratized and individuals began to "count" for something. Sampling was also well advanced and widely practiced, especially in the agricultural sciences (Porter 1986, 23–25). Even opinion polling in political campaigns was actually tried at least as early as 1892, albeit over the objections of many defenders of the sanctity of elections (Jensen 1969, 228–229)—and was picked up by advertising companies and newspapers soon after. Yet public opinion did not become the hegemonic subdiscipline of political science until the Second Republic.

Public policy as a subdiscipline of political science has an even longer genealogy than public opinion although it was more than a decade later in emerging as a hegemonic subdiscipline. The study of public policy begins, of course, with the study of legislation, whose history is usually traced out from divine law through common law to something called positive law, to indicate the demystification of law and the deliberateness of modern laws. There is, then, one later stage called public policy, indicating the intervention of administration between legislature and citizen. Public policy is a term of art reflecting the interpenetration of liberal government and society, suggesting greater flexibility and reciprocity than such unilateralist synonyms as *law, statute, ordinance, edict,* and so on. Public policy began to gain some currency in public administration in the 1930s; and public administration had been one of the hegemonic subdisciplines in the political science of the stateless polity I refer to as the First Republic. The decline and transfiguration of public administration gives us the key to public policy. Traditional public administration was almost driven out of the APSA by the work of a single, diabolical mind, that of Herbert Simon. Simon transformed the field by lowering the discourse. He reduced the bureaucratic phenomenon to the smallest possible unit, the decision, and introduced rationality to tie decisions to a system—not to any system but to an economic system. His doctorate was in political science; his Nobel award was in economics.

Now, Simon did not accomplish this all by himself. His intellectual tour de force was made possible by actual changes in the administrative institutions of the Second Republic. Administrative authority in the First Republic partook of a fairly well established tradition of separating public from private life by a variety of legal rules and procedures that comprise what Joseph Vining calls the "masterful myth of the 'rule of law'"; in the Second Republic, these rules and myths broke down—not spontaneously, but in face of the rise of economic thinking in the corporate world, as well as in government (1978, 27).

It is in this context that modern public policy became a hegemonic subdiscipline in political science, overshadowing behavioralism itself. The study of public policy in the political science of the First Republic drew upon public law and institutional economics. Some of that old-fashioned public policy study exists today. But the modern approach is more appropriately called public policy analysis, which draws upon macroeconomic methods and economic systems thinking. The best way to demonstrate the size and character of this new subdiscipline of political science is to point to the presence of the policy analysis courses within political science departments and the explosive growth of the separate policy analysis programs and the economics requirements in the schools of public affairs and public policy and in the law schools. All the students in those places are learning the new language of the state.

It does no disservice to the subdiscipline of public choice to tie it to another of Karl Mannheim's observations dating from 1929, namely, that in the political science of a bureaucratic state "an economic man, a political man, etc., irrespective of time and race, could be constructed on the basis of a few axiomatic characteristics" (1936, 167–68). Mannheim continues: "Only what could be known by the application of these axioms was considered as knowable. Everything else was due to the perverse 'manifoldness of the real', concerning which 'pure' theory need not worry itself" (p. 168). Compare this to Kenneth Arrow's assertion made in a boastful spirit nearly 40 years later that any assumption other than the rational actor leads to mysticism and irrationality (Goldfield and Gilbert 1990, 14–15). This gives us a start toward a political explanation for why public choice has become probably the hottest thing going in political science today.

Quite aside from whatever merits it may have as a method and however true its truths may be, public choice is hegemonic today for political reasons or (to be more dignified about it) for reasons of state. Let me dramatize this in quite tangible rational actor terms: most of the luminaries in this subfield of political science came from, serve in, or are substantially associated with the same freshwater universities that kept burning the flame of laissez-faire ideology: Chicago, Rochester, Washington University of Saint Louis (nor should we overlook the Saint Louis Federal Reserve staff) (Johnson 1991). Here, again, we are confronting not political opportunism but institutional consonance—a symbiotic relationship between state and political science.

The affinity between modern bureaucratic government and economics—already strong—was further strengthened by the revival of the political popularity of laissez-faire ideology within the Republican party. For most of this century, laissez-faire liberalism (erroneously called conservative) had been the Republican party's center of gravity; but after the Depression, it had had little effect on voters and even less on intellectuals in the social sciences. Few intellectuals figured in national Republican party circles. *Conservative intellectual* was just another oxymoron. Today, of course, Republican administrations are overflowing with intellectuals, as are affiliated think tanks and the op-ed pages of the major newspapers. I see no signs yet of a Republican takeover of the APSA; but I do see one beneficiary of the Republican party era in political science, namely, public choice. People of merit inhabit this subfield, but its hegemony has little to do with their merit. Their success as a group was entirely fortuitous.

We political scientists enjoy the primitive wisdom of Mr. Dooley; and probably Mr. Dooley's best-known scientific proposition was, "No matter whether th' constitution follows th' flag or not, th' supreme court follows th' iliction returns." A more dignified Dooley would say, "The APSA follows Leviathan." I conclude with what are to me the three principal consequences of following Leviathan too closely. First, we have as a consequence failed to catch and evaluate the significance of the coming of economics as the language of the state. Second, we have failed to appreciate how this language made *us* a dismal science like economics. Third, having been so close to Leviathan, we failed to catch, characterize, and evaluate the great ideological sea changes accompanying the changes of regime.

First, then, why economics? Of what use is economic analysis to politics? Since economics was always a deeply flawed predictive science, why was it so attractive to policymakers and bureaucrats in the new state? Why was it so attractive to political science? My evaluation was inspired in part by an observation made 30 years ago by the distinguished economic philosopher Joan Robinson: "Economics . . . has always been partly a vehicle for the ruling ideology of each period as well as partly a method of scientific investigation" (1962, 1). My answer is that economic analysis is politically useful because it closes off debate, especially in a highly public representative assembly like Congress. The rise of economics as the language of the state parallels the decline of Congress as a creative legislature. (I argue this point more extensively in Lowi 1991.) Policymaking powers are delegated less to the agency and more to the decisionmaking formulas residing in the agency. The use of economic analysis to close off debate was strengthened as Republicans discovered that economic analysis could be used as effectively for them as for the Democrats—by manipulating the cost, rather than the benefit, side of cost–benefit analysis. I recommend John Schwarz's evaluation of Murray Weidenbaum's outrageous manipulation of the "costs of regulation" that supported the Reagan administration's commitment to deregulation (1988, 90–99). But I must confess that both the Democratic and the Republican politicians were smarter than the political scientists, because they took the stuff as weaponry, while we took it as science. We swallowed economics before subjecting it to a political analysis.

We should have seen that economics rarely even pretends to speak truth to power. If substantive truths were claimed, there would be room for argument. But economics, particularly as a policy science, Stresses method above all. And the key to the method is the vocabulary of economics, which is the *index*. An index is not a truth but an agreement or convention among its users about what will be the next best thing to truth. M_1, the Dow, the CPI, unemployment, GNP: This is the new representative government—an index representing a truth. Indices have analytic power because they fit into defined systems; and of course, systems are also not truths but only useful fictions. (This, by the way, is not an attack on indices *or* systems. It is just a political evaluation of indices and systems.)

Now to the second of my consequences, that is, that the modern bureaucratic state has made political science just another dismal science. By *dismal* I do not mean merely the making of gloomy forecasts, in the Malthusian tradition: I mean the absence of *passion*.

During my pilgrimage, the most frequent complaints I heard were against the *American Political Science Review*. I join in at least one of these, which I do not limit to the *APSR*. Too few of the articles seek to transcend their analysis to join a more inclusive level of discourse. There is consequently little substantive controversy. The response is that a scientific journal must be dedicated to replication and disproof. But actually, very few pieces independently replicate anything: and even if they did, replication alone is dismal stuff. Political science is a harder science than the so-called hard sciences because we confront an *un*natural universe that requires judgment and evaluation. Without this, there can be no love of subject, only vocational commitment to method and process. The modern state has made us a dismal science, and we have made it worse by the scientific practice of removing ourselves two or three levels away from sensory experience. Political scientists have always quantified whatever and whenever they could, and most tried to be rigorous; but they stayed close to sensory experience. Even with our original mechanical helper, the counter-sorter device, it was possible to maintain a sensory relation to the data. What a pleasure it was to watch the cards seek their slots! And what a pity today that the empiricists have only their printout!

Finally, I turn to our failure to catch or evaluate adequately the ideological sea changes accompanying the changes of regime. Time permits only the barest inventory of missed opportunities, but I think they will speak for themselves.

The perspective of nearly 50 years makes it easy to see what we did not catch about the New Deal as a regime change. Although political scientists caught the new liberalism in the air, they failed to evaluate whether all the elements of this ideology were consistent with liberalism or with constitutionalism. They failed, for example, to capture and evaluate the significance of "administrative law." They noticed, but merely celebrated, the delegation of power from Congress to the executive branch. At the time it meant only the fulfillment of the New Deal program. Even as time passed, our tendency was to render each change consistent with our existing model of the political system. There was virtually no serious political science inquiry into whether the changes in constitutional doctrine, governmental structure, and policy commitments constituted a regime change. Some Republicans suggested that the United States had become a socialist regime, but political science did not respond to this challenging formulation. It should be a matter of ultimate interest, as well as enjoyment, to fight intensely over the identification of criteria for determining when a political change is sufficient to constitute a regime change. The New Deal helped give us a new political science but did not provide sufficient inclination to evaluate what was new.

We are at this moment in the presence of another failure, namely, a failure to catch the nature and significance of the ideological shift accompanying the current Republican era. The inability of the Reagan administration to terminate any important New Deal programs should at least have led to a reflection on the nature of the New Deal as a regime change. Even a post hoc evaluation would be useful. Meanwhile, the Republican era has brought with it some profound ideological changes that political science is failing to capture even though our own public opinion polls are sensing them. Political science has failed to catch and evaluate the two separate components of the Republican coalition: the old, laissez-faire liberalism and the genuine, native conservatism. Political science has stood by and permitted Republican candidates and staff intellectuals to treat the traditional laissez-faire core of the Republican party as conservative and then to compound the felony by stigmatizing liberalism as an alien belief system akin to socialism. This profound misuse of rich terminology is literally poisoning political discourse in the United States, and political science has to take a lot of the blame for this. We also did not catch the rise of the genuine conservatism; although our polls were picking up significant reactionary movements, we continued to treat the Falwell phenomenon and such predecessors as the Christian Anti-communist Crusade as aberrant. And we have passively witnessed the joining of laissez-faire liberalism with genuine right-wing conservatism as though they are consistent in their opposition to big government. Laissez-faire liberal Republicans, supported by their economists, embrace an ideal of radical individualism and view all government as a threat to freedom. In contrast, genuine conservatives are not individualists but statists. The state they want consists of tight and restrictive police control by state and local governments, but they are statists nevertheless. Genuine conservatives were never really at home with purely market relations; and they have never espoused the ideal (much less the methodology) of rational individualism. (Many conservative Catholic lay intellectuals have tried in vain to establish a comfortable concordance with free market liberalism.) Conservative intellectuals are now writing the poetry of executive power and are the authors of most of the writing that bashes Congress and the politics of representative government. Just as political scientists did not catch the ideological significance of the propresidential power writings of the New Deal supporters in the 1950s and early 1960s, we are now not catching the significance of the fact that most of the current propresidential power writing is by the Far Right. The far right-wing intellectuals are also writing a significant proportion of the new work on the founding intended not only to contribute to historical scholarship but to reconstitute the constitution in such a way as to place the presidency above the law and affirmative action beneath it.

No effort has been made to camouflage my antagonism to Republican era ideology. But my own personal position is irrelevant. Political scientists of the left, Right, and center are a unity in their failure to maintain a clear and critical consciousness of political consciousness. Causal and formal analyses of the relations among clusters of variables just will not suffice. Nor will meticulous analysis of original intent. It is time we became intellectuals.

At the end of my pilgrimage, I have come to the conclusion that among the sins of omission of modern political science, the greatest of all has been the omission of passion. There are no qualifications for membership in the APSA; but if I had the power to establish such standards, they would be that a member should love politics, love a good constitution, take joy in exploring the relation between the two, and be prepared to lose some domestic and even some foreign policy battles to keep alive a positive relation between the two. I do not speak for the passion of ideology, though I do not count it out. I speak for the pleasure of finding a pattern, the inspiration of a well-rounded argument, the satisfaction in having made a good guess about what makes democracy work and a good stab at improving the prospect of rationality in human behavior.

Regime changes throughout the world since 1989 ought to give us a clearer perspective on some new sciences of politics. Although only a few 6f the world's regime changes will be liberal democracies, they are stimulating tremendous demand for transferable insights about the workings of liberal democratic institutions, especially U.S. institutions. May this demand draw U.S. political scientists out of the shadow of Leviathan upward and outward toward a level of discourse worthy of the problem. This is not an opportunity to play philosopher-king. It is an opportunity to meet our own intellectual needs while serving the public interest. And we need not worry how to speak truth to power. It is enough to speak truth to ourselves.

REFERENCES

Bensel, Richard F. 1990. *Yankee Leviathan—the Origins of Central State Authority in America, 1859–1877.* New York: Cambridge University Press.

Goldfield, Michael, and Alan Gilbert. 1990. "The Limits of Rational Choice Theory." Presented at the annual meeting of the American Political Science Association, San Francisco.

Jensen, Richard. 1969. "American Election Analysis." in *Politics and the Social Sciences,* ed. Seymour Martin Lipset. New York: Oxford University Press.

Lowi, Theodore J. 1991. "Knowledge, Power, and the Congress. In *Knowledge, Power, and the Congress,* ed. William H. Robinson and H. Wellborn Clay. Washington: Congressional Quarterly.

Mannheim, Karl. 1936. *Ideology and Utopia.* New York: Harcourt Braoe Jovanovich.

Mills, C. Wright. 1959. *The Sociological Imagination.* New York: Oxford University Press.

Porter, Theodore M. 1986. *The Rise of Statistical Thinking, 1820–1900.* Princeton: Princeton University Press.

Robinson, Joan. 1962. *Economic Philosophy.* New York: Doubleday Anchor Books.

Ross, Dorothy. 1991. *The Origins of American Social Science.* New York: Cambridge University Press.

Schwarz, John E. 1988. *America's Hidden Success.* New York: W. W. Norton.

Seidelman, Raymond. 1985. *Disenchanted Realists: Political Science and the American Crisis. 1884–1984.* Albany: State University of New York Press.

Skowronek, Stephen. 1982. *Building a New American State: The Expansion of National Administrative Capacities, 1877–1920.* New York: Cambridge University Press.

Somit, Albert, and Joseph Tannenhaus. 1967. *The Development of Political Science: From Burgess to Behavioralism.* Boston: Allyn & Bacon.

Vining, Joseph. 1978. *Legal Identity: The Coming of Age of Public Law.* New Haven: Yale University Press.

Wiebe, Robert. 1967. *The Search for Order, 1877–1920.* New York: Hill & Wang.

Wilson, Woodrow. 1887. "The Study of Administration." *The Political Science Quarterly* 2:202–17.

Wilson, Woodrow. 1911. "The Law and the Facts." *American Political Science Review* 5:1–11.

Wood, Gordon S. 1969. *The Creation of the American Republic, 1776–1787.* New York: W. W. Norton.

4

Feminist Challenges
to Political Science

Susan J. Carroll and Linda M. G. Zerilli

The study of women and politics within the discipline of political science was stimulated by and has evolved simultaneously with the contemporary feminist movement. Prior to the emergence of the feminist movement in the mid-1960s, few books or articles pertaining to women were written by political scientists (a notable exception being Duverger 1955), and from 1901 to l966 only eleven dissertations focusing on women were completed (Shanley and Schuck 1974). The Women's Caucus for Political Science, founded in 1971, began in 1972 to sponsor several papers on gender at the annual meetings of the American Political Science Association, and during the early to mid-1970s the first few path-breaking books on women and politics were published (e.g., Amundsen 1971; Kirkpatrick 1974; Jaquette 1974; Freeman 1975).

From such humble origins, the subfield of women and politics grew at a rapid pace. By the early 1990s the numbers of papers, articles, and books written by political scientists focusing on women and politics or feminist theory had grown considerably. For example, more than 60 gender-related papers were presented at the 1992 Annual Meeting of the American Political Science Association, and in 1991, *Women & Politics,* a scholarly journal devoted to publishing empirical and theoretical work on women and politics, published 24 articles and reviewed 21 books on women and politics and feminist theory. The growth of a body of scholarship focusing on women and gender within the discipline of political science has paralleled similar (although frequently more rapid) patterns of growth in other disciplines in the humanities and social sci-

Carroll, Susan J., and Linda G. Zerilli. 1993. "Feminist Challenges to Political Science," in *Political Science: The State of the Discipline II,* edited by Ada W. Finifter. Washington, D.C.: American Political Science Association, pp. 55–76.

ences (DuBois et al. 1985). In addition, work on gender in political science has been strongly influenced by the rapid development of interdisciplinary work in women's studies.

The study of women and politics also became more institutionalized within the discipline throughout the 1970s and 1980s. Two of the most important developments were the establishment in 1981 of the journal *Women & Politics* and the formation of an Organized Section on Women and Politics Research within the American Political Science Association in 1986. In addition, in 1986 the political science department at Rutgers University became the first in the country to offer women and politics as both a major and minor field of study toward a Ph.D. Most of the larger political science departments now have at least one faculty member who specializes in gender politics, and many departments now offer women and politics courses as a regular part of their undergraduate curriculum.

The work being done in this rapidly growing field has important implications for all political scientists, not just those who are specialists in women and politics. Feminist scholarship poses a set of questions that challenge the theoretical and epistemological foundation on which the discipline is constructed. Sometimes implicitly and sometimes explicitly, the work being done by feminist scholars raises important questions about both *what* we study as political scientists and *how* we study it.

FRAMEWORK

This essay will examine the questions posed by women and politics research about what we study as political scientists and how we study it in the context of three analytically distinct categories of research on women and politics. The first category consists of critiques of the ways in which political theory and empirical research in political science have traditionally excluded women as political actors and rendered them either invisible or apolitical. The second category consists of research that has attempted to add women into politics, to make them visible as political actors, while accepting the existing dominant frameworks of political analysis. The third category consists of research that calls existing frameworks and assumptions into question; work within this category suggests that our dominant frameworks cannot accommodate the inclusion of women as political actors and that many of the frameworks, assumptions, and definitions central to political science must be reconceptualized.

We would not argue that these categories of work on women and politics are chronologically distinct or that research in any one category is more important than research in another. Although much of the early research on women and politics falls into the first two categories while the third category is of more recent vintage, all three categories of research are apparent in current work. Similarly, all three have made important contributions to our understanding of the ways in which gender and assumptions about gender have permeated the discipline. While we treat these three categories of research as analytically distinct for purposes of this essay, the demarcations among them are admittedly fuzzy. One category tends to flow into another, and the work of a single scholar sometimes cuts across two or even all three categories.

We do not intend to provide a comprehensive review of the literature on women and politics; given the proliferation of work in recent years, such a review would be a monumental task, which fortunately is beyond the scope of this essay. Instead, in discussing the three categories of research, we draw largely on literature from political theory and from American politics both because our specializations are in those fields and because these are the two areas in political science where the greatest amount of work on gender has taken place. Through this review we hope to demonstrate that both feminist theory and more empirically oriented work on gender have posed serious and often similar questions about what we study in political science and how we study it.

WOMEN AS INVISIBLE OR APOLITICAL

In political science as in other disciplines, feminist scholarship had its origins in critiques of the ways in which the philosophical canon of political theory and the empirical canon of behavioral political science excluded women and women's activity from their subject matter, often rendered women invisible, and employed stereotypical assumptions about women's apolitical "nature" and their behavior. Although several important critiques appeared in the 1970s (e.g., Bourque and Grossholtz 1974; Shanley and Schuck 1974; Jaquette 1974; Iglitzin 1974; Goot and Reid 1975; Boals 1975; Okin 1979; Elshtain 1979a)[1] recent critiques continue to add to our understanding of the ways that the discipline as a whole and specific subfields within the discipline either have failed to deal with women or have treated women in a stereotyped manner (e.g., Randall 1991; Ackelsberg and Diamond 1987; Nelson 1989; Sapiro 1989; Grant 1991; Halliday 1991).

Inasmuch as political science is interested in questions of citizenship, many feminists have turned their attention to the historical tradition of Western political theory to explain both the invisibility of women as political actors and the sexist attitudes toward women that have permeated much of the discipline. The earliest feminist critiques were concerned with breaking the silence about women that had characterized—and to some extent still does characterize—the scholarly literature on the canon of political theory. Even as feminists found that the majority of past political theorists had excluded women from participation in the public sphere, they also found that these theorists had not simply neglected women in their texts (Okin 1979; Elshtain 1981;

Sazonhouse 1985; Eisenstein 1981; Shanley 1982). On the contrary, the classic theorists were deeply worried about what they deemed most often to be the disorderly influence of women on political affairs. Women were not simply missing in the canonical texts; rather, they had been read out of the Western tradition by political theory scholars (Jones and Jonasdottir 1988).

In important respects, then, feminist political theorists set out from the start to make visible what their academic colleagues had made invisible, namely women. Although women were present as a subject of no small concern for the classic theorists, they were absent as political actors. Thus feminists were intent to show, first, how the tradition has justified women's exclusion from participation in the public sphere, and, second, how that exclusion has defined what counts as citizenship across a wide historical range of political theories, up to and including modern democratic theory. Because women bad been a virtual non-topic within the scholarly literature in political theory, many feminists were concerned initially with chronicling what past political theorists had said about women and showing how what they had said had been used to justify women's banishment from civic life. Focusing on the "patriarchal attitudes" of political theorists from Plato to Hegel, feminists found that most theorists had portrayed women as not fully human or fully rational or fully political beings (Figes 1970; Mahowald 1978; Brennan and Pateman 1979; Clarke and Lange 1979; Pateman 1980a). Whether women were defined in terms of their disruptive sexuality, lack of justice, incapacity for reason, or all of the above and more, the classic theorists had cast them as being utterly deficient in those qualities that were deemed necessary for active participation in the civic community. "Women *qua* women," in short, were "excluded from the public, political, and economic spheres" (Clarke and Lange 1979, viii).

Those feminists who focused on the "blatantly anachronistic or flatly misogynist elements" of the classic texts (Brown 1988, 11) decried "the sexism of political theory" and declared the Western tradition "utterly bankrupt" as a means for advancing feminist theories of citizenship and sexual equality (Clarke and Lange 1979, xvii; Figes 1970). Even feminists who did not advocate such an outright dismissal of the canon agreed that the classic theorists offered little in the way of a political analysis of the sexual division of labor in the family (Okin 1979; Elshtain 1981; Eisenstein 1981). Part of the problem, as Susan Moller Okin argued, was that political theorists naturalized the family and women's place within it. They viewed women in strictly functionalist terms: "Philosophers who, in laying the foundation for their political theories, have asked 'What are men like?' 'What is man's potential?' have frequently, in turning to the female sex, asked, 'What are women *for*?'" (Okin 1979, 10).

Susan Moller Okin was one among a growing number of feminists who came increasingly to view the less than flattering images of women found throughout the Western tradition as being more than merely incidental to representations of the political. What a theorist said about women, feminists came to argue, was absolutely crucial to how he conceptualized the terms of citizenship (Pateman 1980b; Eisenstein 1981; Elshtain 1981; Saxonhouse 1985). Not only were concepts such as justice, rights, and consent articulated in the absence of women as political actors, but also their meaning was constituted through that absence. This core insight, although not fully developed in the feminist literature of the late 1970s and early 1980s, was crucial for the scholarship on gender for at least three reasons: one, it enabled feminists to contest the "add women and stir" approach to political theory; two. it offered a way of thinking through women's contemporary status as second-class citizens; and, three, it suggested that the legacy of the Western tradition on the discipline of political science has been to treat women as political outsiders whose proper place is in the family.

Critiques of the empirical canon of behavioral political science research have in many respects echoed the themes that have characterized critiques of the political theory canon. Feminists have examined and found problematic the treatment of women in such classic works as: Angus Campbell et al., *The American Voter*; Robert Lane, *Political Life*; Fred Greenstein, *Children and Politics*; Gabriel Almond and Sidney Verba, *The Civic Culture*; Robert Dahl, *Who Governs?*; and Hans Morgenthau, *Politics Among Nations* (Bourque and Grossholtz 1974; Sapiro 1979; Tickner 1991).

Perhaps the most striking observation about the traditional behavioral political science literature is how seldom women are mentioned and how little serious and sustained attention is devoted to explaining their behavior. Regardless of whether women were physically present or absent among the population studied, they are invisible in much of the pre-feminist literature. Even when women were present among the subjects studied, and even when an examination of their experiences would have contradicted the main conclusions of a study (as, for example, Virginia Sapiro maintains would have been the case for Robert Dahl's *Who Governs?*), women were most often ignored (Sapiro 1979).

Nevertheless, a clear and coherent picture of women and their behavior emerges from works in the empirical canon, including several of the books mentioned above, that do explicitly (even if only briefly) examine women's behavior. The portrait is one of women as apolitical at worst and politically deficient at best. Women are portrayed as lacking in political interest and involvement (e.g. Berelson, Lazarsfeld, and McPhee 1954, 25; Campbell et al. 1960, 489–90). They have low political efficacy and belief systems that lack conceptual sophistication (e.g., Campbell et al. 1960, 490–2). They vote less often than men, and when they do vote, they tend to defer to and vote like their husbands (e.g., Campbell et al., 485–6, 492–3). They "personalize" politics, paying more attention to personalities than to issues (e.g., Greenstein 1965, 108; Almond and Verba 1963, 535). They are more conservative in their political preferences and voting (despite the fact that they vote like their husbands) (e.g., Almond and Verba 1963, 535) and less tolerant of left-wing polit-ical groups such as Communists and socialists (e.g., Stouffer 1955,131–55).

Feminist scholars have shown that this political portrait of women is based on research riddled with untested assumptions and methodological flaws (see especially Jaquette 1974; Bourque and Grossholtz 1974; Goot and Reid 1975). Because of the problems that characterize the analysis of women in much of this literature, it is impossible to ascertain fully the extent to which the research reflects an accurate portrayal of women's political behavior at the time and the extent to which the portrayal of women as far less politically engaged and sophisticated than men is a product of gender-related biases on the part of researchers. At a minimum, it seems fair to conclude that the assumptions and biases that are reflected in this research (as discussed below) led to an exaggerated portrayal of differences between women and men.

Early behavioral political scientists accepted unquestioningly the public-private split and the definition of woman as primarily oriented toward respon-sibilities and activities in the private sphere evident in much of Western polit-ical thought (Elshtain 1974). The family was viewed as a monolithic unit (Sapiro 1989; Goot and Reid 1975) with the male as the family head and dom-inant political representative. A woman's primary obligations were assumed to be to her roles as wife and mother. Men's political behavior became the norm against which women's political behavior was measured and found lacking (Bourque and Grossholtz 1974). These assumptions not only were untested, but also seem to have been accepted as "natural," with change in women's and men's roles viewed as either inconceivable or undesirable.

This series of interrelated assumptions affected both *what* questions were asked (and, more importantly, not asked) about women's political behavior and *how* women's political behavior was studied by pre-feminist behavioral political scientists. Because women were viewed as apolitical and oriented primarily toward the private sphere of home and family, findings about women's lower levels of involvement and interest in politics were not con-sidered problematic. Political scientists did not empirically investigate the question of why women in the general population did not show higher levels of engagement with politics; rather, they assumed they knew why. Similarly, the near-absence of women from positions in political elites, particularly as public officeholders, was not a question that intrigued or disturbed political sci-entists. Rather, the underrepresentation of women among political elites became a question worthy of investigation only after the advent of feminism both outside and inside the discipline.

The ways in which the assumptions of pre-feminist behavioral political scientists affected their work are even more evident when it comes to *how* women's political behavior was studied. Feminist critics have devoted con-siderable attention to showing that the application of supposedly objective research methods to the study of women's political behavior in the empirical canon was hardly value-free.

Feminists have pointed to a number of ways in which behavioral political scientists can be accused of practicing "bad science" in investigating women's attitudes and involvement. Several scholars have provided examples demonstrating that political scientists exaggerated or even misconstrued their findings to fit their preconceived notions about women's nature and the ways that women and men differ (e.g., Goot and Reid 1975; Bourque and Grossholtz 1974).

When researchers found legitimate differences between females and males, they almost always interpreted the differences in such a way as to make females appear apolitical. For example, Fred Greenstein asked children what they would do if they could change the world; he noted that girls were more likely to suggest "a distinctly nonpolitical change" such as "Get rid of all the criminals and bad people" (Greenstein 1965, 116; Bourque and Grossholtz 1974, 243). Similarly, Susan C. Bourque and Jean Grossholtz pointed out that findings of lower levels of political efficacy for women when compared with men were interpreted as a sign of men's political competence and women's incompetence. They suggested alternatively that such findings might reflect women's "perceptive assessment of the political process" and that perhaps men "express irrationally high rates of efficacy because of the limitations of their sex role which teaches them that they are masterful and capable of affecting the political process" (Bourque and Grossholtz 1974, 231).

Researchers sometimes asked questions which were clearly biased in such a way as to elicit responses that would construe males as political and females as apolitical. For example, Lynne B. Iglitzin, who examined questionnaires used in three classic political socialization studies (Greenstein 1965; Hess and Torney 1968; Andrain 1971), concluded that in many of the questions, "Politics is portrayed as a male-only world by the unvarying use of the male gender, the pictures chosen, and the limited and stereotyped choices of answers provided" (1974, 33).

Finally, political scientists engaged in a practice that Bourque and Grossholtz termed "fudging the footnotes" (1974). Bourque and Grossholtz found that some political scientists cited sources for statements about the political attitudes and behavior of women that, when checked, did not really say what had been attributed to them. For example, they noted how Robert Lane's contention in *Political Life* that political conflict between husbands and wives is usually resolved by the wife being persuaded by the husband was contradicted by the study he cited in support of his contention. Instead of persuasion by the husband, the study found mutual influence between husbands and wives and a tendency for children to follow the mother's partisan predisposition in cases where parents disagreed on political party preference (1974, 234–5). Bourque and Grossholtz provide other examples showing that early behavioral researchers sometimes "fudged the footnotes" by citing data from earlier studies without the qualifications and context that had accompanied them in the original text, thus misrepresenting the original findings.

While the "bad science" that characterized the examination of women's behavior in some of the classic studies can be corrected by eliminating the biases of the past and practicing "good science" in future research, some feminists have raised criticisms of behavioral political science research that are more fundamental and not nearly as easily addressed as are mere charges of bias. One of these critics is Jean Bethke Elshtain, who has claimed that the problem lies with an epistemology that separates facts and values. She has explained:

> The problem is more complex and fundamental than any charge of bias. *It is that every explanatory theory of politics supports a particular set of normative conclusions.* To have an explanatory theory, the analyst must adopt a framework linked, implicitly if not explicitly, to notions of human nature and human purposes. This framework sets the boundaries of the phenomena to be investigated. Some factors of social life will be incorporated, and others will be expunged from view before research begins (1979a, 242).

In Elshtain's view (a view shared by many other feminist political scientists), behavioral political science has adopted a framework that excludes much of what women do from political analysis and relegates most women to a private realm outside of politics. Elshtain has observed.

> Within mainstream political science, what has been described traditionally as politics tends to factor women out of the activity and has excluded for many years the questions raised by feminists. Such questions are relegated to a sphere outside organized political activity and are dismissed as private "troubles" (1979a, 243).

Like Elshtain, Barbara Nelson has also pointed to problems with both the epistemology and the content of political science. While acknowledging that many feminist political scientists would wish to retain the systematic study of events as one type of research, she has argued that feminist critics raise questions about "the universalism of the findings and disinterestedness and unconnectedness of the observer" that cannot be corrected simply by acknowledging or attempting to remove values or biases from empirical research (1989, 22). She has observed:

> The study of gender is revolutionary because it threatens the belief that most existing research is gender neutral and universalistic. In political science, like the. social sciences in general, women may not fit into existing social theories, which suggests that in many cases social knowledge believed to be cumulative may not be cumulative at all (1989, 22).

As for content, Nelson has concluded, based on her analysis of three popular introductory textbooks and two recent self-reflective volumes on the state of the discipline, that an overemphasis on electoral politics is one of the reasons why political science has devoted so little attention to women and their experiences. She has urged that as a discipline we must:

. . . include in the study of politics not only the recognition of the exclusion of women from what is traditionally political, but also the inclusion of politics in what women have traditionally done. We shall have gone a long way to creating a more inclusive political discourse if we give attention to families, communities, voluntary groups, social movements, and the welfare state, just to name a few topics. The discipline needs a two-fold strategy, emphasizing that all political subjects are gendered while also giving attention to those areas and concerns where women have traditionally put their political energy (1989, 21).

Feminist critiques of both the philosophical canon of political theory and the empirical canon of behavioral political science suggest that contemporary political scientists should regard much of what was written about women prior to the 1970s with skepticism. The pre-feminist empirical literature is so heavily influenced by assumptions about women's apolitical nature that it is difficult to separate scientific fact from fiction. The end result is that we know relatively little about women's political behavior prior to the development of feminist scholarship both because women were so seldom studied in any serious and sustained way, and because when they were studied, they were examined through a biased lens.

The feminist critiques of the empirical canon also provide evidence that a positivist epistemology can (and perhaps always does) mask an underlying set of normative assumptions about human nature and, in particular, about women's nature. Many feminist scholars within the discipline today are very wary of claims to objective, value-free research and universal truths. Their wariness stems, in part, from the discovery of strong biases in pre-feminist scientific research regarding women's political behavior. Their wariness also stems, in part, from the realization that women's absence from the subject matter of much behavioral research means that the universal truths supposedly being discovered through this research are, in fact, gendered—i.e., based on men's experiences of politics, not women's.

Finally, feminist critiques of the philosophical canon of political theory and the empirical canon of behavioral political science call into question our conception of politics with its foundation in the split between public and private life. Rather than take that split at face value, feminists have endeavored to analyze it historically and to show how a more critical conceptualization of it would significantly alter how we think about the meaning of citizenship and about women as citizens.

DEBUNKING THE MYTH OF THE INVISIBLE, APOLITICAL WOMAN

Much of the theoretical and empirical work undertaken by women and politics scholars during the 1970s and 1980s was aimed at making women visible in political theory and behavioral research and correcting the biases of the past; this type of work continues into the present. Women and politics scholars utilized existing disciplinary (and sometimes nongendered interdisciplinary) frameworks and approaches to examine both the portrayal of women in the works of major political theorists and women's political behavior at citizen and elite levels. These scholars attempted to dispel both the notion that women were apolitical beings and the idea that women's (and men's) roles in society were dictated by nature and thus immutable.

This body of women and politics literature is important because it demonstrates the importance of gender as a category of analysis within mainstream political theory and political science. However, it is also important for another reason. In subjecting women and women's experience to political analysis, in applying existing disciplinary frameworks and approaches to women, this research pointed to possible limitations and inadequacies in those frameworks and approaches. Focusing on women and women's experience in an attempt to fit women into the picture often revealed that important adjustments were necessary; women did not always fit simply and neatly into the existing picture. In some respects this research suggested that important material was left out and that the existing picture was only a partial representation of political reality; a wider-angle lens was needed. In other respects this research suggested that the picture itself needed to be recomposed in order to encompass women's experience.

In an effort to complicate the familiar image of public man and private woman, several feminist political theorists have rethought the development of the modern public sphere through the historical lens of women's political participation and experience. For example, Joan Landes (1988) has argued that the emergence of the bourgeois public sphere in enlightenment France cannot be understood adequately without attending to the enormous social influence of salon women in the Old Regime. No mere ornament to the Royal Court, the salon "belonged to a wider urban culture," and was "distinguished by its 'worldliness' and cosmopolitan character" (1988, 25). As key players in the "system of advancement for merit" (1988, 24), salon women were crucial to the social changes that brought about the demise of the landed aristocracy.

By making gender a central category of her analysis, Landes has enriched our understanding of the class struggles that altered the face of eighteenth-century Europe. She has shown that an ideology of female domesticity was crucial to the social ascendancy of the middle classes, and that the modern public sphere was historically constructed through the exclusion of women. When women and their interests are properly accounted for, Landes has argued, "enlightenment begins to look suspiciously like counterenlightenment, and revolution like counterrevolution" (1988, 204). The implications of her claim that the eighteenth-century citizen was not a generic but rather a gendered category are far-reaching: "the [contemporary] women's movement cannot 'take possession' of a public sphere that has been enduringly reconstructed along masculinist lines" (1988, 202).

The tension that Landes has located between political equality and sexual equality has been taken up by several other feminist theorists, who have been concerned to challenge conventional tales about the historical emergence of modern democracies. Mary Lyndon Shanley (1989) has pursued a similar line of investigation into Victorian debates about universal suffrage and female domesticity. Shanley has found that political women challenged nineteenth-century liberalism to live up to its promise of equal rights for all. While recognizing the failure of most Victorian feminists to question the sexual division of labor in the family and to advocate economic equality for the laboring masses, Shanley has also called our attention to how they exploited the tenets of liberal ideology to serve a wide range of progressive ends. In contrast to Landes, she has suggested that the contemporary women's movement can continue to do so.

One of the most important contributions of feminists who have integrated gender into their work on the origins of liberal society has been to highlight the tension between women as rights-bearing citizens and women as an oppressed sex-class. Some scholars have argued that this tension is the very motor behind liberal feminism and that it has the potential to radicalize the mainstream women's movement (Eisenstein 1981; Shanley 1989). As Zillah Eisenstein has observed:

> Liberal feminism involves more than simply achieving the bourgeois male rights earlier denied women, although it includes this. Liberal feminism is not feminism merely added onto liberalism. Rather, there is a real difference between liberalism and liberal feminism in that feminism requires a recognition . . . of the sexual-class identification of women as women. . . . This recognition of women as a sexual class lays the subversive quality of feminism for liberalism because liberalism is premised upon women's exclusion from public life on this basis. The demand for the real equality of women with men, if taken to its logical conclusion, would dislodge the patriarchal structure necessary to a liberal society (1981, 6).

In a later book, *Feminism and Sexual Equality* (1984), Eisenstein concluded that the more American liberal feminists radicalize their agenda in response to an unresponsive state—which has sought, at least since 1980, to curtail the most fundamental political demands brought by the mainstream women's movement (e.g., the ERA and abortion rights)—the more the tension between women as a sex-class and women as citizens would be exposed. Liberal feminists, in short, would be forced to recognize the limits of liberalism.

Other feminists have argued that the problem for liberal feminism lies in its appeal "to the bureaucratic apparatus of the state and of the corporate world to integrate women into the public sphere through programs seeking equal opportunity and affirmative action'" (Ferguson 1984, 4). This reliance on the bureaucratic state to obtain feminist ends, critics have maintained, is antithetical to an anti-hierarchical "vision of individual and collective life" (Ferguson 1984, 5; Elshtain 1981; Ruddick 1989; Denhardt and Perkins 1976).

Many feminists are wary about enhancing the power of a state whose surveillance capacities, they have argued, are cause for alarm. According to Carole Pateman, liberal feminism comes into an uneasy alliance with the state when it relies on the idea of the contract to promote social equality for women. In a time when "the influence of contract doctrine is extending into the last, most intimate nooks and crannies of social life," Pateman has written, feminists have every reason to worry about "the conjuncture of the rhetoric of individual rights and a vast increase of state power" (1988, 232). Pateman rejects the notion that the liberal discourse of rights alone can further feminist struggles for social, economic, and political equality. The putatively autonomous individual who has property in himself and who makes contracts, she has argued, has never applied fully to women. On the contrary, the proprietal self is a masculinist construction that has historically assumed and continues to assume men's property in women. For women, the freedom to contract has always been constrained by their sexual subordination to and economic dependence on men. Arguing that "a free social order cannot be a contractual order," Pateman has urged feminists to develop "other forms of free agreement through which women and men can constitute political relations" (1988, 232).

In contrast to the skepticism of those feminist political theorists who maintain that the women's movement cannot attain its goals of sexual equality through mainstream politics, many empirical feminist political scientists have suggested that women must enter the formal political arena in order to achieve equality. Thus, a significant body of empirical work conducted by women and politics scholars in the 1970s and 1980s focused on electoral politics. In particular, several of the first books to be published on women and politics focused on women public officials and party activists (e.g., Kirkpatrick 1974, 1976; Diamond 1977; Githens and Prestage 1977). Other early work focused on women's collective efforts to influence the policy-making process (e.g., Freeman 1975).

One of the primary tasks undertaken by the earliest research on women in political elites was that of challenging the near invisibility of women in the empirical canon of political science by demonstrating the presence of women among officeholders and activists. Thus, Jeane J. Kirkpatrick began the conclusion to her path-breaking study of 50 women state legislators serving in the early 1970s with the statement, "The most important finding of this study is that political woman exists" (1974, 217). Countering the image of women as apolitical, as by nature different from men, she then went on to assert that the political women she studied were similar in many respects to male politicians, in particular in their social backgrounds sod psychological characteristics (1974, 220). However, to reassure those who at the time might have thought that any woman similar to a male politician could not be "normal,". Kirkpatrick explained:

> . . . *"political woman" is not grossly deviant from her female peers.* She is not necessarily "masculine" in appearance or manner; she has not necessarily rejected traditional female roles and interests. Quite the contrary. The political women on

whom this book is based are . . . [almost all] wives and mothers. . . . Well-groomed, well-mannered, decorous in speech and action, these are "feminine" women in the traditional sex-stereotyped sense of that word (1974, 219).

When viewed from the perspective of the 1990s, Kirkpatrick's book, like other early empirical work on women and politics, appears cautious, conservative, and restricted in scope. However, when considered in its proper historical context, i.e., as a response to the invisibility and apolitical (or politically deficient) image of women within the existing behavioral political science research of the time, the importance and the (at least implicitly) challenging nature of *Political Woman* and other similar works are immediately apparent.

Women and politics scholars have attempted to make political women visible not only as individuals, but also as an organized, collective political force. Working within traditional disciplinary frameworks, women and politics scholars have analyzed both the feminist and anti-feminist movements and their successes and failures in affecting public policy outcomes (e.g., Freeman 1975; Costain 1980, 1982; Gelb and Palley 1982; Gelb 1989; Boles 1979; Mansbridge 1986; Mathews and De Hart 1990; Klatch 1987).

Like Kirkpatrick and others who studied women in political elites, women and politics scholars who studied mass political behavior conducted research that countered the image of women as apolitical or politically deficient. While some researchers continued to find evidence of notable differences between women and men in political orientations and behavior in the U.S. and other countries (e.g., Jennings and Farah 1980; Rapoport 1982, 1985), most researchers in the 1970s and early 1980s found little evidence that women in the United States differed greatly from men in their political orientations or behavior. In part, the findings of few sex differences in these studies resulted from the elimination of much of the gender bias which had influenced both the methodology and the interpretation of findings in earlier research and which had led to a portrayal of women as more politically different from men than they undoubtedly were. However, in part, the lack of significant sex differences in most of the studies conducted in the 1970s and 1980s also reflected actual changes in political behavior that had taken place as differences between men's and women's social roles, education, and employment decreased.

Research conducted in the 1970s and 1980s demonstrated that women were as likely or almost as likely as men to participate in political activities such as working in campaigns, writing letters to public officials, attending political meetings, and contributing money to candidates or parties (Hansen, Franz, and Netemeyer-Mays 1976; Welch 1977; Baxter and Lansing 1980; Beckwith 1986). In addition, Sandra Baxter and Marjorie Lansing found women in all age groups to be as interested as men in following campaigns—a finding that they noted "contrasts sharply with the myth of nonpolitical woman" (Baxter and Lansing 1980, 46). Research on childhood socialization conducted during the 1970s suggested that politically relevant differences between boys and girls also seemed to be few in number and limited primarily to political interest and knowledge (Orum et al. 1974; Sapiro 1983, 38).[1] Berenice A. Carroll, writing in 1979, summed up the feminist empirical research on women in American politics as follows:

> ... the picture which emerges is ... one ... of women holding political attitudes and engaging in political behaviors very similar to those of men, at all levels from school children to party activists and local officeholders. On almost all measures of voting, participation, efficacy, activism, ideology, and performance, sex differences between men and women, if present at all, are small (1979, 292).

In contrast to both the philosophical canon of political theory and the empirical canon of behavioral political science, which viewed differences between women and men as natural, women and politics scholars writing in the 1970s and 1980s generally attributed those sex differences which did occur to gender role socialization and/or adult gender roles. Differences between women and men, whether in elites or mass publics, were viewed as socially constructed and thus changeable rather than as natural and immutable. As the socialization of women and the opportunities and roles that were open to them in society changed, so too would their political behavior.

In this vein, studies of women's political orientations and participation examined the effects of education, finding increased education to be related to increased participation for women as well as to higher levels of political interest and efficacy (e.g., Sapiro 1983; Hansen, Franz, and Netemeyer-Mays 1976; Welch 1977; Baxter and Lansing 1983; Poole and Zeigler 1985). Working outside the home also was found to be related to women's involvement in conventional forms of participation. with employed women participating at rates similar to those of men, and women who were full-time homemakers participating at notably lower rates (Andersen 1975; Welch 1977, 724–5).[2] Finally, studies suggested that having children had an adverse effect on both political participation and various political orientations (Sapiro 1983, 177; Jennings and Niemi 1981, 296–7). The implication of these findings was that women's levels of participation would be likely to increase further as women increased their educational attainment, entered the labor force in larger numbers, spent a smaller proportion of their lives raising children, and received more help with child care. Thus, the few existing sex differences in political orientations and participation might well diminish as changes took place in women's roles and their socialization into those roles.

At the elite level, women and politics scholars devoted considerable attention to examining the question of why so few women held public office, and here, too, early feminist explanations often focused on gender role socialization and adult gender roles. Several studies focused on delegates to national party conventions and other party activists, who were considered a potential pool of future candidates for public office. These studies consistently found that women were less ambitious for public officeholding than their male counterparts (Jennings and Thomas 1968: Costantini and Craik 1977; Kirkpatrick 1976; Fowlkes, Perkins, and Rinehart 1979; Sapiro and Farah 1980; Jennings and

Farah 1981; Costantini and Bell 1984). Women's lower levels of political ambition were generally explained in terms of gender differences in political socialization and gender roles although the explanations were sometimes linked to lack of political opportunities. M. Kent Jennings and Barbara G. Farah, for example, observed, "For the present . . . cultural norms and structural conditions—especially the dual demands of homemaking and career plus inequities in the opportunity structure—continue to exert a dampening influence on the political life expectancies of women" (1981, 480).

The emphasis on gender role socialization and the effects of gender roles in explaining why few women held public office was prevalent in literature examining other politically active women as well. In a frequently cited study, Marcia Manning Lee examined the factors that kept women who were active in their communities from running for office. In addition to fear of sex discrimination, the two factors which held women back were their responsibility for care of young children (a factor that held few men back) and their perceptions of appropriate and inappropriate roles for women; most viewed holding public office as improper behavior for a woman (Lee 1976).

Research on women officeholders also emphasized the constraining effect of gender roles and gender role socialization (Diamond 1977; Stoper 1977; Mandel 1981). Kirkpatrick, for example, noted that traditional sex role requirements were the principal constraints preventing women from running for office. She observed that the women legislators in her study were remarkable precisely because they had managed to blend their political lives with traditional roles. She asked:

> If these women can do it, why can't/don't others? Perhaps because they lack high self-esteem and broad identifications, habits of participation, a desire to influence public policy, political skills needed to do so, a husband willing to cooperate, the empathy, flexibility, self-knowledge, and energy needed to live a busy and complicated life when so many less demanding alternatives are so readily available (1974, 240).

As this passage from Kirkpatrick's *Political Woman* illustrates, much of the literature stressing gender role socialization and gender roles implied that individual women themselves had to change their lives in order for women's representation in public office to increase. Observing this tendency in the literature, Berenice Carroll wrote in 1979, "There is still a heavy focus on sex-role socialization, with its implicit tendency to 'blame the victim' (or her mother) and to place on women the burden of changing sex roles without changing the system which requires the existing sex-role patterns, rewards those who conform to it, and punishes those who defy it" (1979, 306). Whether in response to this observation by Carroll and others or for other reasons, a change in emphasis occurred in the 1980s within the literature on political elites, especially that material dealing with the question of why women were underrepresented numerically among public officeholders. Many researchers turned their focus away from examining how gender role socialization and adult gender roles kept women from being more like the "political men" who held public office. Instead, they focused squarely on the operation of the political system itself as an explanatory variable helping to account for women's underrepresentation (e.g., Carroll 1985; Darcy et al. 1987).

These researchers demonstrated that the staying power of incumbents and the lack of winnable open seats are major obstacles to women's electoral success in the United States and elsewhere (Andersen and Thorson 1984; Darcy et al. 1987; Carroll 1985; Studlar et al. 1988). Electoral arrangements also are very important (see Rule and Zimmerman 1992; see also Welch and Studlar 1990 for a particularly good review of the research on the impact of electoral arrangements on women's electability). At the state legislative level in the U.S., women run in a greater proportion of multimember than single-member districts, and women who run in multimember districts win at a higher rate than those who run in single-member districts (Darcy et al. 1987, 119; Carroll 1985, 110; Rule 1990). Moreover, when states change from multimember to single-member districts as several states have done during the past three decades, the proportion of women running and winning decreases compared to national trends (Darcy et al. 1987, 119–22). Although differences in electoral arrangements are probably less important at the municipal level, there is evidence that women fare slightly better when cities have at-large rather than district elections (Darcy et al. 1987, 117–8; MacManus and Bullock 1989; Welch and Karnig 1979).[3]

Comparative research has demonstrated that women's representation in national legislatures is greater in countries with proportional representation, especially those utilizing party lists, than in countries like the U.S., which elect representatives on the basis of plurality voting (Randall 1987, 140–2; Rule 1981; Norris 1985; Lovenduski 1986; Haavio-Mannila et al. 1985). The institution and implementation of quotas for women on the party list for election within some European political parties has further enhanced women's representation in those countries (e.g., Dahlerup 1988, 297; Kolinsky 1991; Phillips 1991, 84–5).

Although this research on the effect of electoral arrangements on women's representation has been conducted utilizing the frameworks, approaches, and techniques of mainstream political science, it nevertheless has important normative implications for behavioral political scientists. Barbara Nelson was quoted earlier in this essay as suggesting, "all political subjects are gendered." Research on the effect of electoral arrangements provides a good example by showing that certain supposedly gender-neutral features of the way the political system operates systematically discriminate against women. Certainly, the existing electoral arrangements of the U.S. are not gender neutral, although the experience of some Western European countries with quota systems suggests that electoral systems can be altered to make them more so. Political analysis that deals with proposed reforms in electoral systems or procedures (e.g., term limits, campaign finance), or that uncritically accepts existing electoral arrangements without explicitly examining the gender implications of those reforms or arrangements, may well end up, however unintentionally, perpetuating women's exclusion from public officeholding.

Empirical studies of women's behavior at mass and elite levels have also posed challenges to what we study as political scientists and how we study it by calling attention to previously unexamined variables and by arguing that in some cases gender-specific models are necessary to better explain political behavior. Empirical studies of women and politics have devoted considerable attention to the ways that women's so-called private lives, especially their responsibilities and connections to partners and children, influence and constrain their behavior. While generally finding family-related factors to be more important for women than for men, some feminist scholars made another important discovery: men have families too! And those families seem to have a significant impact on men's as well as on women's behavior. For example, Diane Kincaid Blair and Ann R. Henry found that family problems are the major factor leading to retirement from office for men as well as women serving in state legislatures; previous research had attributed legislative turnover primarily to low salaries and had failed to investigate the possible importance of family-related variables (Blair and Henry 1981). Similarly, Sapiro found that conflicts between family commitments and public commitments, although resolved differently by the two sexes, were experienced at least as often by men as by women among partisan elites (Sapiro 1982). Thus, the empirical women and politics literature would suggest that the possible influence of so-called private life considerations be given more serious attention in future research on political behavior.

Although much of the research on women and politics has suggested that some variables have a more important influence on women's political behavior while others are more important for men, a few recent studies have taken this argument one stop further. These studies have suggested that the *process* and *calculus* of political decision making differs for women and men; some factors are more critical to women's decisions and other factors are more critical to men's. An example of such work is a study conducted by Linda L. M. Bennett and Stephen Earl Bennett examining gender differences in political interest and the impact of apathy on voting behavior. They concluded:

> . . . the process leading women to the voting booth differs from that of men. While men are motivated more out of interest and partisanship, age and SES are the prime determinants among women. The top political disposition discriminating among women is citizen duty. In short, while men went to the polls in 1984 mainly because they were interested, to the degree that political dispositions were involved in their calculus of voting, women went to the polls because they thought they ought to go (1989, 119).

There is evidence that women and men employ a different calculus not only in deciding whether to vote, but also in deciding how to vote. For example, Ethel Klein's analysis of 1980 election data indicated that the voting calculus of women and men was very different in that election, with women's rights issues influencing women's votes far more than they influenced men's (1984, 161–2). In a more recent study, Susan Welch and John Hibbing (1992) have demonstrated that economic considerations are less important in women's voting calculus than in men's; moreover, while men are more likely to vote on the basis of egocentric economic judgments, women more often utilize sociotropic economic considerations in making their voting decisions.

In a similar vein, Timothy Bledsoe and Mary Herring have argued that different factors affect the decisions of women and men serving on city councils regarding the pursuit of higher office. They have suggested, "If the situation of women in electoral politics is unique, the decision-making process for these women may be unique as well" (1990, 213). They found that the decisions of women were more likely than those of men to be influenced by the strength of their current political position and their self-perceptions of political vulnerability. However, women's decisions were not influenced by ambition; in fact, ambitious women were less likely than those without ambition to seek office. In contrast, men's decisions were little affected by their current circumstances but strongly affected by political ambition. In fact, ambition seemed to be the only variable that really mattered for men (1990).

Perhaps Janneke Van der Roe (1917) has carried the argument about differences in women's and men's political behavior and decision making further than anyone else. She has suggested that gender-specific explanatory models be used whenever relevant in behavioral studies, and she has taken the first steps toward developing such models.

Not all women and politics scholars agree on the desirability of creating sender-specific models of political behavior. Some would rather see the development of nongendered models that would encompass all of human behavior. Others would suggest that we should reject completely the idea of models that try to generalize across all or even half of humanity and move instead in the direction of greater historical, cultural, and situational specificity in our investigation of political behavior. Nevertheless, studies which suggest that we need gender-specific models of political behavior are important because they call into question the universality of our existing knowledge and reveal it to be rooted in men's experience. Although feminist scholars may not be in agreement over the desirability of universals, they most certainly are in agreement that current empirical knowledge does not adequately reflect women's experiences.

RETHINKING TRADITIONAL FRAMEWORKS AND ASSUMPTIONS

In recent years many women and politics scholars and feminist theorists have produced work that more explicitly confronts and challenges the dominant frameworks and assumptions of the discipline. Often influenced by the interdisciplinary perspectives of women's studies, these scholars have raised new questions and introduced new frameworks into the study of gender and politics. Their work suggests that we need to rethink and reconceptualize various approaches, assumptions, and concepts that are central to the discipline.

Empirically oriented feminist political scientists have challenged conventional definitions of politics by adopting an approach to their research that puts the perspectives of women and women's experiences at the center of their analysis. As one example, in contrast to earlier research that documented the effect that women's private lives had on their public lives but nevertheless did not question the basic assumption underlying much of western political thought and practice that life is, and can be, divided into public and private spheres, some recent research has through its focus on women's experiences called into question this assumption of a split between public and private life. For example, examining women state legislators' decisions to run for office and their private life situations, Susan L Carroll found no evidence of a split between public and private in these women's lives and suggested that we need a new conceptualization. Finding that women's personal life choices had affected public careers and that their public life choices had had an impact on their private life situations, Carroll concluded, "A dualistic conception of public and private as largely separate and mutually exclusive spheres of existence does not adequately portray the reality of these women's lives; rather, public and private in the lives of women officeholders seem to constitute a holistic system of interrelated social relations where any action taken or choice made has repercussions throughout the system" (1989, 63).

Although they have not focused as explicitly on the relationship between public and private, several other scholars have questioned dominant conceptions of politics by using women's perspectives as a point of departure for their analysis of politics. One example is Diane Fowlkes, who interviewed 27 white women activists with diverse political backgrounds. Fowlkes acknowledged that her purpose was "not to test theory but to present and explicate the political worlds of the diverse white women in this study," and that the generalizations that she drew from her interviews were "intended to explicate the various meanings that *these women* give to their political worlds and the various dynamics that shape their political actions" (1992, 27). As part of her study, Fowlkes allowed the women to speak in open-ended fashion about how they defined "the political." The ways in which these activists defined politics were both rich and varied. Some viewed the political as political scientists often do—as working for candidates for public office, holding office, governing, or advocating issues. However, others viewed the political in ways that suggested a broader or an alternative conception of politics—as linking the private and public spheres, as developing power to bring about change, and as bringing change through the lives they lead on a daily basis. While most of the women activists' conceptions touched in one way or another on the theme of power, Fowlkes noted that the themes of educating and consciousness-raising, perhaps less often considered to be part of politics by contemporary political scientists, also cut across their conceptions of politics (1992, 184–214). By allowing women to speak from their own perspectives in their own terms, Fowlkes's work suggests that the discipline of political science must expand its conception of politics if it is to encompass the ways that the women she interviewed think about the political.

Like Fowlkes, Cynthia Enloe in *Bananas, Beaches, and Bases* also used women's perspectives as a point of departure for rethinking politics—in this case international politics. Enloe noted that she "began this book thinking about Pocahontas and ended it mulling over the life of Carmen Miranda" (1990, xi). She readily admitted that:

> These women were not the sorts of international actors I had been taught to take seriously when trying to make sense of world affairs. But the more I thought about Pocahontas and Carmen Miranda, the more I began to suspect that I had been missing an entire dimension of international politics—I got an inkling of how relations between governments depend not only on capital and weaponry, but also on the control of women as symbols, consumers, workers and emotional comforters (1989, xi).

In some ways Cynthia Enloe's work does for international relations what the work of Jeane Kirkpatrick and others helped to do for American politics—it makes women visible. However, Enloe's work differs significantly from that of Kirkpatrick and others discussed earlier in this essay in that Enloe has not adopted the dominant assumptions and frameworks of work in political science; rather, she has set them aside and used instead the perspective of women's experiences, specifically the experiences of Pocahontas and Carmen Miranda, as her point of departure for examining international politics. She has examined some topics (e.g., nationalism, diplomacy, militaries, and international debt) that are familiar to those who study international politics. However, all have been analyzed through the lens of gender and from the perspective of women's experiences with them. Enloe has concluded:

> Conventional analyses stop short of investigating an entire area of international relations, an area that women have pioneered in exploring: how states depend on particular constructions of the domestic and private spheres. If we take seriously the politics of domestic servants or the politics of marketing fashions and global corporate logos, we discover that international politics is more complicated than non-feminist analysts would have us believe. We especially have to take culture—including commercialized culture—far more seriously (1939, 197).

Like Carroll, Fowlkes, and Enloe, scholars who have taken women's experiences as a starting point for their analyses but adopted a more historical approach have suggested that we need to rethink and reconceptualize the way we view politics. Much of what women have done historically has been viewed as "philanthropy" or "service" or "disorderly conduct," but it has rarely been seen as politics (Lebsock 1990, 35). In large part, this has been the result of the public/private split; men's activities have been viewed as public activities while women's have been seen as extensions of their domestic roles. Mary Beth Norton has described the transition that took place in the field of women's history, where scholars initially accepted a "male definition of politics," one clearly linked to the public/private split. Historians who focused on women's experiences quickly discovered that this definition was too narrow to encompass women's political activities. As Norton has explained, "Drawing on the feminist movement's insight that 'the personal is political,' women's historians broadened the category to include women's attempts to gain control over their own lives—both inside and outside marriage—and to have an impact on the society in which they lived" (1986, 40). Consistent with this redefinition of the "political," feminist historians focused on women's participation in voluntary associations, the temperance movement, the women's club movement, the social settlement movement, and the trade union movement among other activities (Norton 1986; Lebsock 1990). Political scientists might well look to the experience of their colleagues in history for guidance in constructing a more gender-inclusive conception of politics.

Some empirical work has moved in a direction similar to the direction suggested by women's history. One example is *Women and the Politics of Empowerment* (1988), edited by Ann Bookman and Sandra Morgen. This volume includes several case studies of the activism of working-class women. It examines the activities of women who are household workers, social service agency workers, hospital union workers, and clerical workers in an insurance office. Included in the volume are studies of women who organized a clerical union, fought to reopen a prenatal and gynecology clinic, organized to obtain better quality education for their children, and led a campaign to obtain improved neighborhood services. While many of these activities might well be considered outside the domain of politics as traditionally defined, the editors have argued that all are politically relevant. As they have explained:

> The articles on community organizing document the political meaning and breadth of women's efforts to transform urban space and public policy. In contrast to the popular view that sees these activities as "voluntary associations" or "mutual aid societies," these cases show women challenging the power of the state and the interests of landlords, developers, and other private institutions. These are certainly political activities (1988, 9–10).

In addition to challenging the ways in which political scientists have traditionally thought about politics, recent empirical work on women and politics has begun to use gender as a category of analysis for studying political structures and processes. This is a relatively new development because, as the previous sections of this essay illustrated, gender has generally been employed as a category of analysis only in studying the behavior of individuals. Perhaps the best example of the application of a gendered analysis to the study of political structures and processes is the recent work on the welfare state and welfare state formation (e.g., Gordon 1990; Sarvasy 1992; Nelson 1990; Diamond 1983). This research has demonstrated that the U.S. welfare state evolved in ways that were clearly gendered (Nelson 1990; Jenson 1990). For example, a two-channel welfare state developed in the U.S., one from the development of Mother's Aid, which was intended for women in the home who had lost their spouses, and the other from the development of Workmen's Compensation, which was intended for men who lost their pay because of work-related disabilities (Nelson 1990). This literature has also demonstrated that the welfare state reinforces inequities based on gender, race, and class at the same time that it provides material aid for those in need (Mink 1990). The welfare state is frequently portrayed as paternalistic and a means of exercising social control over women, but some have argued that it also constitutes a political resource which makes women more secure and less powerless than they otherwise would be (Piven 1990). Regardless, it is clear that the new feminist scholarship on the welfare state has challenged political scientists to think more seriously about the role that gender has played in its formation and operation.

Recent research on women's voting behavior and women in public office, while often employing the same behavioral methodologies that have traditionally characterized research on voting and officeholding, has nevertheless posed a new challenge to the discipline. While much of the earliest empirical research on women and politics worked to counter the image of women as different from men and to convince political scientists that women and men were in most respects politically similar, this new research challenges political scientists to think once again about gender difference. Unlike in its previous incarnation, in its new incarnation gender difference is generally viewed as an asset, not a deficiency; women are seen as bringing perspectives to politics which are currently lacking.

For example, scholars who have examined the so-called gender gap in voting behavior and public opinion have frequently attributed it to differences in women's and men's values and priorities (Conover 1988; Frankovic 1982; Shapiro and Mahajan 1986: Klein 1985; Norris 1985; Mueller 1988). Although they disagree about whether the gender gap is caused by women's greater pacifism, compassion for the needy, nurturance, feminism, commitment to the welfare state, or other qualities, feminist researchers have generally agreed that the gender gap is a manifestation of differing perspectives between women and men (Carroll 1988). Similarly, research on women in public office has found that women public officials give greater priority than men both to so-called women's issues and to issues related to women's traditional roles as care-givers in the family and in society more generally (Dodson and Carroll 1991; Carroll, Dodson, and Mandel 1991; Dodson 1991; Saint-

Germain 1989; Thomas 1991; Thomas and Welch 1991). The authors of these studies have suggested that women's greater involvement with policies in such issue areas as reproductive rights, violence against women, child care, health care, children's welfare, and education reflects the different experiences and perspectives that women bring to office with them. Moreover, the addition of these different experiences and perspectives to the policy-making process is viewed as a positive development that will enhance the overall quality of representation. Debra L. Dodson and Susan J. Carroll, for example, have argued:

> . . . significant change is taking place—change that has important long-term implications. As more women enter legislatures, the policy agenda is being reshaped to better reflect the concerns brought into the legislature by women. The end result is likely to be an agenda that is more responsive not only to the specific needs of women, but also to the needs of a broader cross-section of our society (including, for example, the economically disadvantaged, children and those who lack access to adequate health care)(1991, 94).

Empirically oriented political scientists who have examined the ways that women both as voters and as officeholders are bringing perspectives to politics that are currently underrepresented have been strongly influenced by the work of so-called "gender difference" theorists (e.g., Gilligan 1982; Chodorow 1978; Ruddick 1989) in women's studies. The work of Carol Gilligan on gender differences in moral reasoning has been especially important for many feminist political scientists. Taking on the scholarship in moral theory from Sigmund Freud to Lawrence Kohlberg, Gilligan challenged the claim that women achieve an attenuated stage of moral development in which "goodness is equated with helping and pleasing others" (1982, 18), and that women have therefore a stunted sense of justice (i.e., the capacity to make impartial judgments according to a set of universal rules). Curiously enough, Gilligan observed, "the very traits that traditionally have defined the 'goodness' of women, their care for and sensitivity to the needs of others, are those that mark them as deficient in moral development" (1982, 18). She drew on the work of Nancy Chodorow (1978) to argue that gender differences in moral reasoning are rooted not in biology but rather in childhood development, specifically in the contrasting relationships that boys and girls have to their primary care-giver, the mother. The abstract rules that govern men's moral reasoning, Gilligan held, reflect the achievement of masculine identity through a radical separation from the mother and the maintenance of firm ego boundaries. The context-based principles that govern women's moral reasoning reflect the achievement of feminine identity through a far less radical form of separation from the mother and the maintenance of empathetic relations to others.

Insofar as the traditional moral standard of impartiality takes for granted the masculine values of separateness and autonomy, wrote Gilligan, "women's failure to separate them becomes by definition a failure to develop [morally]" (1982, 9). Gilligan refuted the notion that the "quality of embeddedness in social interaction and personal relationships that characterize women's lives" was a "developmental liability" (1982, 9). She took that quality as an occasion to advance an alternative moral theory, one that would give legitimacy to women's "different voice":

> When one begins with the study of women and derives developmental constructs from their lives, the outline of a moral conception different from that described by Freud, Piaget, and Kohlberg begins to emerge and informs a different description of development. In this conception, the moral problem arises from conflicting responsibilities rather than from competing rights and requires for its resolution a mode of thinking that is contextual and narrative rather than formal and abstract. This conception of morality as concerned with the activity of care centers moral development around the understanding of responsibility and relationships, just as the conception of morality as fairness ties moral development to the understanding of rights and rules (1982, 19).

The argument that women have a different sense of morality grounded in a sense of everyday life and the web of human relationships (Belenky et al. 1986; Miller 1976; Gilligan 1982) has had a profound influence on the work of many feminist theorists who are concerned with challenging a wide variety of abstract models in the social sciences. As Sara Ruddick has put it in *Maternal Thinking*: "Given the value that is placed on abstraction in academic life, concreteness can become a combative insistence on looking, talking, and asking troublesome questions" (1989, 95).

Ruddick has maintained that "abstraction is central to militarist thinking." Like several other feminists working in the area of peach studies, she has argued that realism, as it is articulated by defense intellectuals, is grounded in universal rules of human behavior which assume that "people and nations will, if they can, dominate and exploit those who are weaker" (Ruddick 1989, 179; Elshtain 1987; Cohn 1987; Enloe 1989). Similarly, Jean Bethke Elshtain has written that the realist model of "professionalized IR discourse" focuses exclusively on the abstract entities called states and ignores the most material facts of human life: "No children are ever born, and nobody ever dies, in this constructed world. There are states, and they are what is" (1987, 91).

Both Elshtain and Ruddick have argued that women's experience, and especially maternal experience, provides the basis for political resistance to authoritarian regimes and for peach activism in democratic countries. Each has insisted that women's role in the maintenance of life offers a vital model of civic participation which treasures "the connectedness of self and other" (Ruddick 1989, 225). For example, the famous resistance of the Madres of Argentina challenges us to rethink conventional notions of peace politics and, not least, of femininity. Ruddick has observed:

> In their protests, these women fulfill traditional expectations of femininity and at the same time violate them. . . . Women who bring to the public plazas of a

police state pictures of their loved ones, like women who put pillowcases, toys, and other artifacts of attachment against the barbed wire fences of missile bases, translate the symbols of mothering into political speech. Preservative love, singularity in connection, the promise of birth and the resilience of hope, the implacable treasure of vulnerable bodily being—these cliches of maternal work are enacted in public. . . . They speak a "woman's language" of loyalty, love, and outrage; but they speak with a public anger in a public place in ways they were never meant to do (1989, 229).

Clearly not all feminists espouse the model of "maternal thinking" or social feminism advanced by Ruddick and Elshtain, and some are intensely critical of it. The lively feminist debate over what is called "gender difference" turns in large part on the skepticism some critics have toward any effort to revalue women's traditional role in the family. Mary Dietz has argued that maternal thinking not only overvalues motherhood and the intimate relations of kin, but also devalues the relations among total strangers or mere acquaintances which are the very basis of large representative democracies. The good mother does not necessarily make the good citizen, and "the bond among citizens is not like the love between a mother and child" (1985, 31; Ferguson 1984). As "citizens are not intimately, but politically involved with each other," writes Dietz, "we look in the wrong place for a model of democratic citizenship if we look to the family" (1985, 31).

Perhaps the most difficult of balancing acts for feminist scholars is how to account for and give value to women's experience without reproducing socially ascribed gender roles. Still, many scholars worry that, so long as gender differences carry social significance, feminists downplay those differences at their peril. Feminist scholarship has clearly shown how the notion that "we are all just people" translates in political science discourse, not to mention in social practices, into "we are all just men." As Susan Moller Okin has argued in her most recent work, *Justice, Gender, and the Family*, gender-neutral language in contemporary political theory effaces the material reality of sexual inequality and reproduces "theories of justice [which], like those of the past, are about men with wives at home" (1989, 13). Like Ruddick, Gilligan, and Elshtain, Okin is critical of theories of justice that offer "some abstract 'view from nowhere'" (1989, 15). Like Dietz, however, she cannot accept the argument that " 'justice' and 'rights' are masculinist ways of thinking about morality that feminists should eschew or radically revise, advocating a morality of care: (1989, 15). For one thing, the evidence that women have a different way of moral reasoning is debatable at best; for another, feminists who make such a claim, all disclaimers notwithstanding, risk playing into the familiar "stereotypes that justify separate spheres" (Okin, 1989, 15).

The legal theorist Martha Minnow has captured the problem we have been describing as follows: "Both focusing on and ignoring difference risk recreating it. This is the dilemma of difference" (1984, 160). Negotiating the "difference dilemma" has been a particularly delicate matter in the area of feminist legal studies (Eisenstein 1988; MacKinnon 1987; Bower 1991). In an essay on the sex-discrimination suit brought by the Equal Employment Opportunity Council in 1978 against the Sears, Roebuck & Company, the historian Joan Scott usefully summarized the "equality-versus-difference" conundrum as follows:

> When difference and equality are paired dichotomously, they structure an impossible choice. If one opts for equality, one is forced to accept the notion that difference is antithetical to it. If one opts for difference, one admits that equality is unattainable. . . . How then do we recognize and use notions of sexual difference and yet make arguments for equality? The only response is a double one: the unmasking of the power relationship constructed by posing equality as the antithesis of difference, and the refusal of its consequent dichotomous construction of political choices (1988, 172).

This is a difficult and tall order for feminist scholars. But Scott has insisted that to avoid treating masculinity and femininity as if they were unchanging essences, feminists must ask: "How are differences being constructed" in specific social, historical, and discursive contexts? (1988, 173).

Scott's suggestion that a "power relationship" is concealed in the difference/equality opposition has been forcefully argued by the feminist legal theorist Catherine MacKinnon. In *Feminism Unmodified*, MacKinnon has called for "a shift in perspective from gender as difference to gender as dominance" (1987, 44). What is taken as women's difference from men, she has maintained, is really the difference created through women's social, political, and economic subordination to men. Sexual difference is at bottom an unequal power relationship between women and men, one whose feminist dismantling is not a matter of asserting women's moral superiority; it is rather a matter of politics. Like Scott, MacKinnon has insisted that feminists need to challenge the idea that sexual difference is *the* fundamental social difference, and that they need to refuse the choice between difference and sameness:

> To define the reality of sex as difference and the warrant of equality as sameness is wrong on both counts. Sex, in nature, is not a bipolarity; it is a continuum. In society it is made into a bipolarity. Once this is done, to require that one be the same as those who set the standard—those which one is already socially defined as different from—simply means that sex equality is conceptually designed never to be achieved. Those who most need equal treatment will be the least similar [e.g., poor women], socially, to those whose situation sets the standard as against which one's entitlement to be equally treated is measured (1988, 44).

So-called "sex equality," according to MacKinnon, is an oxymoron. To be sexed is to be a woman (or rather a wo-man) and to be a woman is to be unequal. As long as sexual difference remains unquestioned, social equality for women will remain impossible.

The only way out of the difference dilemma, these critics have argued, is to refuse sexual difference (man versus woman) and to affirm instead what Zillah Eisenstein has termed "the plurality of differences among women" (1988, 223). In *The Female Body and the Law,* she has called for "a radical pluralist and feminist theory of equality," one that would "recognize the specificity of the female body and the variety of ways this is expressed: individually (as in differences of health, age, body strength, and size) and in terms of a woman's race and economic class" (1988, 222). Eisenstein has taken up the most monolithic of all representations of the female body, the pregnant body, and has radically redeployed it throughout her book to undercut the sameness/difference opposition:

> A middle-class, black, pregnant woman's body is not one and the same as a working-class, white, pregnant woman's body. The pregnant body of a woman in her midthirties is not identical to the pregnant body of a woman in her early twenties. A welfare woman's pregnant body may not be the same as an upper-middle-class woman's pregnant body. [And so forth.] (1988, 222–223).

What Eisenstein has called for is a far more complicated approach to the very category of women and of sexual difference than that which has been advanced thus far in the scholarly literature on women and politics. She has asked feminists, in effect, to question the very terms that they use in their work because those terms tend to reproduce the very thing that feminists want to critique: sexual inequality. If one is a woman, surely that is not all that one is. And those other race and class identities (to name but two) shape how one experiences being a woman and—this is crucial—how one is seen by others as a woman. African-American women are not (and have not been) seen as "women" in the same way that white women are seen (hooks 1981; Spelman 1988). Working-class women are not (and have not been) viewed as "women" in the same way that domesticated middle-class women are viewed (Riley 1988; Zerilli 1993). We shall have more to say about the category "women" in our concluding section.

Another problem for feminist scholars who wish to advance a gender-sensitive approach to politics but are wary of monolithic claims about "women's difference" is how to theorize "women's experience." Nancy Hartsock has tackled this problem in her influential work on "feminist standpoint theory." Hartsock wanted to develop an epistemology and a theory of power that would take account of gender differences without universalizing them. She distinguished:

> ... between what Sara Ruddick has termed "invariant or *nearly* unchangeable" features of human life, and those that, despite being *"nearly* universal" are "certainly changeable." Thus that women and not men *bear* children, is not (yet) a social choice, but that women and not men rear children ... is clearly a social choice (1985, 223).

Hartsock read women's experience through the lens of Marxist historical materialism. She argued that it is not enough to talk about "women's standpoint," their sense of interconnectedness with others and with nature (*pace* Gilligan, Ruddick, or Elshtain); rather, one must examine the development of a "feminist standpoint" as it emerges in the context of political activism, that is to say, its "achieved character" and "liberatory potential" (Hartsock 1983, 232).

Hartsock's approach has the advantage of thinking through not only how women's experiences shape their political consciousness but also how their political consciousness shapes their experiences as women. It thus broaches the question of how feminine identity is socially constructed and radically challenged through political activism. Rather than treat "women's experience" as if it were a stable and unified category, she has called for a political analysis of how the experience of "being a woman" is given meaning in and through the political practices of feminism.

SOME THOUGHTS ON CHALLENGES FOR THE 1990s

We have argued that a persistent problem for feminist scholars has been how to develop alternative theoretical and empirical models that would take into account women's experiences and perspectives, but that would avoid both reproducing socially ascribed gender differences and effacing the social diversity among women. For these reasons, the category of women has come under question in the work of some feminist scholars.

Yet feminists have good reason to worry about throwing into question the very category that has enabled both their collective resistance to oppression and their scholarship. Giving voice to women "as women" in social life and political practice has been absolutely crucial for contesting women as invisible, apolitical, or simply as the (deficient) other from men. As Elizabeth Spelman has written, "Feminists have long been aware of the levels at which male privilege operates to erase women's lives and perspectives from view" (1988, 4). "Nevertheless," she has added, "our distancing ourselves from the views of blatant sexists keeps us from recognizing the extent to which we may in fact share elements of their views" (1988, 5). That is to say, feminists also often have a blind spot in their research—one that ignores other categories of social difference (e.g., class, race, and sexual orientation) by working with the category of women as *if* it encompassed the experiences of all women. "This," Spelman has said, "leads us to the paradox at the heart of feminism":

> Any attempt to talk about all women in terms of something we have in common undermines attempts to talk about the differences among us, and vice versa. Is it possible to give the things women have in common their full significance without thereby implying that the differences among us are less important? How can we describe those things that differentiate women without eclipsing what we share in common? (1988, 3).

In our view, Spelman formulates precisely the key dilemma confronting feminist political science today. While enormous strides have been made by feminist scholars, few would doubt that there is still much work to be done. Can that work be accomplished if we treat the differences among women as if they were as significant as what women have in common? How can one make women visible, not to mention challenge the frameworks that render them invisible, if one overly complicated the term "women" that makes the feminist project possible?

There are, needless to say, no easy answers to these questions despite the fact that they are, in our view, some of the most important questions confronting feminist political scientists, and indeed feminist scholars across all disciplines, in the early 1990s. Nevertheless, in this concluding section, we would like to suggest why feminist scholars ought to keep asking these questions, to offer some possible ways of beginning to think through them, and to indicate why we think these questions are important to the discipline.

The first reason why feminists do well to interrogate the category (women) that seems at first glance to be the theoretical foundation of their own research concerns the matter of what is meant by "what women have in common as women." In her book, *Feminist Theory: from Margin to Center,* bell hooks has pondered this very phrase as follows:

> A central tenet of modern feminist thought has been the assertion that "all women are oppressed." This assertion implies that women share a common lot, that factors like class, race, religion, sexual preference, etc. do not create a diversity of experience that determines the extent to which sexism will be an oppressive force in the lives of individual women. Sexism as a system of domination is institutionalized but it has never determined in an absolute way the fate of all women in this society (1984, 5).

This "ideology of 'common oppression'" (1984, 8), hooks has argued, is based on a "one-dimensional perspective on women's reality"—a white, heterosexual, middle-class woman's perspective (1984, 3). When feminists invoke phrases like women's oppression, women's experience, and women's difference, they "conflate the condition of one group of women with the condition of all women and . . . threat the differences of white middle-class women as if they were not differences" (Spelman 1988, 3). The term "women," in other words, effaces the diversity of its purported social referent; its true referent is a far more partial social reality.

As we argue in more detail below, even when feminists try to take account of women's diversity by factoring into their analyses such variables as race and class, they do not tackle properly the problem of the category of women that we have been describing. Just as feminists have shown that one cannot treat gender as a mere variable, neither can one treat race and class as mere variables. Just as feminists have shown that to make gender an analytic category of their research is to rethink traditional political science frameworks, so do critics like Spelman (1988), hooks (1984), Evelyn Brooks Higginbotham (1992), Patricia Hill Collins (1989), and Julianne Malveaux (1990) insist that when race and class are treated as analytic categories of feminist theory, then existing feminist frameworks themselves must be rethought.

For some feminist political theorists, this rethinking has entailed the development of new strategies for interrogating historical and contemporary inscriptions of sexual difference which examine the lived relation of social subjects to socio-symbolic configurations of masculinity and femininity (Brown 1988; Lorraine 1990; Di Stefano 1991; Zerilli 1991; Zerilli 1993). As Christine Di Stefano has written recently, "gender must be approached as simultaneously 'real' and 'false'; that is, as a set of representations that (in conjunction and tension with other representations [e.g., of race and class]) creates a world of fixed, yet also unstable, meanings, relations, and identities, which simultaneously produce and do violence to specific subjects in specific ways" (1991, xiv). The challenge for feminists, she argues, is to disrupt cultural representations of an incommensurable sexual difference which organize "the world 'as if' women stood in a derivative (but also opposed) relation to 'man'" (1991, xiv), and, we would add, "as if" that relation were not only immutable but also more socially significant than the relations of race and class.

The instability of the category "women" and of naturalized sexual difference, as demonstrated in the works of feminist theorists, has important implications not only for political theorists, but also for more empirically oriented political scientists. Although these implications will become clearer as the debate over the category "women" continues to play itself out over the next several years, we can put forth a few preliminary observations from the vantage point of the early 1990s.

The work of feminist theorists suggests that researchers in the 1990s should be more cautious and self-reflective about their use of the category "women" than they have been in the past. Most empirical work focusing on women or gender (or even including sex as a control variable) has assumed that the category "women" has an inherent political meaning, that there is something politically relevant, most commonly "interests" (see Sapiro 1981 for a discussion of issues involved in defining women's interests), that all women share. Most empirical researchers believe that by controlling statistically for variables such as race, age, income, and education, they can isolate and measure the effects due to gender. However, applying statistical controls to isolate the effects of gender is not sufficient to deal with the problem of the category "women" as it is posed by feminist theorists. Rather, feminists who have interrogated the category "women" question whether such gender effects, free from the influence of other confounding variables, exist at all—whether there is any commonality, any essence, or even any interests that all women share after variations in their race, age, education, income, and the like are taken into consideration. Instead, they suggest that race, class, and gender, for example, are so intertwined that all work together to shape identity (or, in this case, political identity). Women exist in an historical and cultural context, and to erase or ignore this context is to gloss over important differences among women.

What does this actually mean for those who do empirical research? First, it means that we should be less concerned with comparing women with men and more concerned with examining how different subgroups of women in different contexts behave politically. If we take the critiques of the category "women" seriously, our research is likely to become more contextual and more historical. It will make visible those women (e.g., women of color, poor women) whose experiences are often erased in the pursuit of scientific generalizations that purportedly apply to all women. Taking seriously critiques of the category "women" will likely move us in the direction of reducing our knowledge claims and our pursuit of universal truths. It will make us less likely to generalize across women (or men) of differing classes, races, cultures, nationalities, ethnicities, or generations. However, what we sacrifice in our ability to generalize (which those who theorize about the category of women would suggest has led only to false or misleading generalizations anyway) will be more than made up for in the depth and richness of our analysis and our understanding.

While empirical researchers who are sensitive to critiques of the category "women" may well become more reflective and self-conscious in their use of the term and more contextual and culturally specific in their approach to research, there are, as we noted earlier, good reasons for researchers not to abandon fully the category that has enabled their work. By using the category "women," feminist political scientists have been able to call into questions some of the central assumptions and frameworks of the discipline. The concerted focus by feminists on women and women's experience has helped us as a discipline to see the biases and the blinders that characterized pre-feminist work and to improve our knowledge base by correcting for these biases and removing the blinders. In the same way, the current feminist interrogation of the category "women" may lead to research that will expand and improve our disciplinary knowledge base through greater historical and cultural specificity and more attention to heretofore neglected segments of the population. A major task for women and politics scholars in the 1990s will be to work through the many questions surrounding the category "women," perhaps finding some middle ground between uncritical acceptance and total abandonment of the category. In doing so, feminist scholars are likely to continue to pose new and important challenges to the discipline of political science.

NOTES

We would like to thank Ada Finifter, Virginia Sapiro, Barbara Crow, Kathleen Casey, and an anonymous reviewer for their careful readings and constructive suggestions regarding this essay.

1. More recent research has suggested that we should not be so quick to discount the impact of childhood socialization in producing politically relevant differences between girls and boys. (See for example, Bennett and Bennett 1989; Owen and Dennis 1988.)
2. More recent research suggests the relationship between working outside the home and political participation may be less straightforward than once thought. For example, McDonagh (1982) has argued that social status variables are more important than employment per se, and Andersen and Cook (1985) failed to find a short-term impact from entry into the paid work force although their findings pointed to the possibility of a long-term impact.
3. In contrast to the results for women, multimember districts and at-large voting systems have been found in many cases to disadvantage African Americans and Latinos. See Parsons (1991) and Fraga (1991) for reviews of this research. Unfortunately, most of the research on women and minorities has not examined the effects of electoral systems on women of color. Notable exceptions are: Karnig and Welch (1979), who found that African-American women do about as well in at-large as in district municipal elections, indicating that the findings for women (dominated by whites) and minorities (dominated by men) cannot be assumed to be true for minority women; Welch and Herrick (1992), who found that African-American, Latino, and white women all fare slightly better with at-large municipal electoral systems, although other factors are more important than electoral structures in explaining the representation of all three groups of women; and Rule (1992), who found that multimember state legislative districts benefit both African-American and white women.

BIBLIOGRAPHY

Ackelsberg, Martha, and Irene Diamond. 1987. "Gender and Political Life: New Directions in Political Science." In *Analyzing Gender: A Handbook of Social Science Research,* ed. Beth B. Hess and Myra Marx Ferree. Newbury, California: Sage.

Almond, Gabriel, and Sidney Verba. 1963. *The Civic Culture.* Princeton: Princeton University Press.

Amundsen, Kirsten. 1971. *The Silenced Majority: Women and American Democracy.* Englewood Cliffs: Prentice Hall.

Andersen, Kristi. 1975. "Working Women and Political Participation, 1952–1972." *American Journal of Political Science* 19:439–53.

Andersen, Kristi, and Elizabeth Cook. 1985. "Women, Work, and Political Attitudes." *American Journal of Political Science* 29:606–25.

Andrain, Charles F. 1971. *Children and Civic Awareness.* Columbus: Merrill.

Baxter, Sandra, and Marjorie Lansing. 1980. *Women and Politics: The Invisible Majority.* Ann Arbor: University of Michigan.

Beckwith, Karen, 1986. *American Women and Political Participation: The Impacts of Work, Generations, and Feminism.* New York: Greenwood.

Belenky, Mary Field et. al. 1986. *Women's Ways of Knowing: The Development of Self, Voice, and Mind.* New York: Basic Books.

Bennett, Linda L. M., and Stephen Earl Bennett. 1989. "Enduring Gender Differences in Political Interest: The Impact of Socialization and Political Dispositions." *American Politics Quarterly* 17:105–22.

Berelson, Bernard R., Paul F. Lazarsfeld, and William N. McPhee. 1954. *Voting*. Chicago: University of Chicago Press.

Blair, Diane Kincaid, and Ann R. Henry. 1981. "The Family Factor in State Legislative Turnover." *Legislative Studies Quarterly* 6:55-68.

Bledsoe, Timothy, and Mary Herring. 1990. "Victims of Circumstances: Women in Pursuit of Political Office." *American Political Science Review* 84:213–23.

Boals, Kay. 1975. "Review Essay: Political Science." *Signs* 1:161–74.

Boles, Janet K. 1979. *The Politics of the Equal Rights Amendment: Conflict and the Decision-Making Process*. New York: Longman.

Bookman, Ann, and Sandra Morgen. 1988. *Women and the Politics of Empowerment*. Philadelphia: Temple University Press.

Bourque, Susan C., and Jean Grossholtz. 1974. "Politics an Unnatural Practice: Political Science Looks at Female Participation." *Politics and Society* 4:225–66.

Bower, Lisa C. 1991. "'Mother in Law': Conceptions of Mother and the Maternal in Feminism and Feminist Legal Theory." *Differences: A Journal of Feminist Cultural Studies* 3:20–38.

Brennan, Teresa, and Carole Pateman. 1979. "Mere Auxiliaries to the Commonwealth: Women and the Origins of Liberalism." *Political Studies* 27:183–200.

Brown, Wendy. 1988. *Manhood and Politics: A Feminist Reading in Political Theory*. Totowa, NJ: Rowman & Littlefield.

Campbell, Angus, Philip Converse, Warren Miller, and Donald Stokes. 1960. *The American Voter*. New York: Wiley.

Carroll, Berenice A. 1979. "Political Science, Part I: American Politics and Political Behavior." *Signs* 5:289–306.

Carroll, Susan J. 1985. *Women as Candidates in American Politics*. Bloomington: Indiana University Press.

Carroll, Susan J. 1988. "Women's Autonomy and the Gender Gap: 1980 and 1982." *In The Politics of the Gender Gap: The Social Construction of Political Influence*, ed. Carol M. Mueller. Newbury Park, CA: Sage.

Carroll, Susan J. 1989. "The Personal Is Political: The Intersection of Private Lives and Public Roles Among Women and Men in Elective and Appointive Office." *Women and Politics* 9:51–67.

Carroll, Susan J., Debra L. Dodson, and Ruth B. Mandel. 1991. *The Impact of Women in Public Office: An Overview*. New Brunswick, NJ: Center for the American Woman and Politics.

Chodorow, Nancy. 1978. *The Reproduction of Mothering: Psychoanalysis and the Sociology of Gender*. Berkeley: University of California Press.

Clarke, Lorenne M. G., and Lynda Lange. 1979. *The Sexism of Social and Political Theory: Women and Reproduction from Plato to Nietzsche*. Toronto: University of Toronto Press.

Cohn, Carol. 1987. "Sex and Death in the Rational World of Defense Intellectuals." *Signs: Journal of Women in Culture and Society* 12:687–718.

Collins, Patricia Hill. 1989. "The Social Construction of Black Feminist Thought." *Signs* 14:745–73.

Conover, Pamela Johnston. 1988. "Feminists and the Gender Gap." *Journal of Politics* 50:985–1010.

Costain, Anne N. 1980. "The Struggle for a National Women's Lobby." *Western Political Quarterly* 33:476–91.

Costain, Anne N. 1982. "Representing Women: The Transition from Social Movement to Interest Group." In *Women, Power and Policy*, ed. Ellen Boneparth. New York: Pergamon Press.

Costantini, Edmond, and Kenneth H. Craik. 1977. "Women as Politicians: The Social Background, Personality, and Political Careers of Female Party Leaders." In *A Portrait of Marginality*, ed. Marianne Githens and Jewel L. Prestage. New York: McKay.

Costantini, Edmond, and Julie Davis Bell. 1984. "Women in Political Parties: Gender Difference in Motives Among California Party Activists." In *Political Women: Current Roles in State and Local Government*, ed. Janet Flammang. Beverly Hills: Sage.

Dahl, Robert. 1961. *Who Governs?* New Haven: Yale University Press.

Dahlerup, Drude. 1988. "From a Small to a Large Minority: Women in Scandinavian Politics." *Scandinavian Political Studies* 11:275–98.

Darcy, R., Susan Welch, and Janet Clark. 1987. *Women, Elections, and Representation.* New York: Longman.

De Lauretis, Teresa. 1987. *Technologies of Gender: Essays on Theory, Film and Fiction.* Bloomington: Indiana University Press.

Denhardt, Robert B., and Jan Perkins. 1976. "The Coming Death of Administrative Man." *Women in Public Administration* 36:379–84.

Diamond, Irene. 1977. *Sex Roles in the State House.* New Haven: Yale University Press.

Diamond, Irene, ed. 1983. *Families, Politics, and Public Policy: A Feminist Dialogue on Women and the State.* New York: Longman

Dietz, Mary G. 1985. "Citizenship with a Feminist Face: The Problem with Maternal Thinking." *Political Theory* 13:19–37.

Di Stefano, Christine. 1991. *Configurations of Masculinity: A Feminist Reading in Modern Political Theory.* Ithaca, NY: Cornell University Press.

Dodson, Debra L. 1991. *Gender and Policymaking: Studies of Women in Office.* New Brunswick, NJ: Center for the American Woman and Politics.

Dodson, Debra L., and Susan J. Carroll. 1991. *Reshaping the Agenda: Women in State Legislatures.* New Brunswick, NJ: Center for the American Woman and Politics.

DuBois, Ellen Carol, Gail Paradise Kelly, Elizabeth Lapovsky Kennedy, Carolyn W. Korsmeyer, and Lillian S. Robinson. 1985. *Feminist Scholarship: Kindling in the Groves of Academe.* Urbana: University of Illinois Press.

Duverger, Maurice. 1955. *The Political Role of Women.* Paris: UNESCO.

Eisenstein, Zillah. 1981. *The Radical Future of Liberal Feminism.* New York: Longman Press.

Eisenstein, Zillah. 1984. *Feminism and Sexual Equality: Crisis in Liberal America.* New York: Monthly Review Press.

Eisenstein, Zillah. 1988. *The Female Body and The Law.* Berkeley: University of California Press.

Elshtain, Jean Bethke. 1974. "Moral Woman and Immoral Man: A Consideration of the Public-Private Split and Its Political Ramifications." *Politics and Society* 4:453–73.

Elshtain, Jean Bethke. 1979a. "Methodological Sophistication and Conceptual Confusion: A Critique of Mainstream Political Science." *In The Prism of Sex: Essays in the Sociology of Knowledge*, ed. Julia A. Sherman and Evelyn Tort Beck. Madison: University of Wisconsin Press.

Elshtain, Jean Bethke. 1981. *Public Man, Private Women: Women in Social and Political Thought.* Princeton: Princeton University Press.

Elshtain, Jean Bethke. 1987. *Women and War.* New York: Basic Books.

Enloe, Cynthia. 1990. *Bananas, Beaches and Bases: Making Feminist Sense of International Politics.* Berkeley: University of California Press.

Ferguson, Kathy E. 1984. *The Feminist Case Against Bureaucracy.* Philadelphia: Temple University Press.

Figes, Eva. 1970. *Patriarchal Attitudes.* Greenwich: Fawcett.

Firestone, Shulamith. 1970. *The Dialectic of Sex.* New York: Bantam.

Fowlkes, Diane L. 1992. *White Political Women: Paths from Privilege to Empowerment.* Knoxville: University of Tennessee Press.

Fowlkes, Diane, Jerry Perkins, and Sue Tolleson Rinehart. 1979. "Gender Roles and Party Roles." *American Political Science Review* 73:772–80.

Fraga, Luis Ricardo. 1991. "Latinos in State Elective Office: Progressive Inclusion in Critical Perspective." In *Women, Black, and Hispanic State Elected Leaders,* ed. Susan J. Carroll. New Brunswick, NJ: Eagleton Institute of Politics.

Frankovic, Kathleen A. 1982. "Sex and Politics—New Alignments, Old Issues." *PS: Political Science & Politics* 15:439–48.

Freeman, Jo. 1975. *The Politics of Women's Liberation.* New York: Longman.

Gelb, Joyce. 1989. *Feminism and Politics: A Comparative Perspective.* Berkeley: University of California Press.

Gelb, Joyce, and Marian Lief Palley. 1982. *Women and Public Policies.* Princeton: Princeton University Press.

Gilligan, Carol. 1982. *In a Different Voice: Psychological Theory and Women's Development.* Cambridge: Harvard University Press.

Githens, Marianne, and Jewel L. Prestage, eds. 1977. *A Portrait of Marginality: The Political Behavior of the American Woman.* New York: McKay.

Goot, Murray, and Elizabeth Reid. 1975. *Women and Voting Studies: Mindless Matrons or Sexist Scientism?* Sage Professional Papers in Contemporary Political Sociology, no. 8. London: Sage.

Gordon, Linda, ed. 1990. *Women, the State, and Welfare.* Madison: University of Wisconsin Press.

Grant, Rebecca. 1991. "The Sources of Gender Bias in International Relations Theory." In *Gender and International Relations,* ed. Rebecca Grant and Kathleen Newland. Bloomington: Indiana University Press.

Greenstein, Fred. 1965. *Children and Politics.* New Haven: Yale University Press.

Halliday, Fred. 1991. "Hidden from International Relations: Women and the International Arena." In *Gender and International Relations,* ed. Rebecca Grant and Kathleen Newland. Bloomington: Indiana University Press.

Hansen, Susan B., Linda M. Franz, and Margaret Netemeyer-Mays. 1976. "Women's Political Participation and Policy Preferences." *Social Science Quarterly* 56:576–90.

Hartsock, Nancy C. M. 1985. *Money, Sex, and Power: Towards a Feminist Historical Materialism.* Boston: Northeastern University Press.

Hasvio-Mannila, Elina et al. 1985. *Unfinished Democracy: Women in Nordic Politics.* Oxford: Pergamon Press.

Hess, Robert D., and Judith V. Torney. 1968. *The Development of Political Attitudes in Children.* Garden City, NY: Doubleday Anchor.

Higginbotham, Evelyn Brooks. 1992. "African-American Women's History and the Metalanguage of Race." *Signs* 17:251–74.

hooks, bell. 1981. *Ain't I a Woman: Black Women and Feminism.* Boston: South End Press.

hooks, bell. 1984. *Feminist Theory: From Margin to Center.* Boston: South End Press.

Iglitzin, Lynne B. 1974. "The Making of the Apolitical Woman: Femininity and Sex-Stereotyping in Girls." In *Women in Politics,* ed. Jane S. Jaquette. New York: Wiley.

Jaquette, Jane S. 1974. "Introduction." In *Women in Politics,* ed. Jane S. Jaquette. New York: Wiley.

Jennings, M. Kent, and Norman Thomas. 1968. "Men and Women in Party Elites: Social Roles and Political Resources." *Midwest Journal of Political Science* 12:469–92.

Jennings, M. Kent, and Barbara G. Farah. 1980. "Ideology, Gender and Political Action: A Cross-National Survey." *British Journal of Political Science* 10:219–40.

Jennings, M. Kent, and Barbara G. Farah. 1981. "Social Roles and Political Researches: An Over-Time Study of Men and Women in Party Elites." *American Journal of Political Science* 25:462–82.

Jennings, M. Kent, and Richard G. Niemi. 1981. *Generations and Politics: A Panel Study of Young Adults and Their Parents.* Princeton: Princeton University Press.

Jenson, Jane. 1990. "Representations of Gender: Policies to 'Protect' Women Workers and Infants in France and the United States before 1914." In *Women, the State, and Welfare,* ed. Linda Gordon. Madison: University of Wisconsin.

Jones, Kathleen B., and Anna G. Jonasdottir. 1988 "Introduction: Gender as an Analytical Category in Political Theory." In *The Political Interests of Gender,* ed. Kathleen B. Jones and Anna G. Jonasdottir. London: Sage.

Karnig, Albert, and Susan Welch. 1979. "Sex and Ethnicity in Municipal Representation." *Social Science Quarterly* 60:465–81.

Kirkpatrick, Jeane J. 1974. *Political Woman.* New York: Basic Books.

Kirkpatrick, Jeane J. 1976. *The New Presidential Elite: Men and Women in National Politics.* New York: Russell Sage Foundation.

Klatch, Rebecca E. 1987. *Women of the New Right.* Philadelphia: Temple University Press.

Klein, Ethel. 1984. *Gender Politics.* Cambridge: Harvard University Press.

Klein, Ethel. 1985. "The Gender Gap: Different Issues, Different Answers." *The Brookings Review* 3:33–7.

Kolinsky, Eva. 1991. "Women's Quotas in West Germany." *Western European Politics* 14:56–72.

Landes, Joan B. 1988. *Women and the Public Sphere in the Age of the French Revolution.* Ithaca, NY: Cornell University Press.

Lane, Robert. 1959. *Political Life.* New York: The Free Press.

Lebsock, Suzanne. 1990. "Women and American Politics, 1880–1920." In *Women, Politics, and Change,* ed. Louise A. Tilly and Patricia Gurin. New York: Russell Sage Foundation.

Lee, Marcia Manning. 1976. "Why Few Women Hold Public Office: Democracy and Sex Roles." *Political Science Quarterly* 91:296–314.

Lorraine, Tamasin E. 1990. *Gender, Identity, and the Production of Meaning.* Boulder, CO: Westview Press.

Lovenduski, Joni. 1981. "Toward the Emasculation of Political Science: The Impact of Feminism." In *Men's Studies Modified: The Impact of Feminism on the Academic Disciplines,* ed. Dale Spender. Oxford: Pergamon Press.

Lovenduski, Joni. 1986. *Women and European Politics: Contemporary Feminism and Pub-

lic Policy. Amherst: University of Massachusetts Press.

MacKinnon, Catherine A. 1987. *Feminism Unmodified: Discourses on Life and Law.* Cambridge: Harvard University Press.

MacManus, Susan A., and Charles S. Bullock III. 1989. "Women on Southern City Councils: A Decade of Change." *Journal of Political Science* 17:32–49.

Mahowald, Mary. 1978. *Philosophy of Women: Classical to Current Concepts.* Indianapolis: Hacket.

Malveaux, Julianne. 1990. "Gender Difference and Beyond: An Economic Perspective on Diversity and Commonality among Women." *In Theoretical Perspectives on Sexual Difference,* ed. Deborah L. Rhode. New Haven: Yale University Press.

Mandel, Ruth B. 1981. *In the Running.* New York: Ticknor and Fields.

Mansbridge, Jane J. 1986. *Why We Lost the ERA.* Chicago: University of Chicago Press.

Mathews, Donald G., and Jane Sherron De Hart. 1990. *Sex, Gender, and the Politics of ERA: A State and the Nation.* New York: Oxford University Press.

McDonagh, Eileen L. 1982. "To Work or Not to Work: The Differential Impact of Achieved and Derived Status upon the Political Participation of Women, 1956–1976." *American Journal of Political Science* 26:280–97.

Miller, Jean Baker. 1976. *Toward a New Psychology of Women.* Boston: Beacon.

Mink, Gwendolyn. 1990. "The Lady and the Tramp: Gender, Race, and the Origins of the American Welfare State." In *Women, the State, and Welfare,* ed. Linda Gordon. Madison: University of Wisconsin.

Minnow, Martha. 1984. "Learning to Live with the Dilemma of Difference: Bilingual and Special Education." *Law and Contemporary Problems* 48:157–211.

Morgenthau, Hans J. 1948. *Politics Among Nations.* New York: Knopf.

Mueller, Carol M., ed. 1988. *The Politics of the Gender Gap: The Social Construction of Political Influence.* Newbury Park, CA: Sage.

Nelson, Barbara J. 1989. "Women and Knowledge in Political Science: Texts, Histories, and Epistemologies." *Women & Politics* 9:1–25.

Nelson, Barbara J. 1990. "The Gender, Race, and Class Origins of Early Welfare Policy and the Welfare State: A Comparison of Workmen's Compensation and Mother's Aid." In *Women, Politics, and Change,* ed. Louise A. Tilly and Patricia Gurin. New York: Russell Sage Foundation.

Norris, Pippa. 1985. "The Gender Gap in Britain and America." *Parliamentary Affairs* 38:192–201.

Norton, Mary Beth. 1986. "Is Clio A Feminist? The New History." *New York Times Book Review,* April 13.

O'Brien, Mary. 1981. *The Politics of Reproduction.* Boston: Routledge & Kegan Paul.

Okin, Susan Moller. 1979. *Women in Western Political Thought.* Princeton: Princeton University Press.

Okin, Susan Moller. 1989. *Justice, Gender, and the Family.* New York: Basic Books.

Orum, Anthony, Roberta Cohen, Sherri Grasmuck, and Amy W. Orum. 1974. "Sex, Socialization and Politics." *American Sociological Review* 39:197–209.

Owen, Diana, and Jack Dennis. 1988. "Gender Differences in the Politicization of American Children." *Women & Politics* 8:23–43.

Pateman, Carole. 1980a. "The Disorder of Women: Women, Love, and the Sense of Justice." *Ethics* 91:20–34.

Pateman, Carole. 1980b. "Women and Consent." *Political Theory* 8:149–68.

Pateman, Carole. 1988. *The Sexual Contract.* Stanford: Stanford University Press.

Persons, Georgia A. 1991. "Blacks in State Elective Office: The Continuing Quest for Effective Representation." In *Women, Black, and Hispanic State Elected Leaders*, ed. Susan J. Carroll. New Brunswick, NJ: Eagleton Institute of Politics.

Phillips, Anne. 1991. *Engendering Democracy.* University Park, PA: Pennsylvania State University.

Piven, Frances Fox. 1990. "Ideology and the State: Women, Power, and the Welfare State." In *Women, the State, and Welfare*, ed. Linda Gordon. Madison: University of Wisconsin Press.

Poole, Keith T., and L. Harmon Zeigler. 1985. *Women, Public Opinion, and Politics.* New York: Longman.

Randall, Vicky. 1987. *Women and Politics: An International Perspective.* 2nd ed. Chicago: University of Chicago.

Randall, Vicky. 1991. "Feminism and Political Analysis." *Political Studies* 39:513–32.

Rapoport, Ronald B. 1982. "Sex Differences in Attitude Expression: A Generational Explanation." *Public Opinion Quarterly* 46:86–96.

Rapoport, Ronald B. 1985. "Like Mother, Like Daughter: Intergenerational Transmission of DK Response Rates." *Public Opinion Quarterly* 49:198–208.

Riley, Denise. 1988. *Am I That Name? Feminism and the Category of "Women" in History.* Minneapolis: University of Minnesota Press.

Ruddick, Sara. 1989. *Maternal Thinking: Towards a Politics of Peace.* Boston: Beacon Press.

Rule, Wilma. 1981. "Why Women Don't Run: The Critical Contextual Factors in Women's Legislative Recruitment." *Western Political Quarterly* 34:60–77.

Rule, Wilma. 1990. "Why More Women Are State Legislators." *Western Political Quarterly* 43:437–48.

Rule, Wilma. 1992. "Multimember Legislative Districts: Minority and Anglo Women's and Men's Recruitment Opportunity." In *United States Electoral Systems: Their Impact on Women and Minorities*, ed. Wilma Rule and Joseph F. Zimmerman. New York: Praeger.

Rule, Wilma, and Joseph F. Zimmerman, eds. 1992. *United States Electoral Systems: Their Impact on Women and Minorities.* New York: Praeger.

Saint-Germain, Michelle A. 1989. "Does Their Difference Make a Difference? The Impact of Women on Public Policy in the Arizona Legislature." *Social Science Quarterly* 70:956–68.

Sapiro, Virginia. 1979. "Women's Studies and Political Conflict." *In The Prism of Sex: Essays in the Sociology of Knowledge*, ed. Julia A. Sherman and Evelyn Tort Beck. Madison: University of Wisconsin Press.

Sapiro, Virginia. 1981. "Research Frontier Essay: When Are Interests Interesting? The Problem of Political Representation of Women." *American Political Science Review* 75:701–16.

Sapiro, Virginia. 1982. "Private Costs of Public Commitments or Public Costs of Private Commitments? Family Roles Versus Political Ambition." *American Journal of Political Science* 26:265–79.

Sapiro, Virginia. 1983. *The Political Integration of Women: Roles, Socialization, and Politics.* Urbana: University of Illinois.

Sapiro, Virginia. 1987. "What Research on the Political Socialization of Women Can Tell Us About the Political Socialization of People." In *The Impact of Feminist Research in the Academy*, ed. Christie Farnham. Bloomington: Indiana University Press.

Sapiro, Virginia. 1989. "Gender Politics, Gendered Politics: The State of the Field." Presented at the annual meeting of the Midwest Political Science Association, Chicago.

Sapiro, Virginia, and Barbara G. Farah. 1980. "New Pride and Old Prejudice: Political Ambitions and Role Orientations Among Female Partisan Elites." *Women & Politics* 1:13–36.

Sarvasy, Wendy. 1992. "Beyond the Difference Versus Equality Policy Debate: Postsuffrage Feminism, Citizenship, and the Quest for a Feminist Welfare State." *Signs* 17:329–62.

Saxonhouse, Arlene W. 1985. *Women in the History of Political Thought: Ancient Greece to Machiavelli.* New York: Praeger.

Scott, Joan Wallach. 1988. *Gender and the Politics of History.* New York: Columbia University Press.

Shanley, Mary L. 1982. "Marriage Contract and Social Contract in Seventeenth-Century English Political Thought." In *The Family in Political Thought,* ed. Jean Bethke Elshtain. Amherst: University of Massachusetts Press.

Shanley, Mary L. 1989. *Feminism, Marriage, and the Law in Victorian England, 1850–1895.* Princeton: Princeton University Press.

Shanley, Mary L., and Victoria Schuck. 1974. "In Search of Political Woman." *Social Science Quarterly* 55:632–44.

Shapiro, Robert Y., and Harpreet Mahajan. 1986. "Gender Differences in Policy Preferences: A Summary of Trends from the 1960s to the 1980s." *Public Opinion Quarterly* 50:42–61.

Spelman, Elizabeth V. 1988. *Inessential Woman: Problems of Exclusion in Feminist Thought.* Boston: Beacon Press.

Stoper, Emily. 1977. "Wife and Politician: Role Strain Among Women in Public Office." In *A Portrait of Marginality,* ed. Marianne Githens and Jewel L. Prestage. New York: McKay.

Stouffer, Samuel A. 1955. *Communism, Conformity and Civil Liberties.* Garden City, NY: Doubleday.

Studlar, Dooley T., Ian McAllister, and Alvaro Ascui. 1988. "Electing Women to the British Commons: Breakout from The Beleaguered Beachhead?" *Legislative Studies Quarterly* 13:515–28.

Thomas, Sue. 1991. "The Impact of Women on State Legislative Policies." *Journal of Politics* 53:958–76.

Thomas, Sue, and Susan Welch. 1991. "The Impact of Gender on Activities and Priorities of State Legislators." *Western Political Quarterly* 44:445–56.

Tickner, J. Ann. 1991. "Hans Morgenthau's Principles of Political Realism: A Feminist Reformulation." In *Gender and International Relations*, ed. Rebecca Grant and Kathleen Newland. Bloomington: Indiana University Press.

Van der Ros, Janpeke. 1987. "Class, Gender, and Participatory Behavior: Presentation of a New Model." *Political Psychology* 8:95–123.

Welch, Susan. 1977. "Women as Political Animals: A Test of Some Explanations for Male-Female Political Participation Differences." *American Journal of Political Science* 21:711–30.

Welch, Susan, and Albert K. Karnig. 1979. "Correlates of Female Office Holding in City Politics." *Journal of Politics* 41:478–91.

Welch, Susan, and Donley T. Studlar. 1990. "Multi-Member Districts and the Representation of Women: Evidence from Britain and the United States." *Journal of Politics* 52:391–412.

Welch, Susan, and Rebekah Herrick. 1992. "The Impact of At-Large Elections on the Representation of Minority Women." In *United States Electoral Systems: Their Impact on Women and Minorities,* ed. Wilma Rule and Joseph F. Zimmerman. New York: Praeger.

Welch, Susan, and John Hibbing. 1992. "Financial Conditions, Gender, and Voting in American Elections." *Journal of Politics* 54:197–213.

Zerilli, Linda M. G. 1991. "Machiavelli's Sisters: Women and the 'Conversation' of Political Theory." *Political Theory* 19:252–76.

Zerilli, Linda M. G. 1993. *Signifying Culture and Chaos: Women in Rousseau, Burke, and Mill.* Ithaca, NY: Cornell University Press.

5

Normative versus Empirical Theory and Method

Rory O'Brien

FROM *THEOREIN* TO THEORY: AN INTRODUCTION

Political science has long been divided as a discipline over the differences between normative and empirical pursuits. Although both rely on theory, the ways in which empirically oriented researchers develop and use theoretical constructs is distinct from the methodology of political theory. Essentially there are two ways that normative and empirical theory building can be seen as differing from one another. In the first place, empirical research is oriented towards finding out about "what is," while normative enquiry is concerned with questions about "what ought to be." Political scientists themselves often argue over whether one is more important than the other. Secondly, a distinction is sometimes drawn between "theory" and "practice," with the implication being that theoretical considerations and conclusions might not have any true practical application. Although it is generally acknowledged by practitioners of the discipline that much of the important work that has been done in the study of politics since the 1960s has either focused on, or owes a great debt to, political thought, the applied study of politics at the same time has been nearly obsessed with its ability to both develop and answer empirical questions.[1]

In terms of method, the political theorist works in a world of relationships between concepts, while the empirical researcher operates in the realm of observables. This distinction underscores the significant differences between these two modes of thought. Historically, most of our knowledge about politics has come from theorists or philosophers. Long before the application of modern methodologies and statistical analyses, political thinkers studied the social order using both the normative and the empirical. Thus, philosophers have been free to develop ideas, for example, about human nature, ethics, "the good life," and justice. All of these conceptually oriented pursuits have helped to inform the empirical research process, for without some form of theoretical framework as their source, we would have no reasons, no justification, for supporting our hypotheses.

Now that we have the ability to pursue our empirical questions through the use of scientific experimentation and sophisticated computer-based data analysis, we can reliably discover answers to our questions about the political world. And, through the answering of our empirical questions we can hope to come closer to a greater understanding of what *ought to be*. Performing optimally, empirically oriented research, then, effectively aids the political scientist by providing the basis for deriving normative conclusions that inform us as to how things *should* be. At the same time, the normative theorist makes reference to what *is* as well as what ought to be as a method for developing prescriptive statements. Normative considerations generally have at their root a question regarding how society might *best* be organized, resulting in a discussion of how society might *ideally* be organized, under the best of circumstances. This feature of normative theory alone distinguishes this pursuit from empirical theory building, but does not in any way imply that our theories cannot have direct application to our understanding of politics.

The most important influence on political philosophy in the western tradition certainly comes from the Greeks. Plato's work has had a tremendous impact on how we view society. In theoretical terms, Plato was an *idealist*, which means that he articulated a philosophy based on the notion that reality was established in a different realm from the world we experience through our senses. In other words, Plato's view of the political order was based on an *ideal* that he created. Although Plato offered his prescriptions to society, he believed that it was probably impossible to attain the ideal in anything experienced on the material level, and that the best we can hope for is to come somewhat closer to it. Since Plato's time, few other political theorists have shared his position in terms of the ideal, but they continued to search for universal generalizations.

Theory Defined

Theory may be defined in many different ways. Surprisingly, theory often means different things depending on the purpose for which it is being employed. Dictionary definitions of the word include "a coherent group of several propositions used as principles of explanation for a class of phenomena" and "a proposed explanation whose status is still conjectural."[2] The Greeks used the word *theorein* (from which we derive our word *theory*), to mean how we look at or contemplate something. In fact, we construe theory, in many instances, to mean a conceptual framework for viewing a social structure or social relationship. For instance, theories are often created so as to better view or understand some aspect of society such as power, or how power is distributed. By focusing on the logical consistencies and inconsistencies of the way power is distributed in society we get a better idea about both what power is and the social relationships to which it pertains.

Political theorists help to provide us with a "symbolic picture of an ordered whole." [3] Instead of just thinking about or looking at discreet portions of the social order, the theorist strives to develop a view of society in its entirety. Through the development of this comprehensive view of society, the theorist is able to do two things: (1) create mental constructs, or models, which we can use to better understand the society in which we live, and (2) critique society by finding out what works and does not work in terms of political ideas, public policies, and political institutions. Working with models of political behavior, the theorist is able to create testable hypotheses. Then, critically examining society, the theorist builds the foundation for our understanding of the social order. It is through the process of critical thinking that we most often find solutions to problems and avenues for the development of alternatives in order to make society better.

At the same time, a theoretical framework can be employed in a manner consistent with our desire to find out how successful, or unsuccessful, earlier ideas about society have been. Consider the following examples: (1) Aristotle highlights his discovery that those constitutions that are not well adapted to the culture of the society from which they arise may be doomed to failure; (2) Thomas Hobbes's concern is that without an authoritarian power structure, a social order quickly breaks down; and (3) Karl Marx views the exploitation of labor under capitalism as irrational.[4] In cases such as these, the political theorist is critiquing society on the broadest, as well as on the most fundamental levels. Theory, then, gives us the opportunity to take a wide rather than a narrow view of society, a long-term versus a short-term view, and to step outside of the structure of our own experience in an attempt to gain greater knowledge about the political realm.

In this chapter, we will argue that although there are useful distinctions to be made in terms of empirical and normative theory building, the actual differences between these two are, in the main, illusory. Typically, political scientists debate the work of theorists on the grounds that political thought is based on certain *nonfalsifiable* assumptions. In other words, empirically oriented political scientists believe that it is impossible for the theorist to test and reject the premises on which they base their arguments. But the fundamental assertions made by theorists are no less falsifiable than are the claims made by the empirically oriented researcher. Empirical projects rest on tenets that are not questioned in a systematic fashion by the social scientist, any more than the foundational aspects of philosophy are questioned by the theorist. Furthermore, as will be discussed below, the theorist works in a world of logical relationships, and, thus, relies in many instances on a more rigorous method of truth testing than does the empiricist.

TRUTH AND ITS CONSEQUENCES

All theory building is ultimately about testing. No theory is created without an end in sight. In other words, theories are made to be tested. The empirical researcher seeks to test the strength or weakness of his or her hypotheses, and the theorist wishes to test the validity of her premises, or assertions. But either way, what might be called a "reality test" is performed. And, in all cases, testing is done in the context of our pursuit of knowledge, or "truth." Just as the empirical researcher can adjust his or her theory upon realizing the weakness of a proposed relationship between variables, so can the theorist tinker with the model, and thus, make it a more realistic reflection of society.

Truth is tested by one of three methods. They are: (1) fact, or observation; (2) subjective values; or (3) logic. Empirically oriented political scientists tend to believe that political theorists work only in a world of subjectivity and value judgments and universals, that, in other words, theory concerns itself only with how an ideal society might always be structured. While it is accurate to characterize political theory as being vitally interested in the normative, the empiricist fails to realize that the analytical theorist operates on the basis of logic. The main methodological difference between theorists and empiricists is that theorists apply logic to questions that have to do with the political order, while empiricists rely on observation and measurement.

The empirical researcher is interested in causal relationships, and tests the "truth" of assertions on the basis of the strength of hypotheses. On the other hand, the political theorist tests the truth of propositions through the application of analytical reasoning. Whereas the social scientist may acknowledge a logic inherent in the research process, it is logic itself that forms the basis for the assertions made by theorists.

The point here is that there are consequences for the ways in which we test our theories. Traditionally, normative work is seen as different from empirical research on the basis of how fundamental assertions are tested. Essentially, the question revolves around the falsifiability of propositions. The empirically oriented social scientist generally sees the project of political theory as one in which basic assertions are not open to the same tests as hypotheses. While theorists undoubtably utilize certain assumptions, so do empirical scientists.

The Fact/Value Distinction

Western scientific methodology has long been based on the distinction between what meets the criteria as being *fact* and that which is construed as *value*. Fact, for the purposes of scientific enquiry, is generally defined as that which can be observed. In other words, facts are what we know about a particular phenomena on the basis of our observation, or experience. This definition raises substantial epistemological questions for philosophers. Epistemology is the theory of knowledge and comprises an entire subfield in philosophy. On even the simplest level, it is easy for us to imagine situations in which reliance on experience alone might confuse or mislead us. Once we begin asking *how* we know *what* we think we know, we run into tremendous problems in terms of using observables as the basis of fact.

At least since the seventeenth century with the work of René Descartes, Western philosophy has been suffused with the underlying notion that our senses can often fool us. In his *Meditations*, Descartes carefully details the ways in which our impressive sensory array (sight, hearing, etc.), allows us to form pictures of the world that may not always be accurate.[5] By relying on our experiences alone we restrict our ability to have any certainty whatsoever about the phenomena we encounter.

Setting aside the problem with facts derived from our sensory experience for the moment, the real controversial aspect of theory, in the minds of empiricists, has been the distinction between observation and subjective judgment. Value has been derided by science as being subjective rather than objective in nature, and has been accorded a level of respect far below that of fact defined on the basis of observation. In evaluating things like social phenomena, political theorists often place them on a scale. When assigning *value,* we make a judgment as to which things are better or worse, and, to the empirically oriented scientist, this sort of behavior is undesirable because value judgments are not only subjective in nature but they are also treated as universals.

All value judgments are seen by the empiricist as either subjective or personal opinion. While data analysis is accepted as a form of subjective reflection, empirical theories are not assumed to be based upon subjective knowledge or opinion. For this reason social science generally views the ideas or models constructed by political theorists as suspect, in that they are often developed through referencing subjective information. In actuality, truth for the political theorist depends on the logical consistency of his or her arguments, and thus, even though based on subjective reflection, is still valid in terms of potentially being consistent with findings in the real world.

Empirical scientists act as theorist in that they lay a groundwork for their hypotheses. But they most often suggest relationships between variables on the basis of prior observation, which is accepted as fact. This is what political scientists mean when they speak of the deductive method of reasoning moving from general conclusions to specific cases. Using facts, the empirically oriented scientist arranges his or her variables in a hypothetical relationship, a statement about how the component elements fit together.

The hypothesis thus developed is then utilized in order to conduct a truth test using specific cases. The truth test is a way to find out if there are reasons to support, or reject, the proposed relationship between variables. The objective testing of hypotheses is a fundamental method for establishing the strength of the relationship proposed by the statement itself. The rigorous social scientist uses the most effective means at her disposal to create a scientifically drawn, representative sample to which some method of testing is applied. Whether the testing method is experimental in nature or survey-based makes little difference as long as the method relies on observables. At the end of the test, quantifiable bits of information are tabulated and cross-tabulated and then analyzed in order to come to some sort of conclusion. This is essentially the project of empirical research.

This methodology can be critiqued on the basis of two fundamental elements. First, the premises for belief in empirical hypotheses can be questioned. On what does the researcher base his or her knowledge about the relationship between variables? If the theory that drives the empirical research project depends merely on observations, it is not much of a theory at all. A collection of conclusions, taken only from various observations, would never serve to fuel empirical social science research. Theory must always, then, depend on the subjective reflection and values of the researcher.

Second, there is a more serious set of questions that arise in consideration of the statistical methods used by social scientists. Statistics is based on the theory that we can learn about the behavior of a large group on the basis of what we know about a small group. This is called *sampling theory,* and it gives rise to the notion that if scientists gather information in the proper manner about a small group of people, they can use that information to tell them something about the larger social group that those individuals came from. Sampling allows social scientists to test small, manageable groups, as it is generally more difficult to measure, or test, a very large group, called a *population.*

The "leap of faith" in statistical theory is to believe that what you discover about a sample drawn from a population is also applicable to the population itself. Said differently, if you were to find that 52 percent of a sample group to which you had administered a survey thought that the government was corrupt, you could conclude (with some great precision in terms of standard deviation and the measurement of confidence level) that some number relatively close to 52 percent of the larger population from which the sample was drawn thought the same way, provided that the sample drawn was a scientific one—that is, it was based on a level of confidence, which then determines probability and the margin of error.

Inductive and Deductive Logic

Political theorists utilize logic so as to gain a greater understanding of the relationship between two variables. Whereas political science, in general, relies on inductive reasoning to drive its research projects, the theorist relies more often on the use of deductive logic. At this point it may be helpful to consider how political scientists define these terms. *Inductive reasoning* is a form of *probable inference* and involves the process of developing scientific generalizations (sometimes called *theories*) from the observation of many cases. Theorists are concerned with testing for *truth*, or conclusions based on complete evidence. But, as conclusive evidence is not always available, the political scientist relies on partial or inferred evidence based on probability. In philosophical terms, an inference, "which from true premises gives us conclusions which are true in most cases, is called probable."[6] *Deductive reasoning* is a process that moves from universal generalizations toward particular cases.

Let us examine the process of inductive reasoning in more detail. As was stated earlier, inductive reasoning is the process of creating generalizations on the basis of knowledge gained about many particular cases. Suppose we were interested in the effect that socioeconomic level has on ideological position. If we had no clear ideas about how these two separate things, or variables, are related, we could go out and measure the socioeconomic levels of many different people and then measure how those same people voted on a variety of political issues. This would form a "real world" test for our very broad and unformed ideas about a particular social phenomena. We could then analyze our findings in an attempt to discover some sort of pattern in terms of voting and socioeconomic level. Let's imagine that we discovered that people of a lower socioeconomic status generally took more liberal views on the social issues on which we focused. We could then develop a certain amount of confidence in there actually being a relationship between low socioeconomic level and liberal positions on those issues.

Based on the knowledge we had gained about the particular cases, we might be able to develop a *generalization* about the relationship between our variables, meaning that we would expect other particular cases to conform to what we had previously observed. On the basis of this expectation, we can infer rules about behavior from what we have studied. Generalizations allow us to use a mental shorthand to better understand groups, institutions, and nations, and they also allow us to predict behavior in the future. We develop generalizations that we believe have application in situations similar to those we have already encountered.

However, generalizations often turn out to be false and this is why we have to rely on probability in our inferences. When, however, we use the rules we have inferred as premises for future investigations, we are able to test whether or not other cases conform to it. If there is a great deal of difference between a proposed rule and what is discovered on the basis of further investigation, then the theorist knows that the generalization must be adjusted to better fit what has been learned about the real world.

Let us now look at the process of deductive reasoning. Actually, the latter part of the process described above is the deductive process. When working on the basis of generalizations (or theories), we look to particular cases in order to answer our questions. As implied above, we utilize our generalizations to make predictions about things that we have not yet observed. Once we believe that we understand the general pattern to which a phenomena may conform, we use our assumptions to fuel hypotheses about future behavior or results. Using the example of socioeconomic status and ideology, armed with our theory about the relationship between these two variables, we could construct hypotheses that could then be used to predict future behavior. By testing those hypotheses, we would further develop our knowledge about the strength between the variables. The demonstrated strength of the hypotheses built on our generalizations helps to support our theories. As noted above, however, if the outcome of the "real world" test demonstrates the weakness of the proposed relationship, we have good reason to adjust our theory.[7]

THE FOUNDATION OF RATIONAL ENQUIRY

The development of Western science and its accompanying view of the world has been based almost entirely on the application of both inductive and deductive logic. At the root of the scientific method is the interplay between these two aspects of logical reasoning. For many centuries after the fall of the Roman Empire, Europe struggled along with only the rudiments of the sophisticated system of logic absorbed by the Romans from the Greeks. Throughout the Middle Ages, the Catholic church and its teachings largely submerged Aristotlean philosophy (including his *Logic*). When Europeans began trading with the Arab Middle East in the twelfth century, the work of Aristotle was finally rediscovered by the Christian world. If it were not for the fact that Aristotle's work had been translated and preserved by the Arabs, who inherited Greek science and philosophy, it would not have survived the Middle Ages.

With the reintroduction of Greek philosophy and logic, European science began to develop more rapidly. It is impossible to imagine the speedy development of European science without the return of ancient Greek thinking, because the new learning during the Renaissance and beyond was the direct result of the application of logic to problems that had hitherto been intractable. By using logic, Europeans were able to eventually develop "science" as we know it, relying heavily on this method of truth testing. Over the course of the past three hundred years, however, practitioners of both the natural and social sciences have moved away from the use of logic in terms of pursuing their research interests. Social science does not approve of using logic to determine the validity of claims, opting instead for verification based on observation.

The Falsification of Theory

The argument put forward by social science is roughly this: because political theorists rely on nonfalsifiable assertions, or assumptions, their conclusions can never be truly objective. All hypotheses are built upon assumptions. If we lacked the capacity to operate on the basis of assumption we would never raise a research question in the first place. And, all research, whether it arises out of normative or empirical theory, is based on how we think things are, or how we *assume* them to be. Even formal empirical theory requires some subjective reasoning (conceptual categories that require judgment are often used here), which in turn, allows for at least the possibility that assumption has crept in.

It is also an error to suppose that all of the reasoning we call scientific proceeds only from facts, or observables. Going back to an example used above, our study of the relationship between socioeconomic level and ideology is predicated on two important assumptions; (1) we have faith in our ability to actually define concepts in a manner that leads to their operationalization, and (2) we assume that we know something about "ideology." When we create mental constructs of the type that allow us to even use language such as "socio-economic level," we are assuming that those labels are useful. Just as we do on a regular basis in our everyday lives, we believe that the way we see the world is an accurate assessment of reality. In terms of studying the social order, however, the belief in any particular world view may influence both our research focus and our conclusions. Furthermore, by accepting the concept "socioeconomic level" we must believe that all of our empirical observations relevant to that term have captured a meaningful descriptive category. Although this does not present a problem for the theorist, the empirical researcher has a difficult time accounting for such vagaries of human endeavor.

We also develop our research projects on a foundation of what can best be characterized as a set of epistemological assumptions. To say that we work on the basis of epistemological assumptions is simply to say that we assume we know what we think we know. We generally assume that we can "know" about anything that we perceive. In other words, we pretty much take observables to be a part and parcel of reality, even if we have no other evidence on which to recommend them.

The application of empirically oriented methodologies in the social sciences has, in many ways, come at the expense of content over form. The formal role that theory generally plays in the research process hampers its ability to speak to the content of research goals. Whereas the empiricist feels most comfortable when theoretical constructs are utilized to outline the parameters of research, the political theorist is more concerned with content oriented issues such as value and intrinsic meaning. In this way, the theorist and the empiricist rely on different sorts of premises. But to establish that one type of premise is falsifiable and the other non-falsifiable would be a difficult project.

Political theorists make claims on the basis of the logical strength of the relationship between variables, while empirically oriented researchers are interested in statistically analyzing the specifics of those relationships. Although the theorist develops concepts such as *human nature* and *justice*, they are really no different than the variables *socioeconomic level* and *ideology*. Both are based on subjective views of what is, or ought to be. And, while political thought may be based on the aspirations and convictions of an individual philosopher, the theorist often acts as representative of many members of their societies. Theorists have reasons for believing the way they do about the political order, but those reasons are no different, in kind, from those utilized by empirical researchers in defense of the premises they assert. Where views of human nature, for instance, are found to be inconsistent with reality, theorists are generally flexible enough to change their positions. But the point is that theorists work to develop universal generalizations while empiricists develop generalizations that may or may not be applicable.

Political Thought and Practical Application

Among the more prominent thinkers of the Western tradition, three stand out in terms of their contributions to modern methodological approaches to the study of politics. Aristotle, Hobbes, and Marx each added conceptually to the development of political science, as we are familiar with it today, on two separate levels. First, these three thinkers helped bring about greater clarity in the study of politics through their contributions to our conception of what analysis means; and, second, they all articulate through their work the view that theory ought to lead to application, or practice. That is to say, they felt that their work formed a universal plan to be applied by future generations. What follows this chapter in the text are selections from these three thinkers. As a prelude to your reading those excerpts, this section will function as an overview of their thought. Additionally, we hope this also functions to further explicate the general notion explored here so far, that the differences between normative thinking and empirical theory building may have been, in the past, exaggerated.

Aristotle: Theory and Practice

The fourth century B.C. philosopher Aristotle is, after Plato, considered one of the most important earlier contributors to the development of what we now call political science. Aristotle is important in this regard because he recognized a distinction between what he referred to as the theoretical, and the practical, sciences. The latter category was made up of areas of study such as mathematics, theology, and physics, whereas the former was concerned only with matters that have to do with humankind. Unlike the theoretical sciences which are concerned with the gaining of knowledge, the purpose of the practical sciences is to make society better. Aristotle sees political science as "a mode of analysis designed less to discover the principles or causes than to articulate the phenomena of human action. . . ."[8]

Unlike his mentor Plato, Aristotle was interested in the real, the actual. His notions about the best social order were tempered with a healthy dose of knowledge of the relative nature of social life. In order to gain a better understanding of governments throughout the Greek city-states, Aristotle undertook a study of over 150 actual governments in order to develop a theory about how close they came to the ideal. He found that "few, if any actual states could be found which measured up to an ideal standard."[9] In this way, Aristotle can be seen as an early political scientist who developed his own methodology for employing inductive logic, and, thus carried out a comparative study of different governments.

In addition to providing us with some of the fundamentals of social research such as the distinction between the theoretical and practical sciences and the comparative study of actual, instead of ideal governments Aristotle also gave us the idea that humans are "social animals." According to Aristotle, each thing in nature has some special purpose, or end, that it is destined to reach. For humans, our end, or *teleology*, can be experienced only through our association with others in society, for it is only in the realm of social interaction that we can express virtue. Our virtue is made manifest when we meet our social obligations. Based on this notion, without society it would be impossible for humans to reach their full potential.[10]

In the selection from Aristotle's *Politics* (chapter 6), he explores the variety of constitutions he found in ancient Greece. Aristotle also takes up a discussion about the best form of government. Overall, Aristotle prefers the rule of an aristocracy headed by a king of superior qualities, but he finds democracy a tolerable form of government, especially if its alternative is either tyranny or oligarchy, both of which he holds in low esteem. In this way, he demonstrates his interest in both the theoretical and the practical. Aristotle's idea of the *best* is tempered and informed by his view of actual governments as he finds them. In other words, Aristotle builds normative, deductive theories on the basis of conclusions drawn through the inductive research he has conducted.

Citizen Hobbes

The seventeenth-century English philosopher Thomas Hobbes was also interested in the scientific analysis of politics. Hobbes took the view that the universe was mechanical in nature, that all of nature operated, more or less, like a giant clockwork. This mechanistic view implies that whatever happens in the universe is determined, so ideas like free will have diminished potency. Additionally, a person "is simply one of the objects making up the universe; he is more complex than such things as rocks and trees, but not essentially different."[11] Writing during the English Civil War, Hobbes' fascination is with peace and security. Times of crisis often give rise to coherent political theories which function as attempts to modify the social order.

For Hobbes, scientific knowledge is synonymous with mathematical knowledge, and again we see the foundations of modern political science. Hobbes' method was mathematical in the sense that it was based on the logical relationships between component elements of society, or variables. Hobbes even wrote of his work as "speculation," which he urged the members of his society to put "into the utility of practice."[12] Once again we encounter the idea that theory finds its expression in the practical. Hobbes' intention in writing *Leviathan*, for example, is obviously to provide a form of guidance for his society in terms of getting through a period of political upheaval and social disorder. But overall, Hobbes seems to think that human society is best served by investing political power in a powerful, centralized government.

In *De Cive*, or *The Citizen* (chapter 7), Hobbes looks at three different forms of government, democracy, aristocracy and monarchy, much as Aristotle had before him. Although Hobbes comes to a similar conclusion to Aristotle, he arrives there for different reasons. Aristotle's practical position in terms of the efficiency of government under a superior monarch is based on notions of justice and the ultimate ends of all things. Hobbes' view of human life without social contract, or the compelling rules of society, as "nasty and short" makes the need for a focused centralized sovereign paramount. In order to bring about social coherence, peace and tranquility, Hobbes is willing to sacrifice all expressions of political freedom as we are familiar with them today.

Praxis: Impetus to Application

In the nineteenth century, Marx brought to the conceptual study of society something which it had previously lacked: a set of testable hypotheses with which to conduct research. Marx focused on the economic sphere and presented a view of the social order predicated on economic conditions. But one of his most important contributions to political theory is the notion that merely "interpreting" the world relegates philosophy to a rather unimportant position in terms of history. On the other hand, if political theories can change the world, then those ideas occupy a much more important, and, potentially, powerful position.

Marx was interested in studying humankind as it is: not in the ideal, but in the real, the actual. This is the important realm for Marx. In essence, he wants to strip away the metaphysical and spiritual aspects of philosophy. For

Marx, it is only through practice, or *praxis*, that change in society can be achieved.[13] And so the practical application of theory becomes nearly an imperative. Political theorists can not remain complacent but instead must participate not only in the study of society but in its fundamental reorientation. This is what Marx refers to as a "reflexive relation" between philosophy and the world. The defect of philosophy, for Marx, is the fact that it is focused on the theoretical rather than the practical. But, through the process of theories' application, theory itself becomes directed toward the pragmatic. Marx sees its consequence in that "the world's becoming philosophical is at the same time philosophy's becoming worldly. . . ."[14]

Marx underscores the importance of the relationship between theory and practice — between philosophy and its application. Throughout our discussion in this chapter, we have been interested in this relationship, for it is in practical application that political theory finds its realization. When theory is able to aid empirical research, both aspects of the process are enriched. Theories that lead to testable hypotheses are useful in fueling research, and hypotheses built on strong logical relationships between variables are more likely to be supported in reality tests.

Ultimately, when acting only in the realm of the "ideal," or in being concerned strictly with what "ought to be," political theorists limit their own projects. It is through the worldly connection that theory goes beyond merely analyzing the political. As Marx says, "The philosophers have only interpreted the world, in various ways; the point, however, is to change it."[15]

NOTES

1. Alan C. Isaak, *Scope and Methods of Political Science: An Introduction to the Methodology of Political Inquiry* (Homewood, Ill.: The Dorsey Press, 1975, pp. 139–143).
2. *Webster's Encyclopedic Unabridged Dictionary of the English Language* (New York: Gramercy Books, 1994).
3. Sheldon S. Wolin, "Political Theory as a Vocation," *American Political Science Review,* 62:1062.
4. See Thomas A. Spragens, Jr., *Understanding Political Theory* (New York: St. Martin's Press, 1976).
5. See René Descartes, *Meditations on First Philosophy* (Indianapolis: Hackett Publishing Co., 1980).
6. Morris R. Cohen and Ernest Nagel, *An Introduction to Logic* (New York: Harcourt, Brace and World, Inc. 1962, pp. 9–11).
7. Ibid., p.13.
8. Carnes Lord, "Aristotle," in *History of Political Philosophy,* 3rd ed., edited by Leo Strauss and Joseph Cropsey (Chicago:The University of Chicago Press, 1987, p. 121).
9. William T. Bluhm, *Theories of the Political System: Classics of Political Thought and Modern Political Analysis,* 3rd ed. (Englewood Cliffs, N.J.: Prentice Hall, 1978, p. 91).

10. Edward Bryan Portis, *Reconstructing the Classics: Political Theory From Plato to Marx* (Chatham, N.J.: Chatham House Publishers, Inc., 1994, p. 23).

11. Glenn Tinder, *Political Thinking: The Perennial Questions,* 2nd ed. (Boston: Little, Brown, 1974, p. 25).

12. Thomas Hobbes, *Leviathan* (New York: E. P. Dutton, 1950, p. 319).

13. See Shlomo Avineri, *The Social and Political Thought of Karl Marx* (New York: Cambridge University Press, 1968).

14. Karl Marx, "Notes to The Doctoral Dissertation," from *Writings of The Young Marx on Philosophy and Society,* edited by Loyd D. Easton and Kurt H. Guddat (Garden City, N.Y.: Anchor Books, 1967).

15. Karl Marx, "Theses on Feuerbach," from *The Marx-Engels Reader,* edited by Robert C. Tucker (New York: W. W. Norton & Co., 1978).

6

Actual Constitutions
and Their Varieties

Aristotle

CHAPTER I

In all arts and sciences which embrace the whole of any subject, and do not come into being in a fragmentary way, it is the province of a single art or science to consider all that appertains to a single subject. For example, the art of gymnastic considers not only the suitableness of different modes of training to different bodies (1), but what sort is absolutely the best (2); (for the absolutely best must suit that which is by nature best and best furnished with the means of life), and also what common form of training is adapted to the great majority of men (3). And if a man does not desire the best habit of body, or the greatest skill in gymnastics, which might be attained by him, still the trainer or the teacher of gymnastic should be able to impart any lower degree of either (4). The same principle equally holds in medicine and shipbuilding, and the making of clothes, and in the arts generally.

Hence it is obvious that government too is the subject of a single science, which has to consider what government is best and of what sort it must be, to be most in accordance with our aspirations, if there were no external impediment, and also what kind of government is adapted to particular states. For the best is often unattainable, and therefore the true legislator and statesman ought to be acquainted, not only with (1) that which is best in the abstract, but also with (2) that which is best relatively to circumstances. We should be able further to say how a state may be constituted under any given conditions (3); both how it is originally formed and, when formed, how it may be

Aristotle. 1976. *The Politics of Aristotle,* edited by Ernest Baker. New York: Oxford University Press, pp. 155–175.

longest preserved; the supposed state being so far from having the best constitution that it is unprovided even with the conditions necessary for the best; neither is it the best under the circumstances, but of an inferior type.

He ought, moreover, to know (4) the form of government which is best suited to states in general; for political writers, although they have excellent ideas, are often unpractical. We should consider, not only what form of government is best, but also what is possible and what is easily attainable by all. There are some who would have none but the most perfect; for this many natural advantages are required. Others, again, speak of a more attainable form, and, although they reject the constitution under which they are living, they extol some one in particular, for example the Lacedaemonian. Any change of government which has to be introduced should be one which men, starting from their existing constitutions, will be both willing and able to adopt, since there is quite as much trouble in the reformation of an old constitution as in the establishment of a new one, just as to unlearn is as hard as to learn. And therefore, in addition to the qualifications of the statesman already mentioned, he should be able to find remedies for the defects of existing constitutions, as has been said before. This he cannot do unless he knows how many forms of government there are. It is often supposed that there is only one kind of democracy and one of oligarchy. But this is a mistake; and, in order to avoid such mistakes, we must ascertain what differences there are in the constitutions of states, and in how many ways they are combined. The same political insight will enable a man to know which laws are the best, and which are suited to different constitutions; for the laws are, and ought to be, relative to the constitution, and not the constitution to the laws. A constitution is the organization of offices in a state, and determines what is to be the governing body, and what is the end of each community. But laws are not to be confounded with the principles of the constitution; they are the rules according to which the magistrates should administer the state, and proceed against offenders. So that we must know the varieties, and the number of varieties, of each form of government, if only with a view to making laws. For the same laws cannot be equally suited to all oligarchies or to all democracies, since there is certainly more than one form both of democracy and of oligarchy.

CHAPTER II

In our original discussion about governments we divided them into three true forms: kingly rule, aristocracy, and constitutional government, and three corresponding perversions—tyranny, oligarchy, and democracy. Of kingly rule and of aristocracy, we have already spoken, for the inquiry into the perfect state is the same thing with the discussion of the two forms thus named, since both imply a principle of virtue provided with external means. We have already determined in what ways aristocracy and kingly rule differ from one another, and when the latter should be established. In what follows we have to describe the so-called constitutional government, which bears the common name of all constitutions, and the other forms, tyranny, oligarchy, and democracy.

It is obvious which of the three perversions is the worst, and which is the next in badness. That which is the perversion of the first and most divine is necessarily the worst. And just as a royal rule, if not a mere name, must exist by virtue of some great personal superiority in the king, so tyranny, which is the worst of governments, is necessarily the farthest removed from a well-constituted form; oligarchy is little better, for it is a long way from aristocracy, and democracy is the most tolerable of the three.

A writer who preceded me has already made these distinctions, but his point of view is not the same as mine. For he lays down the principle that when all the constitutions are good (the oligarchy and the rest being virtuous), democracy is the worst, but the best when all are bad. Whereas we maintain that they are in any case defective, and that one oligarchy is not to be accounted better than another, but only less bad.

Not to pursue this question further at present, let us begin by determining (1) how many varieties of constitution there are (since of democracy and oligarchy there are several); (2) what constitution is the most generally acceptable, and what is eligible in the next degree after the perfect state; and besides this what other there is which is aristocratical and well-constituted, and at the same time adapted to states in general; (3) of the other forms of government to whom each is suited. For democracy may meet the needs of some better than oligarchy, and conversely. In the next place (4) we have to consider in what manner a man ought to proceed who desires to establish some one among these various forms, whether of democracy or of oligarchy; and lastly, (5) having briefly discussed these subjects to the best of our power, we will endeavor to ascertain the modes of ruin and preservation both of constitutions generally and of each separately, and to what causes they are to be attributed.

CHAPTER III

The reason why there are many forms of government is that every state contains many elements. In the first place we see that all states are made up of families, and in the multitude of citizens there must be some rich and some poor, and some in a middle condition; the rich are heavy-armed, and the poor not. Of the common people, some are husbandmen, and some traders, and some artisans. There are also among the notables differences of wealth and property—for example, in the number of horses which they keep, for they cannot afford to keep them unless they are rich. And therefore in old times the cities whose strength lay in their cavalry were oligarchies, and they used cavalry in wars against their neighbors; as was the practice of the Eretrians and Chalcidians, and also of the Magnesians on the river Maeander, and of other peoples in Asia. Besides differences of wealth there are differences of rank and merit, and there are some other elements which were mentioned by us when in treating of aristocracy we enumerated the essentials of a state. Of these elements, sometimes all, sometimes the lesser and sometimes the greater number, have a share in the government. It is evident then that there must be many forms of government, differing in kind, since the parts of which they are composed differ from each other in kind. For a constitution is an organization of offices, which all the citizens distribute among themselves, according to the power which different classes possess, for example the rich or the poor, or according to some principle of equality which includes both. There must therefore be as many forms of government as there are modes of arranging the offices, according to the superiorities and differences of the parts of the state.

There are generally thought to be two principal forms: as men say of the winds that there are but two—north and south, and that the rest of them are only variations of these, so of governments there are said to be only two forms—democracy and oligarchy. For aristocracy is considered to be a kind of oligarchy, as being the rule of a few, and the so-called constitutional government to be really a democracy, just as among the winds we make the west a variation of the north, and the east of the south wind. Similarly of musical modes there are said to be two kinds, the Dorian and the Phrygian; the other arrangements of the scale are comprehended under one or other of these two. About forms of government this is a very favorite notion. But in either case the better and more exact way is to distinguish, as I have done, the one or two which are true forms, and to regard the others as perversions, whether of the most perfectly attempered mode or of the best form of government: we may compare the severer and more overpowering modes to the oligarchical forms, and the more relaxed and gentler ones to the democratic.

CHAPTER IV

It must not be assumed, as some are fond of saying, that democracy is simply that form of government in which the greater number are sovereign, for in oligarchies, and indeed in every government, the majority rules; nor again is oligarchy that form of government in which a few are sovereign. Suppose the whole population of a city to be 1300, and that of these 1000 are rich, and do not allow the remaining 300 who are poor, but free, and in an other respects their equals, a share of the government—no one will say that this is a democracy. In like manner, if the poor were few and the masters of the rich who outnumber them, no one would ever call such a government, in which the rich majority have no share of office, an oligarchy. Therefore we should rather say that democracy is the form of government in which the free are rulers, and oligarchy in which the rich; it is only an accident that the free are the many and the rich are the few. Otherwise a government in which the offices were given according to stature, as is said to be the case in Ethiopia, or according to beauty, would be an oligarchy; for the number of tall or good-looking men is small. And yet oligarchy and democracy are not sufficiently distinguished merely by these two characteristics of wealth and freedom. Both of them contain many other elements, and therefore we must carry our analysis further, and say that the government is not a democracy in which the freemen, being few in number, rule over the many who are not free, as at Apollonia, on the Ionian Gulf, and at Thera; (for in each of these states the nobles, who were also the earliest settlers, were held in chief honor, although they were but a few out of many). Neither is it a democracy when the rich have the government because they exceed in number; as was the case formerly at Colophon, where the bulk of the inhabitants were possessed of large property before the Lydian War. But the form of government is a democracy when the free, who are also poor and the majority, govern, and an oligarchy when the rich and the noble govern, they being at the same time few in number.

I have said that there are many forms of government, and have explained to what causes the variety is due. Why there are more than those already mentioned, and what they are, and whence they arise, I will now proceed to consider, starting from the principle already admitted, which is that every state consists, not of one, but of many parts. If we were going to speak of the different species of animals, we should first of all determine the organs which are indispensable to every animal, as for example some organs of sense and the instruments of receiving and digesting food, such as the mouth and the stomach, besides organs of locomotion. Assuming now that there are only so many kinds of organs, but that there may be differences in them—I mean different kinds of mouths, and stomachs, and perceptive and locomotive organs—the possible combinations of these differences will necessarily furnish many varieties of animals. (For animals cannot be the same which have different kinds of mouths or of ears.) And when all the combinations are exhausted, there will be as many sorts of animals as there are combinations of the necessary organs. The same, then, is true of the forms of government which have been described; states, as I have repeatedly said, are composed, not of one, but of many elements. One element is the food-producing class, who are called husbandmen; a second, the class of mechanics who practice the arts without which a city cannot exist; of these arts some are absolutely necessary, others contribute to luxury or to the grace of life. The third class is that of traders, and by traders I mean those who are engaged in buying and selling, whether in commerce or in retail trade. A fourth class is that of the serfs or laborers. The warriors make up the fifth class, and they are as necessary as any of the others, if the country is not to be the slave of every invader. For how can a state which has any title to the name be of a slavish nature? The state is independent and self-suffing, but a slave is the reverse of independent. Hence we see that this subject, though ingeniously, has not been satisfactorily treated in the Republic. Socrates says that a state is made up of four sorts of people who are absolutely necessary; these are a weaver, a husbandman, a shoemaker, and a builder; afterwards, finding that they are not enough, he adds a smith, and again a herdsman, to look after the necessary animals; then a merchant, and then a retail trader. All these together form the complement of the first state, as if a state were established merely to supply the necessaries of life, rather than for the sake of the good, or stood equally in need of shoemakers and of husbandmen. But he does not admit into the state a military class until the country has increased in size, and is beginning to encroach on its neighbor's land, whereupon they go to war. Yet even amongst his four original citizens, or whatever be the number of those whom he associates in the state, there must be some one who will dispense justice and determine what is just. And as the soul may be said to be more truly part of an animal than the body, so the higher parts of states, that is to say, the warrior class, the class engaged in the administration of justice, and that engaged in deliberation, which is the special business of political common sense—these are more essential to the state than the parts which minister to the necessaries of life. Whether their several functions are the functions of different citizens, or of the same—for it may often happen that the same persons are both warriors and husbandmen—is immaterial to the argument. The higher as well as the lower elements are to be equally considered parts of the state, and if so, the military element at any rate must be included. There are also the wealthy who minister to the state with their property; these form the seventh class. The eighth class is that of magistrates and of officers; for the state cannot exist without rulers. And therefore some must be able to take office and to serve the state, either always or in turn. There only remains the class of those who deliberate and who judge between disputants; we were just now distinguishing them. If presence of all these elements, and their fair and equitable organization, is necessary to states, then there must also be persons who have the ability of statesmen. Different functions appear to be often combined in the same individual; for example, the warrior may also be a husbandman, or an artisan; or, again, the councillor a judge. And all claim to possess political ability, and think that they are quite competent to fill most offices. But the same persons cannot be rich and poor at the same time. For this reason the rich and the poor are regarded in an especial sense as parts of a state. Again, because the rich are generally few in number, while the poor are many, they appear to be antagonistic, and as the one or the other prevails they form the government. Hence arises the common opinion that there are two kinds of government—democracy and oligarchy.

I have already explained that there are many forms of constitution, and to what causes the variety is due. Let me now show that there are different forms both of democracy and oligarchy, as will indeed be evident from what has preceded. For both in the common people and in the notables various classes are included; of the common people, one class are husbandmen, another artisans; another traders, who are employed in buying and selling; another are the seafaring class, whether engaged in war or in trade, as ferrymen or as fishermen. (In many places any one of these classes forms quite a large population; for example, fishermen at Tarentum and Byzantium, crews of triremes at Athens, merchant seamen at Aegina and Chios, ferrymen at Tenedos.) To the classes already mentioned may be added day-laborers, and those who, owing to their needy circumstances, have no leisure, or those who are not of free birth on both sides; and there may be other classes as well. The notables again may be divided according to their wealth, birth, virtue, education, and similar differences.

Of forms of democracy first comes that which is said to be based strictly on equality. In such a democracy the law says that it is just for the poor to have no more advantage than the rich; and that neither should be masters, but both equal. For if liberty and equality, as is thought by some, are chiefly to be found in democracy, they will be best attained when all persons alike share in the government to the utmost. And since the people are the majority, and the opinion of the majority is decisive, such a government must necessarily be a democracy. Here then is one sort of democracy. There is another, in which the magistrates are elected according to a certain property qualification, but a low one; he who has the required amount of property has a share in the government, but he who loses his property loses his rights. Another kind is that in which all the citizens who are under no disqualification share in the government, but still the law is supreme. In another, everybody, if he be only a citizen, is admitted to the government, but the law is supreme as before. A fifth form of democracy, in other respects the same, is that in which, not the law, but the multitude, have the supreme power, and supersede the law by their decrees. This is a state of affairs brought about by the demagogues. For in democracies which are subject to the law the best citizens hold the first place, and there are no demagogues; but where the laws are not supreme, there demagogues spring up. For the people becomes a monarch, and is many in one; and the many have the power in their hands, not as individuals, but collectively. Homer says that "it is not good to have a rule of many," but whether he means this corporate rule, or the rule of many individuals, is uncertain. At all events this sort of democracy, which is now a monarch, and no longer under the control of law, seeks to exercise monarchical sway, and grows into a despot; the flatterer is held in honor; this sort of democracy being relatively to other democracies what tyranny is to other forms of monarchy. The spirit of both is the same, and they alike exercise a despotic rule over the better citizens. The decrees of the demos correspond to the edicts of the tyrant; and the demagogue is to the one what the flatterer is to the other. Both have great power; the flatterer with the tyrant, the demagogue with democracies of the kind which we are describing. The demagogues make the decrees of the people override the laws, by referring all things to the popular assembly. And therefore they grow great, because the people have an things in their hands, and they hold in their hands the votes of the people, who are too ready to listen to them. Further, those who have any complaint to bring against the magistrates say, "Let the people be judges"; the people are too happy to accept the invitation; and so the authority of every office is undermined. Such a democracy is fairly open to the objection that it is not a constitution at all; for where the laws have no authority, there is no constitution. The law ought to be supreme over all, and the magistracies should judge of particulars, and only this should be considered a constitution. So that if democracy be a real form of government, the sort of system in which all things are regulated by decrees is clearly not even a democracy in the true sense of the word, for decrees relate only to particulars.

These then are the different kinds of democracy.

CHAPTER V

Of oligarchies, too, there are different kinds: one where the property qualification for office is such that the poor, although they form the majority, have no share in the government, yet he who acquires a qualification may obtain a share. Another sort is when there is a qualification for office, but a high one, and the vacancies in the governing body are fired by co-optation. If the election is made out of all the qualified persons, a constitution of this kind inclines to an aristocracy, if out of a privileged class, to an oligarchy. Another sort of oligarchy is when the son succeeds the father. There is a fourth form, likewise hereditary, in which the magistrates are supreme and not the law. Among oligarchies this is what tyranny is among monarchies, and the last-mentioned form of democracy among democracies; and in fact this sort of oligarchy receives the name of a dynasty (or rule of powerful families).

These are the different sorts of oligarchies and democracies. It should, however, be remembered that in many states the constitution which is established by law, although not democratic, owing to the education and habits of the people may be administered democratically, and conversely in other states the established constitution may incline to democracy, but may be administered in an oligarchical spirit. This most often happens after a revolution: for governments do not change at once; at first the dominant party are content with encroaching a little upon their opponents. The laws which existed previously continue in force, but the authors of the revolution have the power in their hands.

CHAPTER VI

From what has been already said we may safely infer that there are so many different kinds of democracies and of oligarchies. For it is evident that either all the classes whom we mentioned must share in the government, or some only and not others. When the class of husbandmen and of those who possess moderate fortunes have the supreme power, the government is administered according to law. For the citizens being compelled to live by their labor have no leisure; and so they set up the authority of the law, and attend assemblies only when necessary. They all obtain a share in the government when they have acquired the qualification which is fixed by the law—the absolute exclusion of any class would be a step towards oligarchy; hence all who have acquired the property qualification are admitted to a share in the constitution. But leisure cannot be provided for them unless there are revenues to support them. This is one sort of democracy, and these are the causes which give birth to it. Another kind is based on the distinction which naturally comes next in order; in this, every one to whose birth there is no objection is eligible, but actually shares in the government only if he can find leisure. Hence in such a democracy the supreme power is vested in the laws, because the state has no means of paying the citizens. A third kind is when all freemen have a right to share in the government, but do not actually share, for the reason which has been already given; so that in this form again the law must rule. A fourth kind of democracy is that which comes latest in the history of states. In our own day, when cities have far outgrown their original size, and their revenues have increased, all the citizens have a place in the government, through the great preponderance of the multitude; and they all, including the poor who receive pay, and therefore have leisure to exercise their rights, share in the administration. Indeed, when they are paid, the common people have the most leisure, for they are not hindered by the care of their property, which often fetters the rich, who are thereby prevented from taking part in the assembly or in the courts, and so the state is governed by the poor, who are a majority, and not by the laws.

So many kinds of democracies there are, and they grow out of these necessary causes.

Of oligarchies, one form is that in which the majority of the citizens have some property, but not very much; and this is the first form, which allows to any one who obtains the required amount the right of sharing in the government. The sharers in the government being a numerous body, it follows that the law must govern, and not individuals. For in proportion as they are further removed from a monarchical form of government, and in respect of property have neither so much as to be able to live without attending to business, nor so little as to need state support, they must admit the rule of law and not claim to rule themselves. But if the men of property in the state are fewer than in the former case, and own more property, there arises a second form of oligarchy. For the stronger they are, the more power they claim, and having this object in view, they themselves select those of the other classes who are to be admitted to the government; but, not being as yet strong enough to rule without the law, they make the law represent their wishes. When this power is intensified by a further diminution of their numbers and increase of their property, there arises a third and further stage of oligarchy, in which the governing class keep the offices in their own hands, and the law ordains that the son shall succeed the father. When, again, the rulers have great wealth and numerous friends, this sort of family despotism approaches a monarchy; individuals rule and not the law. This is the fourth sort of oligarchy, and is analogous to the last sort of democracy.

CHAPTER VII

There are still two forms besides democracy and oligarchy; one of them is universally recognized and included among the four principal forms of government, which are said to be (1) monarchy, (2) oligarchy, (3) democracy, and (4) the so-called aristocracy or government of the best. But there is also a fifth, which retains the generic name of polity or constitutional government; this is not common, and therefore has not been noticed by writers who attempt to enumerate the different kinds of government; like Plato, in their books about the state, they recognize four only. The term 'aristocracy' is rightly applied to the form of government which is described in the first part of our treatise; for that only can be rightly called aristocracy which is a government formed of the best men absolutely, and not merely of men who are good when tried by any given standard. In the perfect state the good man is absolutely the same as the good citizen; whereas in other states the good citizen is only good relatively to his own form of government. But there are some states differing from oligarchies and also differing from the so-called polity or constitutional government; these are termed aristocracies, and in them the magistrates are certainly chosen, both according to their wealth and according to their merit. Such a form of government differs from each of the two just now mentioned, and is termed an aristocracy. For indeed in states which do not make virtue the aim of the community, men of merit and reputation for virtue may be found. And so where a government has regard to wealth, virtue, and numbers, as at Carthage, that is aristocracy; and also where it has regard only to two out of the three, as at Lacedaemon, to virtue and numbers, and the two principles of democracy and virtue temper each other. There are these two forms of aristocracy in addition to the first and perfect state, and there is a third form, viz., the constitutions which incline more than the so-called polity towards oligarchy.

7

Of the Three Kinds of Government: Democracy, Aristocracy, Monarchy

Thomas Hobbes

DOMINION

Chapter VII.

I. We have already spoken of a City by institution in its Genus; we will now say somewhat of its species. As for the difference of Cities, it is taken from the difference of the Persons, to whom the Supreme Power is committed; this Power is committed either to one Man, or Council, or some one Court consisting of many men. Furthermore, a Council of many men, consists either of all the Citizens, (insomuch as every man of them hath a Right to Vote, and an interest in the ordering of the greatest affaires, if he will himself) or of a part only; from whence there arise three sorts of Government: The one, when the Power is in a Council, where every Citizen hath a right to Vote, and it is called a DEMOCRACY. The other, when it is in a Council, where not all, but some part only have their suffrages, and we call it an ARISTOCRACY. The third is that, when the Supreme Authority rests only in one, and it is styled a MONARCHY. In the first, he that governs is called demos, The PEOPLE. In the second, the NOBLES. In the third, the MONARCH.

II. Now, although Ancient Writers of Politics have introduced three other kinds of Government opposite to these, to wit, Anarchy or confusion to Democracy, Oligarchy, that is, the command of some few, to Aristocracy, and Tyranny to Monarchy, yet are not these three distinct formes of Government, but three diverse Titles given by those who were either displeased with that present Government, or those that bare Rule. For men, by giving names, doe usually,

Hobbes, Thomas. 1949. *De Cive,* edited by Sterling P. Lamprecht. New York: Appleton-Century-Crofts, pp. 87–99.

not only signifie the things themselves, but also their own affections, as love, hatred, anger, and the like, whence it happens that what one man calls a Democracy, another calls an Anarchy; what one counts an Aristocracy, another esteems an Oligarchy. and whom one titles a King, another stiles him a Tyrant; so as we see these names betoken not a diverse kind of Government, but the diverse opinions of the Subjects concerning him who hath the Supreme Power. For first, who sees not that Anarchy is equally opposite to all the forenamed Formes? For that word signifies that there is no Government at all, that is, not any City. But how is it possible that no City should be the species of a City? Furthermore, what difference is there between an Oligarchy, which signifies the Command of a few, or Grandees, or an Aristocracy, which is that of the Prime, or Chief Heads, more then that men differ so among themselves, that the same things seem not good to all men? Whence it happens, that those persons, who by some are looked on as the best, are by others esteemed to be the worst of all men.

III. But men, by reason of their passions, will very hardly be persuaded that a Kingdom, and Tyranny, are not diverse kinds of Cities, who though they would rather have the City subject to one, then many, yet doe they not believe it to be well governed unless it accord with their judgements: But we must discover by Reason, and not by Passion, what the difference is between a King, and a Tyrant: but first, they differ not in this, That a Tyrant hath the greater Power, for greater then the Supreme cannot be granted; nor in this, That one hath a limited power, the other not; for he, whose authority is limited, is no King, but his Subject that limits him. Lastly, neither differ they in their manner of acquisition; for if in a Democratical, or Aristocratically Government some one Citizen should, by force, possess himself of the Supreme Power, if he gain the consent of all the Citizens, he becomes a legitimate Monarch; if not, he is an Enemy, not a Tyrant. They differ therefore in the sole exercise of their command, insomuch as he is said to be a King, who governs well, and he a Tyrant that doth otherwise. The case therefore is brought to this passe, That a King legitimately constituted in his Government, if he seem to his Subjects to Rule well, and to their liking, they afford him the appellation of a King, if not, they count him a Tyrant. Wherefore we see a Kingdom, and Tyranny, are not diverse Formes of Government, but one and the self-same Monarch hath the name of a King given him in point of Honor, and Reverence to him, and of a Tyrant in way of contumely, and reproach. But what we frequently find in books said against Tyrants, took its original from Greek, and Roman Writers, whose Government was partly Democratical, and partly Aristocratically, and therefore not Tyrants only, but even Kings were odious to them.

IV. There are, who indeed doe think it necessary, That a Supreme Command should be somewhere extant in a, City. but if it should be in any one, either Man, or Council, it would follow (they say) that all the Citizens must be slaves. Avoiding this condition, they imagine that there may be a certain Form of Government compounded of those three kinds we have spoken of, yet different from each particular, which they call a mixed Monarchy, or mixed Aristocracy, or mixed Democracy, according as any one of these three sorts shall be more eminent then the rest: For example, if the naming of Magistrates, and the arbitration of War, and Peace, should belong to the King, Judicature to the Lords, and contribution of Monies to the People, and the power of making Laws too altogether, this kind of State would they call a mixed Monarchy forsooth. But if it were possible that there could be such a State, it would no whit advantage the liberty of the subject; for as long as they all agree, each single Citizen is as much subject as possibly he can be; but if they disagree, the State returns to a Civil War, and the Right of the private Sword, which certainly is much worse then any subjection whatsoever: But that there can be no such kind of Government hath been sufficiently demonstrated in the foregoing Chapter, Arctic: 6, 7, 8, 9, 10, 11, 12.

But that there can be no such kind of Government. Most men grant, That a Government ought not to be divided, but they would have it moderated, and bounded by some limits. Truly it is very reasonable it should be so; but if these men, when they speak of moderating, and limiting, do understand dividing it, they make a very fond distinction. Truly, for my part, I wish that not only Kings, but all other Persons endued with Supreme Authority would so temper themselves as to commit no wrong, and only minding their charges contain themselves within the limits of the natural, and divine Laws: But they who distinguish thus, they would have the chief Power bounded, and restrained by others; which, because it cannot be done, but that they who doe set the limits, must needs have some part of the Power, whereby they may be enabled to doe it, the Government is properly divided, not moderated.

V. Let us see a little now in the constituting of each Form of Government, what the constitutors doe. Those who met together with intention to erect a City, were almost in the very act of meeting a Democracy; for in that they willingly met, they are supposed obliged to the observation of what shall be determined by the major part: which, while that convent lasts, or is adjourned to some certain days, and places, is a clear Democracy; for that convent, whose will is the will of all the Citizens, hath the Supreme Authority; and because in this Convent every man is supposed to have a Right to give his voice, it follows, that it is a Democracy by the definition given in the first Article of this Chap. But if they depart, and break up the Convent, and appoint no time, or place, where, and when they shall meet again, the public weal returns to Anarchy, and the same state it stood in before their meeting, that is, to the state of all men warring against all. The People therefore retains the supreme power no longer then there is a certain day and place publicly appointed, and known, to which whosoever will, may resort. For except that be known and determined, they may either meet at divers times, and places, that is in factions, or not at all; and then it is no longer demos, the People, but a dissolute multitude, to whom we can neither attribute any Action, or Right: Two things therefore frame a Democracy, whereof one (to wit the perpetual prescription of Convents) makes demos, the People, the other (which is a plurality of voices) to *kratos* or the power.

VI. Furthermore, it will not be sufficient for the People, so as to maintain its supremacy, to have some certain known times, and places of meeting, unless that either the intervals of the times be of less distance, then that any thing may in the mean time happen whereby (by reason of the defect of power) the City may be brought into some danger, or at least that the exercise of the supreme authority be, during the interval, granted to some one man, or Council. For unless this be done, there is not that wary care, and heed taken for the defense and Peace of single men which ought to be, and therefore will not deserve the name of a City, because that in it for want of security, every mans Right of defending himself at his own pleasure, returns to him again.

VII. Democracy is not framed by contract of particular persons with the People, but by mutual compacts of single men each with other. But hence it appears in the first place, that the Persons contracting, must be in being before the contract itself. But the People is not in being before the constitution of government, as not being any Person, but a multitude of single Persons; wherefore there could then no contract passe between the People and the Subject. Now, if after that government is framed, the subject make any contract with the People, it is in vain, because the People contains within its will, the will of that subject to whom it is supposed to be obliged; and therefore may at its own will and pleasure disengage itself, and by consequence is now actually free. But in the second place, that single Persons doe contract each with other may be inferred from hence, that in vain sure would the City have been constituted, if the Citizens had been engaged by no contracts to doe, or omit what the City should command to be done or omitted. Because therefore such kind of compacts must be understood to passe as necessary to the making up of a City, but none can be made (as is already shewed) between the Subject and the People; it follows, that they must be made between single Citizens, namely that each man contract to submit his will to the will of the major part, on condition that the rest also doe the like, as if every one should say thus, I give up my Right unto the People for your sake, on condition, that you also deliver up yours, for mine.

VIII. An Aristocracy, or Council of Nobles endued with supreme authority, receives its original from a Democracy, which gives up its Right unto it; where we must understand that certain men distinguished from others, either by eminence of title, blood, or some other Character, are propounded to the People, and by plurality of voices are elected; and being elected, the whole Right of the People, or City, is conveyed on them, insomuch as whatsoever the People might doe before, the same by Right may this Court of elected Nobles now doe. Which being done, it is clear that the People, considered as one Person, (its supreme authority being already transferred on these) is no longer now in being.

IX. As in Democracy the People, so in an Aristocracy the Court of Nobles is free from all manner of obligation; for seeing subjects not contracting with the People, but by mutual compacts among themselves, were tied to all that the People did, hence also they were tied to that act of the People in resigning up its Right of government into the hands of Nobles. Neither could this Court, although elected by the People, be by it obliged to any thing; for being erected, the People is at once dissolved, as was declared above, and the authority it had as being a Person utterly vanisheth. Wherefore the obligation which was due to the Person must also vanish, and perish together with it.

X. Aristocracy hath these considerations, together with Democracy; First, that without an appointment of some certain times, and places, at which the Court of Nobles may meet, it is no longer a Court, or one Person, but a dissolute multitude without any supreme power; Secondly, that the times of their assembling cannot be disjoined by long intervals, without prejudice to the supreme power, unless its administration be transferred to some one man: Now the reasons why this happens, are the same which we set down in the fifth Article.

XI. As an Aristocracy, so also a monarchy is derived from the Power of the People, transferring its Right, (that is) its Authority on one man: Here also we must understand, that some one man, either by name, or some other token, is propounded to be taken notice of above all the rest, and that by a plurality of voices the whole Right of the People is conveyed on him, insomuch as whatsoever the People could doe before he were elected, the same in every Respect may he by Right now do, being elected; which being done, the People is no longer one Person, but a rude multitude, as being only one before by virtue of the supreme command, whereof they now have made a conveyance from themselves on this one Man.

XII. And therefore neither doth the Monarch oblige himself to any for the command he receives, for he receives it from the People; but as hath been shewed above, the People, as soon as that act is done, ceaseth to be a Person; but the Person vanishing, all obligation to the Person vanisheth. The subjects therefore are tied to perform obedience to the Monarch, by those compacts only by which they mutually obliged themselves to the observation of all that the People should command them, (that is) to obey that Monarch, if he were made by the People.

XIII. But a Monarchy differs as well from an Aristocracy, as a Democracy, in this chiefly, that in those there must be certain set times and places for deliberation, and consultation of affaires, that is, for the actual exercise of it in all times, and places; For the People, or the Nobles not being one natural Person must necessarily have their meetings. The Monarch who is one by nature, is always in a present capacity to execute his authority.

XIV. Because we have declared above in the 7. 9. and 12. Articles, that they who have gotten the supreme command are by no compacts obliged to any man, it necessarily follows, that they can doe no injury to the subjects; for injury according to the definition made in the third Article of the third

Chapter, is nothing else but a breach of contract: and therefore where no contracts have part, there can be no injury. Yet the People, the Nobles, and the Monarch may diverse ways transgress against the other Laws of nature, as by cruelty, iniquity, contumely, and other like vices, which come not under this strict, and exact notion of injury. But if the subject yield not obedience to the supreme, he will in propriety of speech be said to be injurious as well to his fellow subjects, because each man hath compacted with the other to obey, as to his chief Ruler, in resuming that Right, which he hath given him, without his consent. And in a Democracy, or Aristocracy, if any thing be decreed against any Law of nature, the City itself, that is, the civil Person sins not, but those subjects only by whose votes it was decreed; for sin is a consequence of the natural express will, not of the political, which is artificial; for if it were otherwise, they would be guilty, by whom the decree was absolutely disliked: But in a Monarchy, if the Monarch make any decree against the Laws of nature, he sins himself, because in him the civil will and the natural are all one.

XV. The people who are about to make a Monarch, may give him the supremacy either simply without limitation of time, or for a certain season; and time determined; if simply, we must understand that he who receives it, hath the self-same power which they had, who gave it, on the same grounds: therefore that the People by Right could make him a Monarch, may he make another Monarch: insomuch as the Monarch to whom the command is simply given, receives a Right not of possession only, but of succession also, so as he may declare whom he pleaseth for his successor.

XVI. But if the power be given for a time limited, we must have regard to somewhat more then the bare gift only: First, whether the People conveying its authority, left it self any Right to meet at certain times, and places, or not. Next, if it have reserved this power, whether it were done, so as they might meet before that time were expired, which they prescribed to the Monarch. Thirdly, whether they were contented to meet only at the will of that temporary Monarch and not otherwise. Suppose now the People had delivered up its Power to some one man for term of life only; which being done, let us suppose in the first place, that every man departed from the Council without making any order at all concerning the place where (after his death) they should meet again to make a new election. In this case it is manifest by the fifth Article of this Chapter, that the People ceaseth to be a Person, and is become a dissolute multitude, every one whereof hath an equal, to wit, a natural Right to meet with whom he lists at divers times, and in what places shall best please him; nay, and if he can, engross the supreme power to himself, and settle it on his own head. What Monarch soever therefore hath a command in such a condition, he is bound by the Law of nature (set down in the Article of the third Chapter of not returning evil for good) prudently to provide, that by his death the City suffer not a dissolution, either by appointing a certain day, & place, in which those subjects of his who have a mind to it may assemble themselves, or else by nominating a successor: whether of these shall to him seem most conducible to their common benefit. He therefore who on this aforesaid manner hath received his command during life, hath an absolute Power, and may at his discretion dispose of the succession. In the next place, if we grant that the people departed not from the election of the temporary Monarch, before they decreed a certain time and place of meeting after his death, then the Monarch being dead, the authority is confirmed in the people, not by any new acts of the subjects, but by virtue of the former Right; for all the supreme command (as Dominion) was in the People, but the use, and exercise of it was only in the temporary Monarch, as in one that takes the benefit, but hath not the Right. But if the People after the election of a temporary Monarch, depart not from the Court before they have appointed certain times, and places to convene, during the time prescribed him (as the Dictators in ancient times were made by the People of Rome) such an one is not to be accounted a Monarch, but the Prime Officer of the People; and if it shall seem good, the People may deprive him of his office even before that time, as the People of Rome did, when they conferred an equal power on Minutius Master of the horse, with Quintus Fabius Maximus, whom before they had made Dictator. The reason whereof is, that it is not to be imagined, that, whether Man or Council who hath the readiest, and most immediate power to act, should hold his command on such terms as not to be able actually to execute it; for command is nothing else but a Right of commanding, as oft as nature allows it possible. Lastly, if the People having declared a temporary Monarch, depart from the Court on such terms, as it shall not be lawful for them to meet without the command of the Monarch, we must understand the People to be immediately dissolved, and that his authority who is thus declared, is absolute; forasmuch as it is not in the power of all the subjects to frame the City anew, unless he give consent who hath now alone the authority. Nor matters it, that he hath perhaps made any promise to assemble his Subjects on some certain times, since there remains no Person now in being, but at his discretion, to whom the promise was made. What we have spoken of these four cases of a People electing a Temporary Monarch will be more clearly explained by comparing them with an absolute Monarch, who hath no heir apparent; for the People is Lord of the subject in such a manner as there can be no Heir but whom it self doth appoint. Besides, the spaces between the times of the subjects meeting may be fitly compared to those times wherein the Monarch sleeps, for in either the Acts of commanding ceases, the Power remains: Furthermore, to dissolve the convent, so as it cannot meet again, is the death of the People; just as sleeping, so as he can never wake more, is the death of a man: As therefore a King, who hath no Heir, going to his rest, so as never to rise again, (i.e.) dying, if he commit the exercise of his Regal Authority to any one till he awake, does by consequence give him the Succession; the People also electing a Temporary Monarch, and not reserving a power to convene, delivers up to him the whole Dominion of the Country: Furthermore, as a King going to sleep for some season, entrusts the administration of his Kingdom to some other, and waking takes it again; so the people having elected a Temporary Monarch, and withal retaining a right to meet at a certain day, and place, at that day receives its supremacy again. And as a King who hath committed the execution of his Authority to another, himself in the mean while waking, can recall this commission again when he pleaseth; so the People, who during the time prescribed to the Temporary Monarch, doth by Right convene, may if they please, deprive the Monarch of his Authority. Lastly, the King, who commits his Authority to another while himself sleeps, not being able to wake again till he whom he entrusted, give consent, loses at once both his power, and his life; so the people, who hath given the Supreme Power to a temporary Monarch in such sort as they cannot assemble without his command is absolutely dissolved, and the power remains with him whom they have chosen.

XVII. If the Monarch promise ought to any one, or many subjects together, by consequence whereof the exercise of his power may suffer prejudice, that Promise or Compact whether made by Oath, or without it, is null: for all Compact is a conveyance of Right, which by what hath been said in the fourth Article of the second Chapter, requires meet, and proper signs of the Will in the conveyer. But he who sufficiently signifies his will of retaining the end, doth also sufficiently declare that he quits not his Right to the means necessary to that end. Now he who hath promised to part with somewhat necessary to the Supreme Power, and yet retains the Power it self, gives sufficient tokens, That he no otherwise promised it then so far forth as the power might be retained without it. Whensoever therefore it shall appear that what is promised cannot be performed without prejudice to the Power, the promise must be valued as not made, (i.e.) of no effect.

XVIII. We have seen how Subjects, nature dictating, have obliged themselves by mutual Compacts to obey the supreme Power. We will see now by what means it comes to pass that they are released from these bonds of obedience. And first of all this happens by rejection, namely, if a man cast off, or forsake, but convey not the Right of his Command on some other; for what is thus rejected, is openly exposed to all alike, catch who catch can; whence again, by the Right of nature, every subject may heed the preservation of himself according to his own judgement. In the second place, If the Kingdom fall into the power of the enemy, so as there can no more opposition be made against them, we must understand that he, who before had the Supreme Authority, hath now lost it: For when the Subjects have done their full endeavor to prevent their falling into the enemies hands, they have fulfilled those Contracts of obedience which they made each with other, and what, being conquered, they promise afterwards, to avoid death, they must, with no less endeavor, labor to perform. Thirdly, in a Monarchy, (for a Democracy, and Aristocracy cannot fail) if there be no successor, all the subjects are discharged from their obligations; for no man is supposed to be tied he knows not to whom, for in such a case it were impossible to perform ought. And by these three ways all subjects are restored from their civil subjection to that liberty, which all men have to all things, to wit, natural, and salvage, (for the natural state hath the same proportion to the Civil, I mean liberty to subjection, which Passion hath to Reason, or a Beast to a Man:) Furthermore, each subject may lawfully be freed from his subjection by the will of him who hath the Supreme Power, namely, if he change his soil, which may be done two ways, either by permission, as he, who gets license to dwell in another Country; or Command, as he, who is Banished: In both cases he is free from the Laws of his former Country, because he is tied to observe those of the latter.

8

Philosophy after Its Completion

Karl Marx

In regard to Hegel, too, it is out of mere ignorance that his disciples explain this or that determination of his system by accommodation and the like or, in a word, *morally*. They forget that a very short time ago they enthusiastically adhered to all aspects of his one-sidedness; clear evidence of this fact is found in their own writings.

If they really were so much affected by the completed scientific knowledge they received that they submitted to it with naïve, uncritical trust, how unconscionable it is to reproach the master with having a hidden motive behind his insight—the master for whom scientific knowledge was not something received but something evolving as his own intellectual life's blood pulsed to its outmost periphery. Doing this, they throw suspicion on themselves, as though formerly they were not serious, and they combat their own former position in the form of ascribing it to Hegel They forget, however, that he stood in direct, substantial relationship to his system, and they in a reflected relationship.

It is conceivable that a philosopher commits this or that apparent non sequitur out of this or that accommodation. He himself may be conscious of it. But he is not conscious that the possibility of this apparent accommodation is rooted in the inadequacy of his principle or in its inadequate formulation. Hence, if a philosopher has accommodated himself, his disciples have to explain *from his inner essential consciousness* what for him had *the form of an exoteric consciousness*. In this way what appears as progress of consciousness *is* progress of knowledge as well. It is not that the particular consciousness of the philosopher is suspect; rather, his essential form of consciousness is constructed, raised to a particular form and meaning, and at the same time superseded.

Incidentally, I regard this unphilosophical turn made by a large segment of the Hegelian school as a phenomenon that will always accompany the transition from discipline to freedom.

It is a psychological law that the theoretical mind, having become free in itself, turns into practical energy. Emerging as *will* from Amenthes' shadow-world, it turns against worldly actuality which exists outside it. (It is important, however, from the philosophical point of view, to specify these aspects more clearly, because deductions about a philosophy's immanent determination and world-historical character can be made from the particular manner of this turn. Here we see, as it were, its curriculum vitae narrowed down, brought to the subjective point.) The *practice [Praxis]* of philosophy, however, is itself *theoretical.* It is *criticism* which measures individual existence against essence, particular actuality against the Idea. But this *direct realization* of philosophy is burdened with contradictions in its innermost essence, and this essence manifests itself in appearance and puts its stamp thereon.

While philosophy, as will, turns toward the apparent world, the system is reduced to an abstract totality, that is, it becomes one side of the world facing another. Its relation to the world is reflexive relation. Enthusiastic in its drive to realize itself, it enters into tension with everything else. The inner self-contentedness and roundedness is broken down. The former inner light becomes a consuming flame turning outward. The consequence, hence, is that the world's becoming philosophical is at the same time philosophy's becoming worldly, that its realization is at the same time its loss, that what it combats outside is its own inner defect, that just in this combat philosophy itself falls into the faults which it combats in its opponent, and that it transcends these faults only by falling victim to them. Whatever opposes it and what philosophy combats is always the very same thing as philosophy, only with reversed factors.

This is the one side, when we look at the matter *purely objectively,* as immediate realization of philosophy. But there is also a *subjective* side—actually only a different form of the other side. This is *the relation of the philosophical system* which is actualized to its intellectual supporters and to the individual self-consciousnesses in which its progress becomes manifest. From the relationship that lies in the realization of philosophy in opposition to the world it is apparent that these individual self-consciousnesses always have a *double-edged demand,* of which one edge turns against the world, the other against philosophy itself. For what appears objectively as a relationship reversed in itself, appears to them as a double, self-contradictory demand and action. Their liberation of the world from nonphilosophy is at the same time their own liberation from the philosophy which fettered it as a definite system. Being themselves involved in action and the immediate energy of development, and hence, as far as theory is concerned, not yet beyond that system, they sense only the contradiction with the plastic self-identity of the system and are unaware that by turning against it, they merely actualize its particular moments.

Finally, this duality of philosophical self-consciousness manifests itself in double directions which arc diametrically opposed. The one, which we may generally call the *liberal* party, adheres to the Concept and the principle of philosophy as its main determination; the other to its *Non-concept*, the element of reality. This second direction is *positive philosophy*. The act of the former is criticism; hence, precisely the turning outward of philosophy. The act of the latter is the attempt to philosophize, thus the turning inward of philosophy. It grasps the deficiency as immanent to philosophy, while the former conceives it as a deficiency of the world to be made philosophical. Each of these parties does exactly what the other wants to do, and what each one itself does not want to do. But the former, with its inner contradiction, is conscious in general of principle and aim. In the second appears perversity, so to speak, insanity as such. In content only the liberal party makes real progress, because it is the party of the Concept while positive philosophy is capable of achieving merely demands and tendencies whose form contradicts its meaning.

What seems to be, first of all, philosophy's wrong relation to and diremption with the world, turns secondly into a diremption of the individual philosophical self-consciousness in itself and finally appears as philosophy's external separation and duality, as two opposed philosophical directions.

It is understood that in addition a lot of subordinate, trifling, unoriginal forms appear, which perhaps hide behind a philosophical giant of the past—but one soon notices the donkey under the lion's skin; the whiny voice of a perennial puppet cries in comic contrast to the mighty voice that fills centuries, say Aristotle's, having made itself his unwelcome mouthpiece; it is, as if a mute person wanted to acquire a voice with the aid of an enormous megaphone—or, armed with double spectacles, some Lilliputian stands on the extremity of the giant's posterior, announces amazedly to the world what an astoundingly new view is offered from his point of vantage and ridiculously endeavors to demonstrate that the Archimedean point, the που στω on which the world hinges, can be found not in the pulsating heart but in the firm and solid area on which he stands. Thus originate hair-, toe-, excrement-philosophers, and others who represent an even worse position in Swedenborg's mystical world-man. According to their nature, however, all these clams fall into the two directions stated, these being their element. In regard to these directions, I shall elsewhere explain completely their relationship to each other and to Hegel's philosophy, as well as the particular historical moments in which this development is manifest.

9

A Role for History
and Progress through Revolutions

Thomas Kuhn

INTRODUCTION: A ROLE FOR HISTORY

History, if viewed as a repository for more than anecdote or chronology, could produce a decisive transformation in the image of science by which we are now possessed. That image has previously been drawn, even by scientists themselves, mainly from the study of finished scientific achievements as these are recorded in the classics and, more recently, in the textbooks from which each new scientific generation learns to practice its trade. Inevitably, however, the aim of such books is persuasive and pedagogic; a concept of science drawn from them is no more likely to fit the enterprise that produced them than an image of a national culture drawn from a tourist brochure or a language text. This essay attempts to show that we have been misled by them in fundamental ways. Its aim is a sketch of the quite different concept of science that can emerge from the historical record of the research activity itself.

Even from history, however, that new concept will not he forthcoming if historical data continue to be sought and scrutinized mainly to answer questions posed by the unhistorical stereotype drawn from science texts. Those texts have, for example, often seemed to imply that the content of science is uniquely exemplified by the observations, laws, and theories described in their pages. Almost as regularly, the same books have been read as saying that scientific methods are simply the ones illustrated by the manipulative techniques used in gathering textbook data, together with the logical operations employed when relating those data to the textbook's theoretical generaliza-

Kuhn, Thomas. 1970. *The Structure of Scientific Revolutions*. Chicago: University of Chicago Press, pp. 1–9, 160–173.

tions. The result has been a concept of science with profound implications about its nature and development

If science is the constellation of facts, theories, and methods collected in current texts, then scientists are the men who, successfully or not, have striven to contribute one or another element to that particular constellation. Scientific development be-comes the piecemeal process by which these items have been added, singly and in combination, to the ever growing stockpile that constitutes scientific technique and knowledge. And history of science becomes the discipline that chronicles both these successive increments and the obstacles that have inhibited their accumulation. Concerned with scientific development, the historian then appears to have two main tasks. On the one hand, he must determine by what man and at what point in time each contemporary scientific fact, law, and theory was discovered or invented. On the other, he must describe and explain the congeries of error, myth, and superstition that have inhibited the more rapid accumulation of the constituents of the modern science text Much research has been directed to these ends, and some still is.

In recent years, however, a few historians of science have been finding it more and more difficult to fulfil the functions that the concept of development-by-accumulation assigns to them. As chroniclers of an incremental process, they discover that additional research makes it harder, not easier, to answer questions like: When was oxygen discovered? Who first conceived of energy conservation? Increasingly, a few of them suspect that these are simply the wrong sorts of questions to ask. Perhaps science does not develop by the accumulation of individual discoveries and inventions. Simultaneously, these same historians confront growing difficulties in distinguishing the "scientific" component of past observation and belief from what their predecessors had readily labeled "error" and "superstition." The more carefully they study, say, Aristotelian dynamics, phlogistic chemistry, or caloric thermodynamics, the more certain they feel that those once current views of nature were, as a whole, neither less scientific nor more the product of human idiosyncrasy than those current today. If these out-of-date beliefs are to be called myths, then myths can be produced by the same sorts of methods and held for the same sorts of reasons that now lead to scientific knowledge. If, on the other hand, they are to be called science, then science has included bodies of belief quite incompatible with the ones we hold today. Given these alternatives, the historian must choose the latter. Out-of-date theories are not in principle unscientific because they have been discarded. That choice, however, makes it difficult to see scientific development as a process of accretion. The same historical research that displays the difficulties in isolating individual inventions and discoveries gives ground for profound doubts about the cumulative process through which these individual contributions to science were thought to have been compounded.

The result of all these doubts and difficulties is a historiographic revolution in the study of science, though one that is still in its early stages. Gradually, and often without entirely realizing they are doing so, historians of science have begun to ask new sorts of questions and to trace different, and often less than cumulative, developmental lines for the sciences. Rather than seeking the permanent contributions of an older science to our present vantage, they attempt to display the historical integrity of that science in its own time. They ask, for example, not about the relation of Galileo's views to those of modem science, but rather about the relationship between his views and those of his group, i.e., his teachers, contemporaries, and immediate successors in the sciences. Furthermore, they insist upon studying the opinions of that group and other similar ones from the viewpoint—usually very different from that of modem science—that gives those opinions the maximum internal coherence and the closest possible fit to nature. Seen through the works that result, works perhaps best exemplified in the writings of Alexandre Koyré, science does not seem altogether the same enterprise as the one discussed by writers in the older historiographic tradition. By implication, at least, these historical studies suggest the possibility of a new image of science. This essay aims to delineate that image by making explicit some of the new historiography's implications.

What aspects of science will emerge to prominence in the course of this effort? First, at least in order of presentation, is the insufficiency of methodological directives, by themselves, to dictate a unique substantive conclusion to many sorts of scientific questions. Instructed to examine electrical or chemical phenomena, the man who is ignorant of these fields but who knows what it is to be scientific may legitimately reach any one of a number of incompatible conclusions. Among those legitimate possibilities, the particular conclusions he does arrive at are probably determined by his prior experience in other fields, by the accidents of his investigation, and by his own individual makeup. What beliefs about the stars, for example, does he bring to the study of chemistry or electricity? Which of the many conceivable experiments relevant to the new field does he elect to perform first? And what aspects of the complex phenomenon that then results strike him as particularly relevant to an elucidation of the nature of chemical change or of electrical affinity? For the individual, at least, and sometimes for the scientific community as well, answers to questions like these are often essential determinants of scientific development. We shall note, for example, in Section II that the early developmental stages of most sciences have been characterized by continual competition between a number of distinct views of nature, each partially derived from, and all roughly compatible with, the dictates of scientific observation and method. What differentiated these various schools was not one or another failure of method—they were all "scientific"—but what we shall come to call their incommensurable ways of seeing the world and of practicing science in it. Observation and experience can and must drastically restrict the range of admissible scientific belief, else there would be no science. But they cannot alone determine a particular body of such belief. An apparently arbitrary element, compounded of personal and historical accident, is always a formative ingredient of the beliefs espoused by a given scientific community at a given time.

That element of arbitrariness does not, however, indicate that any scientific group could practice its trade without some set of received beliefs. Nor does it make less consequential the particular constellation to which the group, at a given time, is in fact committed. Effective research scarcely begins before a scientific community thinks it has acquired firm answers to questions like the following: What are the fundamental entities of which the universe is composed? How do these interact with each other and with the senses? What questions may legitimately be asked about such entities and what techniques employed in seeking solutions? At least in the mature sciences, answers (or full substitutes for answers) to questions like these are firmly embedded in the educational initiation that prepares and licenses the student for professional practice. Because that education is both rigorous and rigid, these answers come to exert a deep hold on the scientific mind. That they can do so does much to account both for the peculiar efficiency of the normal research activity and for the direction in which it proceeds at any given time. When examining normal science in Sections III, IV, and V, we shall want finally to describe that research as a strenuous and devoted attempt to force nature into the conceptual boxes supplied by professional education. Simultaneously, we shall wonder whether research could proceed without such boxes, whatever the element of arbitrariness in their historic origins and, occasionally, in their subsequent development.

Yet that element of arbitrariness is present, and it too has an important effect on scientific development, one which will be examined in detail in Sections VI, VII, and VIII. Normal science, the activity in which most scientists inevitably spend almost all their time, is predicated on the assumption that the scientific community knows what the world is like. Much of the success of the enterprise derives from the community's willingness to defend that assumption, if necessary at considerable cost. Normal science, for example, often suppresses fundamental novelties because they are necessarily subversive of its basic commitments. Nevertheless, so long as those commitments retain an element of the arbitrary, the very nature of normal research ensures that novelty shall not be suppressed for very long. Sometimes a normal problem, one that ought to be solvable by known rules and procedures, resists the reiterated onslaught of the ablest members of the group within whose competence it falls. On other occasions a piece of equipment designed and constructed for the purpose of normal research fails to perform in the anticipated manner, revealing an anomaly that cannot, despite repeated effort, be aligned with professional expectation. In these and other ways besides, normal science repeatedly goes astray. And when it does—when, that is, the profession can no longer evade anomalies that subvert the existing tradition of scientific practice—then begin the extraordinary investigations that lead the profession at last to a new set of commitments, a new basis for the practice of science. The extraordinary episodes in which that shift of professional commitments occurs are the ones known in this essay as scientific revolutions. They are the tradition-shattering complements to the tradition-bound activity of normal science.

The most obvious examples of scientific revolutions are those famous episodes in scientific development that have often been labeled revolutions before. Therefore, in Sections IX and X, where the nature of scientific revolutions is first directly scrutinized, we shall deal repeatedly with the major turning points in scientific development associated with the names of Copernicus, Newton, Lavoisier, and Einstein. More clearly than most other episodes in the history of at least the physical sciences, these display what all scientific revolutions are about. Each of them necessitated the community's rejection of one time-honored scientific theory in favor of another incompatible with it. Each produced a consequent shift in the problems available for scientific scrutiny and in the standards by which the profession determined what should count as an admissible problem or as a legitimate problem-solution. And each transformed the scientific imagination in ways that we shall ultimately need to describe as a transformation of the world within which scientific work was done. Such changes, together with the controversies that almost always accompany them, are the defining characteristics of scientific revolutions.

These characteristics emerge with particular clarity from a study of, say, the Newtonian or the chemical revolution. It is, however, a fundamental thesis of this essay that they can also be retrieved from the study of many other episodes that were not so obviously revolutionary. For the far smaller professional group affected by them, Maxwell's equations were as revolutionary as Einstein's, and they were resisted accordingly. The invention of other new theories regularly, and appropriately, evokes the same response from some of the specialists on whose area of special competence they impinge. For these men the new theory implies a change in the rules governing the prior practice of normal science. Inevitably, therefore, it reflects upon much scientific work they have already successfully completed. That is why a new theory, however special its range of application, is seldom or never just an increment to what is already known. Its assimilation requires the reconstruction of prior theory and the re-evaluation of prior fact, an intrinsically revolutionary process that is seldom completed by a single man and never overnight. No wonder historians have had difficulty in dating precisely this extended process that their vocabulary impels them to view as an isolated event.

Nor are new inventions of theory the only scientific events that have revolutionary impact upon the specialists in whose domain they occur. The commitments that govern normal science specify not only what sorts of entities the universe does contain, but also, by implication, those that it does not. It follows, though the point will require extended discussion, that a discovery like that of oxygen or X-rays does not simply add one more item to the population of the scientist's world. Ultimately it has that effect, but not until the professional community has re-evaluated traditional experimental procedures, altered its conception of entities with which it has long been familiar, and, in the process, shifted the network of theory through which it deals with the world. Scientific fact and theory are not categorically separable, except perhaps within a single tradition of normal-scientific practice. That is why the unexpected discovery is not simply factual in its import and why the scientist's world is qualitatively transformed as well as quantitatively enriched by fundamental novelties of either fact or theory.

This extended conception of the nature of scientific revolutions is the one delineated in the pages that follow. Admittedly the extension strains customary usage. Nevertheless, I shall continue to speak even of discoveries as revolutionary, because it is just the possibility of relating their structure to that of, say, the Copernican revolution that makes the extended conception seem to me so important. The preceding discussion indicates how the complementary notions of normal science and of scientific revolutions will be developed in the nine sections immediately to follow. The rest of the essay attempts to dispose of three remaining central questions. Section XI, by discussing the textbook tradition, considers why scientific revolutions have previously been so difficult to see. Section XII describes the revolutionary competition between the proponents of the old normal-scientific tradition and the adherents of the new one. It thus considers the process that should somehow, in a theory of scientific inquiry, replace the confirmation or falsification procedures made familiar by our usual image of science. Competition between segments of the scientific community is the only historical process that ever actually results in the rejection of one previously accepted theory or in the adoption of another. Finally, Section XIII will ask how development through revolutions can be compatible with the apparently unique character of scientific progress. For that question, however, this essay will provide no more than the main outlines of an answer, one which depends upon characteristics of the scientific community that require much additional exploration and study.

Undoubtedly, some readers will already have wondered whether historical study can possibly effect the sort of conceptual transformation aimed at here. An entire arsenal of dichotomies is available to suggest that it cannot properly do so. History, we too often say, is a purely descriptive discipline. The theses suggested above are, however, often interpretive and sometimes normative. Again, many of my generalizations are about the sociology or social psychology of scientists; yet at least a few of my conclusions belong traditionally to logic or epistemology. In the preceding paragraph I may even seem to have violated the very influential contemporary distinction between "the context of discovery" and "the context of justification." Can anything more than profound confusion be indicated by this admixture of diverse fields and concerns?

Having been weaned intellectually on these distinctions and others like them, I could scarcely be more aware of their import and force. For many years I took them to be about the nature of knowledge, and I still suppose that, appropriately recast, they have something important to tell us. Yet my attempts to apply them, even *grosso modo*, to the actual situations in which knowledge is gained, accepted, and assimilated have made them seem extraordinarily problematic. Rather than being elementary logical or methodological distinctions, which would thus be prior to the analysis of scientific knowledge, they now seem integral parts of a traditional set of substantive answers to the very questions upon which they have been deployed. That circularity does not at all invalidate them. But it does make them parts of a theory and, by doing so, subjects them to the same scrutiny regularly applied to theories in other fields. If they are to have more than pure abstraction as their content, then that content must be discovered by observing them in application to the data they are meant to elucidate. How could history of science fail to be a source of phenomena to which theories about knowledge may legitimately be asked to apply?

PROGRESS THROUGH REVOLUTIONS

The preceding pages have carried my schematic description of scientific development as far as it can go in this essay. Nevertheless, they cannot quite provide a conclusion. If this description has at all caught the essential structure of a science's continuing evolution, it will simultaneously have posed a special problem: Why should the enterprise sketched above move steadily ahead in ways that, say, art, political theory, or philosophy does not? Why is progress a perquisite reserved almost exclusively for the activities we call science? The most usual answers to that question have been denied in the body of this essay. We must conclude it by asking whether substitutes can be found.

Notice immediately that part of the question is entirely semantic. To a very great extent the term "science" is reserved for fields that do progress in obvious ways. Nowhere does this show more clearly than in the recurrent debates about whether one or another of the contemporary social sciences is really a science. These debates have parallels in the pre-paradigm periods of fields that are today unhesitatingly labeled science. Their ostensible issue throughout is a definition of that vexing term. Men argue that psychology, for example, is a science because it possesses such and such characteristics.

Others counter that those characteristics are either unnecessary or not sufficient to make a field a science. Often great energy is invested, great passion aroused, and the outsider is at a loss to know why. Can very much depend upon a *definition* of "science"? Can a definition tell a man whether he is a scientist or not? If so, why do not natural scientists or artists worry about the definition of the term? Inevitably one suspects that the issue is more fundamental. Probably questions like the following are really being asked: Why does my field fail to move ahead in the way that, say, physics does? What changes in technique or method or ideology would enable it to do so? These are not, however, questions that could respond to an agreement on definition. Furthermore, if precedent from the natural sciences serves, they will cease to be a source of concern not when a definition is found, but when the groups that now doubt their own status achieve consensus about their past and present accomplishments. It may, for example, be significant that economists argue less about whether their field is a science than do practitioners of some other fields of social science. Is that because economists know what science is? Or is it rather economics about which they agree?

That point has a converse that, though no longer simply semantic, may help to display the inextricable connections between our notions of science and of progress. For many centuries, both in antiquity and again in early modern Europe, painting was regarded as *the* cumulative discipline. During those years the artist's goal was assumed to be representation. Critics and historians, like Pliny and Vasari, then recorded with veneration the series of inventions from foreshortening through chiaroscuro that had made possible successively more perfect representations of nature.[1] But those are also the years, particularly during the Renaissance, when little cleavage was felt between the sciences and the arts. Leonardo was only one of many men who passed freely back and forth between fields that only later became categorically distinct.[2] Furthermore, even after that steady exchange had ceased, the term "art" continued to apply as much to technology and the crafts, which were also seen as progressive, as to painting and sculpture. Only when the latter unequivocally renounced representation as their goal and began to learn again from primitive models did the cleavage we now take for granted assume anything like its present depth. And even today, to switch fields once more, part of our difficulty in seeing the profound differences between science and technology must relate to the fact that progress is an obvious attribute of both fields.

It can, however, only clarify, not solve, our present difficulty to recognize that we tend to see as science any field in which progress is marked. There remains the problem of understanding why progress should be so noteworthy a characteristic of an enterprise conducted with the techniques and goals this essay has described. That question proves to be several in one, and we shall have to consider each of them separately. In all cases but the last, however, their resolution will depend in part upon an inversion of our normal view of the relation between scientific activity and the community that practices it. We must learn to recognize as causes what have ordinarily been taken to be effects. If we can do that, the phrases "scientific progress" and even "scientific objectivity" may come to seem in part redundant. In fact, one aspect of the redundancy has just been illustrated. Does a field make progress because it is a science, or is it a science because it makes progress?

Ask now why an enterprise like normal science should progress, and begin by recalling a few of its most salient characteristics. Normally, the members of a mature scientific community work from a single paradigm or from a closely related set. Very rarely do different scientific communities investigate the same problems. In those exceptional cases the groups hold several major paradigms in common. Viewed from within any single community, however, whether of scientists or of non-scientists, the result of successful creative work *is* progress. How could it possibly be anything else? We have, for example, just noted that while artists aimed at representation as their goal, both critics and historians chronicled the progress of the apparently united group. Other creative fields display progress of the same sort. The theologian who articulates dogma or the philosopher who refines the Kantian imperatives contributes to progress, if only to that of the group that shares his premises. No creative school recognizes a category of work that is, on the one hand, a creative success, but is not, on the other, an addition to the collective achievement of the group. If we doubt, as many do, that nonscientific fields make progress, that cannot be because individual schools make none. Rather, it must be because there are always competing schools, each of which constantly questions the very foundations of the others. The man who argues that philosophy, for example, has made no progress emphasizes that there are still Aristotelians, not that Aristotelianism has failed to progress.

These doubts about progress arise, however, in the sciences too. Throughout the pre-paradigm period when there is a multiplicity of competing schools, evidence of progress, except within schools, is very hard to find. This is the period described in Section II as one during which individuals practice science, but in which the results of their enterprise do not add up to science as we know it. And again, during periods of revolution when the fundamental tenets of a field are once more at issue, doubts are repeatedly expressed about the very possibility of continued progress if one or another of the opposed paradigms is adopted. Those who rejected Newtonianism proclaimed that its reliance upon innate forces would return science to the Dark Ages. Those who opposed Lavoisier's chemistry held that the rejection of chemical "principles" in favor of laboratory elements was the rejection of achieved chemical explanation by those who would take refuge in a mere name. A similar, though more moderately expressed, feeling seems to underlie the opposition of Einstein, Bohm, and others, to the dominant probabilistic interpretation of quantum mechanics. In short, it is only during periods of normal science that progress seems both obvious and assured. During those periods, however, the scientific community could view the fruits of its work in no other way.

With respect to normal science, then, part of the answer to the problem of progress lies simply in the eye of the beholder. Scientific progress is not different in kind from progress in other fields, but the absence at most times of competing schools that question each other's aims and standards makes the progress of a normal-scientific community far easier to see. That, however, is only part of the answer and by no means the most important part. We have, for example, already noted that once the reception of a common paradigm has freed the scientific community from the need constantly to reexamine its first principles, the members of that community can concentrate exclusively upon the subtlest and most esoteric of the phenomena that concern it. Inevitably, that does increase both the effectiveness and the efficiency with which the group as a whole solves new problems. Other aspects of professional life in the sciences enhance this very special efficiency still further.

Some of these are consequences of the unparalleled insulation of mature scientific communities from the demands of the laity and of everyday life. That insulation has never been complete—we are now discussing matters of degree. Nevertheless, there are no other professional communities in which individual creative work is so exclusively addressed to and evaluated by other members of the profession. The most esoteric of poets or the most abstract of theologians is far more concerned than the scientist with lay approbation of his creative work, though he may be even less concerned with approbation in general. That difference proves consequential. Just because he is working only for an audience of colleagues, an audience that shares his own values and beliefs, the scientist can take a single set of standards for granted. He need not worry about what some other group or school will think and can therefore dispose of one problem and get on to the next more quickly than those who work for a more heterodox group. Even more important, the insulation of the scientific community from society permits the individual scientist to concentrate his attention upon problems that he has good reason to believe he will be able to solve. Unlike the engineer, and many doctors, and most theologians, the scientist need not choose problems because they urgently need solution and without regard for the tools available to solve them. In this respect, also, the contrast between natural scientists and many social scientists proves instructive. The latter often tend, as the former almost never do, to defend their choice of a research problem—e.g., the effects of racial discrimination or the causes of the business cycle—chiefly in terms of the social importance of achieving a solution. Which group would one then expect to solve problems at a more rapid rate?

The effects of insulation from the larger society are greatly intensified by another characteristic of the professional scientific community, the nature of its educational initiation. In music, the graphic arts, and literature, the practitioner gains his education by exposure to the works of other artists, principally earlier artists. Textbooks, except compendia of or handbooks to original creations, have only a secondary role. In history, philosophy, and the social sciences, textbook literature has a greater significance. But even in these fields the elementary college course employs parallel readings in original sources, some of them the "classics" of the field, others the contemporary research reports that practitioners write for each other. As a result, the student in any one of these disciplines is constantly made aware of the immense variety of problems that the members of his future group have, in the course of time, attempted to solve. Even more important, he has constantly before him a number of competing and incommensurable solutions to these problems, solutions that he must ultimately evaluate for himself.

Contrast this situation with that in at least the contemporary natural sciences. In these fields the student relies mainly on textbooks until, in his third or fourth year of graduate work, he begins his own research. Many science curricula do not ask even graduate students to read in works not written specially for students. The few that do assign supplementary reading in research papers and monographs restrict such assignments to the most advanced courses and to materials that take up more or less where the available texts leave off. Until the very last stages in the education of a scientist, textbooks are systematically substituted for the creative scientific literature that made them possible. Given the confidence in their paradigms, which makes this educational technique possible, few scientists would wish to change it. Why, after all, should the student of physics, for example, read the works of Newton, Faraday, Einstein, or Schrödinger, when everything he needs to know about these works is recapitulated in a far briefer, more precise, and more systematic form in a number of up-to-date textbooks?

Without wishing to defend the excessive lengths to which this type of education has occasionally been carried, one cannot help but notice that in general it has been immensely effective. Of course, it is a narrow and rigid education, probably more so than any other except perhaps in orthodox theology. But for normal-scientific work, for puzzle-solving within the tradition that the textbooks define, the scientist is almost perfectly equipped. Furthermore, he is well equipped for another task as well—the generation through normal science of significant crises. When they arise, the scientist is not, of course, equally well prepared. Even though prolonged crises are probably reflected in less rigid educational practice, scientific training is not well designed to produce the man who will easily discover a fresh approach. But so long as somebody appears with a new candidate for paradigm—usually a young man or one new to the field—the loss due to rigidity accrues only to the individual. Given a generation in which to effect the change, individual rigidity is compatible with a community that can switch from paradigm to paradigm when the occasion demands. Particularly, it is compatible when that very rigidity provides the community with a sensitive indicator that something has gone wrong.

In its normal state, then, a scientific community is an immensely efficient instrument for solving the problems or puzzles that its paradigms define. Furthermore, the result of solving those problems must inevitably be progress. There is no problem here. Seeing that much, however, only highlights the second main part of the problem of progress in the sciences. Let us therefore turn to it and ask about progress through extraordinary science. Why should progress also be the apparently universal concomitant of scientific revolutions? Once again, there is much to be learned by asking what else the result of a revolution could be. Revolutions close with a total victory for one of the two opposing camps. Will that group ever say that the result of its victory has been something less than progress? That would be rather like admitting that they had been wrong and their opponents right. To them, at least, the outcome of revolution must be progress, and they are in an excellent position to make certain that future members of their community will see past history in the same way. [A previous section] described in detail the techniques by which this is accomplished, and we have just recurred to a closely related aspect of professional scientific life. When it repudiates a past paradigm, a scientific community simultaneously renounces, as a fit subject for professional scrutiny, most of the books and articles in which that paradigm had been embodied. Scientific education makes use of no equivalent for the art museum or the library of classics, and the result is a sometimes drastic distortion in the scientist's perception of his discipline's past. More than the practitioners of other creative fields, he comes to see it as leading in a straight line to the discipline's present vantage. In short, he comes to see it as progress. No alternative is available to him while he remains in the field.

Inevitably those remarks will suggest that the member of a mature scientific community is, like the typical character of Orwell's *1984*, the victim of a history rewritten by the powers that be. Furthermore, that suggestion is not altogether inappropriate. There are losses as well as gains in scientific revolutions, and scientists tend to be peculiarly blind to the former.[3] On the other hand, no explanation of progress through revolutions may stop at this point. To do so would be to imply that in the sciences might makes right, a formulation which would again not be entirely wrong if it did not suppress the nature of the process and of the authority by which the choice between paradigms is made. If authority alone, and particularly if nonprofessional authority, were the arbiter of paradigm debates, the outcome of those debates might still be revolution, but it would not be *scientific* revolution. The very existence of science depends upon vesting the power to choose between paradigms in the members of a special kind of community. Just how special that community must be if science is to survive and grow may be indicated by the very tenuousness of humanity's hold on the scientific enterprise. Every civilization of which we have records has possessed a technology, an art, a religion, a polit-ical system, laws, and so on. In many cases those facets of civilization have been as developed as our own. But only the civilizations that descend from Hellenic Greece have possessed more than the most rudimentary science. The bulk of scientific knowledge is a product of Europe in the last four centuries. No other place and time has supported the very special communities from which scientific productivity comes.

What are the essential characteristics of these communities? Obviously, they need vastly more study. In this area only the most tentative generalizations are possible. Nevertheless, a number of requisites for membership in a pro-fessional scientific group must already be strikingly clear. The scientist must, for example, be concerned to solve problems about the behavior of nature. In addition, though his concern with nature may be global in its extent, the prob-lems on which he works must be problems of detail. More important, the solu-tions that satisfy him may not be merely personal but must instead be accepted as solutions by many. The group that shares them may not, however, be drawn at random from society as a whole, but is rather the well-defined community of the scientist's professional compeers. One of the strongest, if still unwritten, rules of scientific life is the prohibition of appeals to heads of state or to the pop-ulace at large in matters scientific. Recognition of the existence of a uniquely competent professional group and acceptance of its role as the exclusive arbiter of professional achievement has further implications. The group's members, as individuals and by virtue of their shared training and experience, must be seen as the sole possessors of the rules of the game or of some equivalent basis for unequivocal judgments. To doubt that they shared some such basis for evaluations would be to admit the existence of incompatible standards of sci-entific achievement. That admission would inevitably raise the question whether truth in the sciences can be one.

This small list of characteristics common to scientific communities has been drawn entirely from the practice of normal science, and it should have been. That is the activity for which the scientist is ordinarily trained. Note, however, that despite its small size the list is already sufficient to set such communities apart from all other professional groups. And note, in addition, that despite its source in normal science the list accounts for many special fea-tures of the group's response during revolutions and particularly during par-adigm debates. We have already observed that a group of this sort must see a paradigm change as progress. Now we may recognize that the perception is, in important respects, self-fulfilling. The scientific community is a supremely efficient instrument for maximizing the number and precision of the problem solved through paradigm change.

Because the unit of scientific achievement is the solved problem and because the group knows well which problems have already been solved, few scientists will easily be persuaded to adopt a viewpoint that again opens to question many problems that had previously been solved. Nature itself must first undermine professional security by making prior achievements seem problematic. Furthermore, even when that has occurred and a new candidate for paradigm has been evoked, scientists will be reluctant to embrace it unless convinced that two all-important conditions are being met. First, the new candidate must seem to resolve some outstanding and generally recognized problem that can be met in no other way. Second) the new paradigm must promise to preserve a relatively large part of the concrete problem-solving ability that has accrued to science through its predecessors. Novelty for its own sake is not a desideratum in the sciences as it is in so many other creative fields. As a result, though new paradigms seldom or never possess all the capabilities of their predecessors, they usually preserve a great deal of the most concrete parts of past achievement and they always permit additional concrete problem-solutions besides.

To say this much is not to suggest that the ability to solve problems is either the unique or an unequivocal basis for paradigm choice. We have already noted many reasons why there can be no criterion of that sort. But it does suggest that a community of scientific specialists will do all that it can to ensure the continuing growth of the assembled data that it can treat with precision and detail. In the process the community will sustain losses. Often some old problems must be banished. Frequently, in addition, revolution narrows the scope of the community's professional concerns, increases the extent of its specialization, and attenuates its communication with other groups, both scientific and lay. Though science surely grows in depth, it may not grow in breadth as well. If it does so, that breadth is manifest mainly in the proliferation of scientific specialties, not in the scope of any single specialty alone. Yet despite these and other losses to the individual communities, the nature of such communities provides a virtual guarantee that both the list of problems solved by science and the precision of individual problem-solutions will grow and grow. At least, the nature of the community provides such a guarantee if there is any way at all in which it can be provided. What better criterion than the decision of the scientific group could there be?

These last paragraphs point the directions in which I believe a more refined solution of the problem of progress in the sciences must be sought. Perhaps they indicate that scientific progress is not quite what we had taken it to be. But they simultaneously show that a sort of progress will inevitably characterize the scientific enterprise so long as such an enterprise survives. In the sciences there need not be progress of another sort. We may, to be more precise, have to relinquish the notion, explicit or implicit, that changes of paradigm carry scientists and those who learn from them closer and closer to the truth.

It is now time to notice that until the last very few pages the term "truth" had entered this essay only in a quotation from Francis Bacon. And even in those pages it entered only as a source for the scientist's conviction that incompatible rules for doing science cannot coexist except during revolutions when the profession's main task is to eliminate all sets but one. The developmental process described in this essay has been a process of evolution *from* primitive beginnings—a process whose successive stages are characterized by an increasingly detailed and refined understanding of nature. But nothing that has been or will be said makes it a process of evolution *toward* any-thing. Inevitably that lacuna will have disturbed many readers. We are all deeply accustomed to seeing science as the one enterprise that draws constantly nearer to some goal set by nature in advance.

But need there be any such goal? Can we not account for both science's existence and its success in terms of evolution from the community's state of knowledge at any given time? Does it really help to imagine that there is some one full, objective, true account of nature and that the proper measure of scientific achievement is the extent to which it brings us closer to that ultimate goal? If we can learn to substitute evolution-from-what-we-do-know for evolution-toward-what-we-wish-to-know, a number of vexing problems may vanish in the process. Somewhere in this maze, for example, must lie the problem of induction.

I cannot yet specify in any detail the consequences of this alternate view of scientific advance. But it helps to recognize that the conceptual transposition here recommended is very close to one that the West undertook just a century ago. It is particularly helpful because in both cases the main obstacle to transposition is the same. When Darwin first published his theory of evolution by natural selection in 1859, what most bothered many professionals was neither the notion of species change nor the possible descent of man from apes. The evidence pointing to evolution, including the evolution of man, had been accumulating for decades, and the idea of evolution had been suggested and widely disseminated before. Though evolution, as such, did encounter resistance, particularly from some religious groups, it was by no means the greatest of the difficulties the Darwinians faced. That difficulty stemmed from an idea that was more nearly Darwin's own. All the well-known pre-Darwinian evolutionary theories—those of Lamarck, Chambers, Spencer, and the German *Naturphilosophen*—had taken evolution to he a goal-directed process. The "idea" of man and of the contemporary flora and fauna was thought to have been present from the first creation of life, perhaps in the mind of Cod. That idea or plan had provided the direction and the guiding force to the entire evolutionary process. Each new stage of evolutionary development was a more perfect realization of a plan that had been present from the start.[4]

For many men the abolition of that teleological kind of evolution was the most significant and least palatable of Darwin's suggestions.[5] *The Origin of Species* recognized no goal set either by God or nature. Instead, natural selection, operating in the given environment and with the actual organisms presently at hand, was responsible for the gradual but steady emergence of more elaborate, further articulated, and vastly more specialized organisms. Even such marvelously adapted organs as the eye and hand of man—organs whose design had previously provided powerful arguments for the existence of a supreme artificer and an advance plan—were products of a process that moved steadily *from* primitive beginnings but *toward* no goal. The belief that natural selection, resulting from mere competition between organisms for survival, could have produced man together with the higher animals and plants was the most difficult and disturbing aspect of Darwin's theory. What could "evolution," "development," and "progress" mean in the absence of a specified goal? To many people, such terms suddenly seemed self-contradictory.

The analogy that relates the evolution of organisms to the evolution of scientific ideas can easily be pushed too far. But with respect to the issues of this closing section it is very nearly perfect. The process described in [a previous section] as the resolution of revolutions is the selection by conflict within the scientific community of the fittest way to practice future science. The net result of a sequence of such revolutionary selections, separated by periods of normal research, is the wonderfully adapted set of instruments we call modern scientific knowledge. Successive stages in that developmental process are marked by an increase in articulation and specialization. And the entire process may have occurred, as we now suppose biological evolution did, without benefit of a set goal, a permanent fixed scientific truth, of which each stage in the development of scientific knowledge is a better exemplar.

Anyone who has followed the argument this far will nevertheless feel the need to ask why the evolutionary process should work. What must nature, including man, be like in order that science be possible at all? Why should scientific communities be able to reach a firm consensus unattainable in other fields? Why should consensus endure across one paradigm change after another? And why should paradigm change invariably produce an instrument more perfect in any sense than those known before? From one point of view those questions, excepting the first, have already been answered. But from another they are as open as they were when this essay began. It is not only the scientific community that must be special. The world of which that community is a part must also possess quite special characteristics, and we are no closer than we were at the start to knowing what these must be. That problem—What must the world be like in order that man may know it?—was not, however, created by this essay. On the contrary, it is as old as science itself, and it remains unanswered. But it need not be answered in this place. Any conception of nature compatible with the growth of science by proof is compatible with the evolutionary view of science developed here. Since this view is also compatible with close observation of scientific life, there are strong arguments for employing it in attempts to solve the host of problems that still remain.

NOTES

1. E. H. Gombrich, *Art and Illusion: A Study in the Psychology of Pictorial Representation* (New York, 1960), pp. 11–12.
2. *Ibid.*, p. 97; and Giorgio de Santillana, "The Role of Art in the Scientific Renaissance," In *Critical Problems in the History of Science,* ed. M. Clagett (Madison, Wis., 1959), pp. 33–65.
3. Historians of science often encounter this blindness in a particularly striking form. The group of students who come to themf rom the sciences is very often the most rewarding group they teach. But it is also usually the most frustrating at the start. Because science students "know the right answers," it is particularly difficult to make them analyze an older science in its own terms.
4. Loren Eiseley, *Darwin's Century: Evolution and the Men Who Discovered It* (New York, 1958), chaps. ii, iv–v.
5. For a particularly acute account of one prominent Darwinian's struggle with this problem, see A. Hunter Dupree, *Asa Gray, 1810–1888* (Cambridge, Mass., 1959), pp. 295–306, 355–83.

10

Scientific Principles in Political Study: Some Enduring Situations

Marcus E. Ethridge

Scientific political inquiry uses principles and methods derived from mathematics and the natural sciences and applies them to politics. This book is based on the premise that such an effort is valuable. The scientific approach to research has generated many new insights and understandings, which have replaced inaccurate suppositions, prejudices, and "common sense" views about political life. This method of studying politics has been a resounding success in many important areas.

From its inception, however, the scientific study of politics has aroused controversy. Critics have argued, and continue to argue, that human behavior, particularly *political* behavior, cannot and should not be studied in the same way we study the natural environment. The purpose of this chapter is to identify and explore some of the more common criticisms of scientific political research. As we understand and acknowledge these arguments, we will see that there may, in fact, be limits on the application of scientific principles to the study of politics.

CRITICISM 1. SCIENTIFIC POLITICAL RESEARCH IS IMPRACTICAL

The basic principles of scientific research were developed in the natural sciences, where the subject matter is very different from that studied by political scientists. For many critics, the special nature of political phenomena makes the scientific method impractical, if not impossible.

From *The Political Research Experience: Readings and Analysis, 2nd Edition* by Marcus E. Ethridge. Copyright © 1994, The Dushkin Publishing Group/Brown & Benchmark Publishers, a division of McGraw-Hill Higher Education Group, Guilford, CT. All rights reserved. Reprinted by permission.

For one thing, both the availability and quality of political data pose severe problems. In the face of such problems, political scientists have devised imaginative, but sometimes questionable, ways of generating usable information. For example, during the height of U.S. competition with the Soviet Union, Kremlin watchers were known to quantify the number and types of applause reported in public transcripts of official speeches, as a way of determining the status of each Soviet leader. A Soviet newspaper report of "long and stormy" applause following a leader's speech was cited as evidence that his standing in the Politburo was higher than that of a leader whose statements were reportedly greeted with "polite applause." To put it in terms of our discussion in [a previous chapter], we often encounter validity problems in operationalizing political variables. Data are much more easily obtained and quantified in the realm of the natural sciences.

Perhaps even more important, the number of influences on political behavior is so large that our hypotheses may be fatally incomplete. Compared to experiments in physics or chemistry, where critical variables can be precisely measured and confounding factors controlled, political research often seems disturbingly imprecise. We suffer from research problems that involve a large number of variables and (usually) a relatively small number of cases. This makes causal inference very difficult. Often, even when a dependent variable appears to have been influenced by a particular independent variable, unknown factors may have been responsible for the observed change.

Of course, the difficulties inherent in the scientific prediction of complex phenomena are not limited to the social sciences. Consider the case of the meteorologist who encountered an interesting problem while using a computer to predict weather patterns. He first constructed a mathematical model that incorporated several basic variables, each weighted in accordance with well-established practice. He then entered a set of initial conditions and ran his model, generating a set of predicted changes in the weather for a specified period. Shortly thereafter, he ran the same program again in an attempt to replicate his initial forecast. To his great surprise, the second set of predictions was identical to the earlier one for only the first few days. Thereafter, they were very different.

Upon further analysis, the meteorologist discovered that the differences in the two sets of predictions were caused by extremely minute differences in rounding the numbers of his initial set of conditions. In a very complex model, this alteration, small enough to be considered irrelevant, profoundly affected the predictions. This discovery led to what has since become known as the "butterfly's wing" problem. The term derives from the idea that the weather some months ahead may be significantly affected by today's movement of a butterfly's wing (Gleick, 1987).

The meteorologist's objectives are similar to those of many political researchers who attempt to anticipate the occurrence or outcome of extremely complex phenomena such as elections, the incidence of coups, and state economic growth rates. if predictions of weather patterns are completely altered as a result of a minute error in specifying a single initial condition, what chance do political scientists have? (In this connection, it must be admitted that political scientists conspicuously failed to predict the dismantling of the Berlin Wall or the demise of communism in even one of the Warsaw Pact nations in 1989, a set of events that was central to research in comparative government, international relations, and political development.) One answer is that they are able to make useful predictions of a less exacting variety. Though they may never construct models that allow them to forecast when and where political coups will occur, their research can significantly improve predictions that would otherwise be made on the basis of hunches or blind intuition. In short, the best empirical studies demonstrate that scientific political research can have value even if it never allows us to foresee the future with complete precision or certainty.

CRITICISM 2. POLITICAL RESEARCH IS SUBJECT TO MISUSE

The issues addressed by political research are necessarily controversial, and the findings may be misinterpreted, sometimes intentionally. A notable example of this problem is the controversy over Arthur Jensen's 1969 research on the relationship between IQ tests and heredity. The original purpose of Jensen's study was to examine the feasibility of compensatory education (programs, such as Head Start, designed to compensate for conditions that lead to under-achievement among certain groups of students). Some people, however, quickly misinterpreted his findings as evidence of the genetic inferiority of African Americans. This controversy has led a few critics to conclude that, at least in some areas, the danger of misuse outweighs the potential benefits of research.

Of course, this problem is hardly unique to the social sciences. Scientific research in the areas of weapons development and pesticides, for example, has resulted in the creation of potentially catastrophic new weapons and chemicals. Whether political research might ever produce equally threatening results is difficult to say. What is clear is that the core issues and terminology of political research are directly involved with values. For this reason, they are highly susceptible to misinterpretation, whether deliberate or accidental.

Nonetheless, a strong case can be made that ignorance of political and social phenomena is at least as damaging as the findings of political scientists. The Nazis proclaimed sociological "truths" that would have been hilarious in their unsophistication if they had not served as the foundation for such unspeakable evils; Hitler once dismissed Einstein's theories as "Jewish Physics." When scientific research corrects error and ignorance, the results are almost always beneficial.

The crucial factor is to maintain an unconfined setting throughout the political research process. As long as the research process is open to those with different points of view, and as long as the results are subject to scrutiny by a diverse community of scholars, the benefits of political research will outweigh the dangers of its misuse.

CRITICISM 3. THE APPLICATION OF SCIENCE TO POLITICAL ISSUES DULLS OUR ETHICAL AND MORAL SENSIBILITIES

Political research is often concerned with revolutionary violence, war, racial injustice, and other matters that have profoundly important moral dimensions. Does the scientific method divert our attention from morality? Lawrence Tribe (1972), for one, has suggested that quantifying aspects of human aspirations and tragedy may be necessary for scientific analysis, but doing so may make us lose sight of their complex moral aspects.

In a similar vein, it has been argued that finding solutions to our major social problems requires an emotional attachment to high moral and even spiritual values. David Easton (1971) has argued that "the contemporary loss or confusion of faith by which men live has been hastened by the growth of scientific reasoning in the natural and social sciences" (p. 19). These are challenging ideas. Essentially, we are told that an emphasis on science is detrimental to ethical, moral, and philosophical analysis. Numbed by his or her pursuit of quantification, the scientific researcher falls victim to the delusion that political issues can be resolved by science.

Interestingly enough, this criticism of scientific research in the social sciences comes from both ends of the political spectrum. Liberals like Tribe argue that social science methods lead us to gloss over the serious human tragedy of, say, joblessness, by diverting our focus from human suffering to the bloodless, impersonal, and "objective" indicators we use to measure unemployment. Similarly, conservatives like James Q. Wilson (1993) contend that social science methodology deflects attention away from traditional social values that lie at the core of a functioning society. Science, they argue, can easily determine if a statistical relationship exists, but it cannot, by itself, provide moral guidance concerning how best to change or manage those relationships. To the extent that the answers to political problems lie in a moral plane, the quest for them is not advanced, and may even be retarded, by the application of science.

The solution is obvious to most social scientists. Good research is enlightening, even for moral discourse. It cannot be seriously argued that judgment is enhanced by ignorance, and we are better able to address moral and ethical problems when we operate from a factual basis. If research is sometimes misleading, poorly designed, and misinterpreted, then we should pay greater attention to improving its quality. Using scientific research methods to resolve factual questions will promote the understanding of political problems, ethical or otherwise.

CRITICISM 4. SCIENTIFIC RESEARCH ON POLITICS IS RESTRICTED BY THE EXISTENCE OF FREE WILL

There is a very old controversy in the social sciences regarding the problem of free will. The general concept is straightforward. When a physicist develops and tests a theory of, say, quantum mechanics, the objects of the study are driven by certain forces. If all the relevant variables are known, arriving at a conclusion becomes possible. However, political research attempts to predict human behavior, and, regardless of the forces that we think encourage certain forms of behavior, human beings can choose to act differently, thereby invalidating our predictions. Nonetheless, political research, like all scientific inquiry, rests on the assumption that behavior is ultimately understandable in terms of general laws. If we could exhaustively identify the variables, political behavior could be fully accounted for and predicted. The concept of free will is inconsistent with this assumption, and Peter Winch (1958) argues on this side of the case with conviction:

> [E]ven given a specific set of initial conditions, one will still not be able to predict any determinate outcome to a historical trend because the continuation or breaking off of that trend involves human decisions which are not determined by their antecedent conditions. . . . Think of the interplay between orthodoxy and heresy in the development of religion; or of the way in which the game of football was revolutionized by the Rugby boy who picked up the ball and ran. It would certainly not have been possible to predict that revolution from knowledge of the preceding state of the game any more than it would have been possible to predict the philosophy of Hume from the philosophies of his predecessors. (pp. 92–93)

The central point here is that many important political events are profoundly affected by the results of human decisions, which we will never be able to predict in detail.

In response, even the staunchest defenders of the scientific approach have been willing to concede that human behavior is more complicated, and therefore less predictable, than the subject matter of the natural sciences where subjects cannot "choose their behavior." Yet, some have argued, perhaps this complexity is not due to free will itself, but to the fact that the number of environmental influences acting upon human beings is so large. An individual who makes a choice based apparently on nothing other than his or her own creative impulses is really being driven by influences that we simply have not identified. Those who hold to this position suggest that, in principle, human behavior *can* be predictable; we simply need to know all of the influences, including remote childhood experiences, that may be acting upon a person's observed behavior.

Happily, we do not have to resolve this thorny philosophical problem so long as we recognize that our predictions about political behavior are inevitably imprecise. Whether this is because of free will or the almost infinite number of influences acting on human behavior is not terribly important. What does matter is that even a limited science of politics is still extremely useful. It may be, for example, that we can predict a person's party affiliation with only 75 percent accuracy from knowledge of his or her income, education level, and other relevant factors. Nonetheless, such information is extremely useful, as both campaign managers and political analysts would be quick to attest.

CRITICISM 5. THE SCIENTIFIC METHOD IGNORES HOLISTIC FACTORS

It is often remarked that a group is more than the sum of its parts. At the most abstract level, this implies that some quality or characteristic of the group cannot be entirely accounted for in terms of the behavior or other characteristics of the group's members. This idea, called holism, is usually offered as a challenge to the principles of empirical research in social science, and is described by Brodbeck (1958):

> If, for instance, the efficiency of a group is not some function of the behavior of its constituent individuals, then there must be something else that exhibits this efficiency, the group itself. And if there be such a superentity as, say, a group mind, then it will have characteristics of its own: allegedly, it may have political opinions. (p. 283)

The implication for scientific research is clear: we cannot effectively study groups, classes, or other wholes by studying the individuals comprising them. The nature of the group itself will be overlooked or distorted in our research. If, as holistic thinkers believe, the group itself is important in some respects, we will have failed to take its effects into account in our observation and analysis of individual behavior.

The problem is that groups are not observable. We observe individuals. Even when we use aggregate-level data, for example, state per capita income, we assume that the values are derived from measurements taken at the individual level. For this reason, most proponents of holism inevitably reject empirical scientific inquiry. Conversely, a scientific approach to political study must reject holism, at least in its more extreme forms.

Consider a discussion of the "German Mind," a notion that many thinkers pondered after World War II and which is now resurfacing with a newly unified Germany. The most appropriate empirical approach to the problem would be to conduct a survey of a representative sample of Germans and compare their answers to those of a sample of persons from other countries (see Almond & Verba, 1963, for a classic study along these lines). If the answers given by our German respondents were significantly different from those of the other group, we might conclude that the former do, indeed, have a distinctive set of attitudes.

Such a conclusion would, however, be based on the opinions of German *individuals.* The holistic analyst could claim that the "German Mind" is an entity that transcends the opinions of individual Germans. If so, we have a serious problem. Since the "German Mind" cannot be observed except by observing individuals, we cannot treat the holistic concept scientifically: "The holistic assumption that there are group properties over and above the individuals making up the group, their properties, and the relations among them is counter to empiricism" (Brodbeck, 1958, p. 283). An empirical, scientific approach requires that we deny the existence of an entity transcending individuals.

This does not mean, however, that we cannot study and compare aggregates, or even that we must reject the study of properties like culture or class consciousness, which are widely shared by many people. Holistic thinkers may, moreover, contribute to our understanding by steering us toward factors that *appear* to transcend individuals; they may help us to see the forest and not only the trees. However, when we embark on empirical research we are limited to those concepts that can be analyzed by observation. In political science, this normally requires that we emphasize individual behavior and concepts derived from it.

CRITICISM 6. POLITICAL RESEARCH IS EXCESSIVELY QUANTIFIED

Political researchers have been criticized for their attraction to quantification in their efforts to use the most advanced statistical tools. According to some critics, "If you cannot count it, it does not count," is the motto of these methodologically sophisticated political scientists.

There are at least two reasons why a bias toward quantification may distort our research findings. The first is that it may lead us to disregard factors that are relevant to the behavior in question but are difficult to quantify. This is an especially intense controversy in comparative politics: Quantifiers argue that political development and stability can be measured by factors such as the number of telephones per 100,000 population, literacy rates, or voting turnout, while their less quantitatively oriented colleagues claim that distinctive cultural characteristics and historical events are of paramount importance. If a penchant for quantification leads the analyst to ignore difficult-to-measure concepts that are nonetheless important to the question at hand, his or her research will be seriously flawed.

Second, quantification can lead to oversimplifying or even trivializing concepts. Abraham Kaplan (1964) illustrated the problem with an amusing anecdote about the famous Kinsey report on sexual behavior:

> One of the subjects of [the Kinsey study] complained bitterly of the injury to his masculine ego. "No matter what I told him," he explained, "he just looked me straight in the eye and asked, 'How many times . . . ?" Plainly the subject felt

that *what* he had done was incomparably more significant than the frequency of its performance. (p. 171)

In a realm as complex as politics, the attempt to quantify unique events inevitably carries with it the risk of distortion. Every violent overthrow of a government, for example, is surely different in many important ways from all others. Yet some researchers have used a simple 3-point rating scheme to classify and count them! The question here is whether an event involving a conspiracy of many important and unique individuals accompanied by acts of violence and intrigue can be meaningfully studied by assigning it a score of 2 while a similar event somewhere else receives a score of 1 or 3. Most observers would say it cannot.

We need not conclude from this that quantification serves no purpose. It seems more reasonable to suggest that (a) we must be creative in devising ways to quantify difficult concepts; (b) we must incorporate qualitative variables into our research where appropriate; and (c) some aspects of politics may lie beyond the reach of quantitative research. Not every concept can be measured, perhaps, but where quantification is possible, a great deal can be done with the scientific method. Progress in political science will, to a large extent, be a matter of how effectively we can extend the limits of quantification while still finding meaningful ways to study important concepts.

CRITICISM 7. SCIENTIFIC POLITICAL RESEARCH OBSCURES SUBJECTIVE JUDGMENT AND BIAS

Prescientific analysis of political issues is unabashedly subjective. We can easily perceive the author's biases and opinions, since they are often explicitly stated as such. It is sometimes argued that scientific analysis, although cloaked with a mantle of objectivity, is in fact no less subjective than any other type of analysis. This appearance of objectivity is highly deceptive and even dangerous. Unwary readers may be misled into assuming that an author's conclusions are the result of objective research, when they are really subjective viewpoints, as is suggested by the well-known expression, "figures don't lie, but liars figure."

The problem here, however, is not so much with the scientific method itself, as with the conduct of researchers and readers. To the extent that prejudices are conveyed as objective fact by deliberate distortion, the only means of counteraction is a thorough knowledge of scientific method. It is difficult to use science to deceive someone who understands statistics, causal inference, sampling, measurement, and operationalization.

Subjective judgments and prejudice actually constitute a more serious problem when they *unintentionally* find their way into a research design. Even a conscientious researcher may select measures and construct hypotheses in ways that enhance the chances of arriving at his or her preferred conclusion.

Since the results are presented as objective, and since the biases and prejudices are normally not made explicit (as they would be in a nonscientific, philosophical discourse), readers may attach undeserved weight to such findings.

Bachrach and Baratz's classic 1962 essay, "The Two Faces of Power," discussed the problem of unintentional bias. In it, they studied the research of Robert Dahl, who, they asserted, hoped to prove that political power was widely distributed in society. Dahl observed the process by which political decisions were publicly debated and decided. As Bachrach and Baratz pointed out, this strategy tended to confirm the researcher's preexisting views. They claimed that Dahl's study would necessarily conclude that no single faction won all the battles, that one faction might defeat another on one issue only to suffer a reverse on the next. Dahl then was able to find that no single elite dominated the decision-making process. According to Bachrach and Baratz, the design of his study (analyzing highly visible political decisions) led him to overlook those important issues that never reached the public agenda, perhaps in part because they were kept from doing so by a very powerful elite. The choice of research design, they contended, had led to a seemingly objective yet predetermined set of results that overstated the extent to which political power is broadly shared in a state or community.

While inadvertent bias is probably a more difficult problem than intentional deception, the solution is the same. As researchers, students, and others become more conversant with research methods and principles, biased research designs will increasingly be perceived as flawed, or, at the very least, their nonneutral elements will be identified and discussed. Moreover, as more analysts are involved in the research process, different approaches to research problems will be developed, and greater balance in perspective will be achieved. Indeed, this is one purpose of the peer review process used by professional associations and publishers to help them identify the material most worthy of publication.

CRITICISM 8. SCIENTIFIC POLITICAL RESEARCH OFTEN VIOLATES ETHICAL STANDARDS

Political research can be unethical in several different ways. The potential for misconduct by political scientists, though, is not as great as in many other areas, primarily because this field rarely has much to do with personal finances, legal liability, or patented inventions. It also avoids the often serious ethical issues encountered in medicine. However, unethical practices in political science are a possibility, and it is important to be aware of the standards that apply.

First, it is essential to respect the privacy and dignity of human subjects. Political research typically does not delve into intimate personal issues in the way that psychological research does, but some studies can violate the privacy of subjects. When subjects are told that their names will not be associated with their responses to a survey, it is unethical to do otherwise. Experimental treatments should not include anything that degrades subjects, or makes them fearful or embarrassed. Human subjects place themselves in a vulnerable position when agreeing to take part in an experiment, and ethical researchers do not exploit this vulnerability.

Second, scientific research should strive toward objectivity. As noted above, this is not wholly possible; an ideological perspective of some kind usually influences our selection of a research problem. However, it is unethical to exploit the stature of scientific method to make readers believe that findings are objective when they are only arguments. A trickier problem has to do with the potential conflict of interests of funding sources. Objectivity requires that ethical researchers reject funding that carries obligations regarding their conclusions and results.

In a provocative extension of this theme, Theodore Lowi, a distinguished political scientist and recent president of the American Political Science Association, claims that political science has always been too closely tied to the interests of the state. In his 1992 presidential address to the association, he claimed that "every regime tends to produce a political science consonant with itself" (p. 1). Lowi's concerns transcend ethics and approach deeper philosophical issues, but, if the state actually does influence what scientists do, certain questions may not be studied and certain issues may not be raised. In light of the heavy dependence of political scientists on government funding, it is essential that the ethical principle of objectivity be strongly guarded. The ethical scientist does not promise or deliver findings that please those who pay the bills.

Third, it is also unethical to keep scientific findings secret. Political scientists, like other academics, are professionally obligated to share their studies through publication in academic journals. Unless there is some legitimate national security interest that makes secrecy necessary, funding relationships that interfere with sharing are unethical.

Strict adherence to ethical standards ensures that political science research will be useful, accessible, and meaningful. Unsound findings can be effectively criticized and challenged only in a genuinely open setting created and engendered by ethical standards.

CONCLUSION

Common sense once told us many things about politics. It told us that political independents know more about politics than do strong party identifiers, that revolutions are more likely to occur when repression is at its worst, that those who are most dependent on government assistance will vote more regularly than more prosperous citizens. Tradition and prejudice once told us that certain racial groups are inferior. A hopeful idealism once told us that corruption and selfishness among public officials could be eliminated by giving women the right to vote. Scientific political research has shown that all of these suppositions are false.

It is my firm conviction that, within important limits, the most reliable and productive, though by no means the only, path to political understanding is through empirical, scientific inquiry. The scientific study of politics has not only helped us set aside some longstanding but incorrect assumptions, but it has also provided a firm foundation for ethical and moral discussion. No informed person can seriously doubt that we know much more about politics now than we did even a few decades ago.

While critics of scientific political research argue that science works best in physics, chemistry, and biology, the quantification and precise thinking associated with scientific principles may be particularly valuable in social science. Herbert Simon, a Nobel Prize winner in economics, made the point in the strongest terms:

> Mathematics has become the dominant language of the natural sciences not because it is quantitative—a common delusion—but primarily because it permits clear and rigorous reasoning about phenomena too complex to handle in words. This advantage of mathematics over cruder languages should prove of even greater significance in the social sciences, which deal with phenomena of the greatest complexity, than it has in the natural sciences. (quoted in Buchanan, 1988, p. 63)

Thus, the principles of scientific method may open doors to even greater progress in political research than they have in other fields. If so, we must consider political science as a discipline in its infancy. We have a long way to go, and the arguments raised in this chapter suggest that we will probably never reach our ultimate objective of a set of universal laws of political behavior. However, a vast range of important questions is clearly within our reach. Striving to answer them scientifically will make us wiser in all our political thinking. When considering the true value of a scientific approach to the study of politics, we would do well to recall the words of Charles Beard:

> No one can deny that the idea is fascinating—the idea of subduing the phenomena of politics to the laws of causation, of penetrating to the mystery of its transformations, of symbolizing the trajectory of its future; in a word, of grasping destiny by the forelock and bringing it prostrate to earth. The very idea itself is worthy of the immortal gods. . . . If nothing ever comes of it, its very existence will fertilize thought and enrich imagination. (quoted in Easton, 1971, p. viii)

REFERENCES

Almond, G. A., and Verba, S. *The Civic Culture* (Boston: Little, Brown, 1963).

American Political Science Association. *Ethical Problems of Academic Political Scientists* (Washington, DC: APSA, 1968).

Bachrach, P., and Baratz, M. S. "The Two Faces of Power," *American Political Science Review* 56, pp. 947–1053, 1962.

Brodbeck, M. "Methodological Individualism," in *Reading in the Philosophy of the Social Sciences* (New York: Macmillian, 1958).

Easton, D. *The Political System* 2nd ed. (New York: Knopf, 1971).

Gleick, J. *Chaos: Making a New Science* (New York: Viking, 1987).

Jensen, A. "How Much Can We Boost IQ and School Achievement," *Harvard Educational Review* 39, pp. 11–12, 1969.

Kaplan, A. *The Conduct of Inquiry* (Scranton, PA: Chandler, 1964).

Lowi, T. J. "The State of Political Science: How We Become What We Study," *American Political Science Review* 86, pp. 1–7, 1992.

Tribe, L. "Political Science: Analysis or Ideology?" *Philosophy and Public Affairs* 2, pp. 66–110, 1972.

Wilson, J. Q. *The Moral Sense* (New York: Free Press, 1993).

Winch, P. *The Idea of the Social Science and It's Relation to Philosophy* (London: Routledge & Kegan Paul, 1958).

11

Starting from Scratch:
The Research Process

Stella Z. Theodoulou

What is research? How is it done? What are "good" research practices? In this chapter we attempt to outline the research process that any student of politics can follow. It is not set in stone, which is to say it is not rigid, but if followed it will produce sound research. The general goal of research is to add to our knowledge. And it does so in three ways: through exploration, description, and explanation.

Undertaking research involves the political scientist in making decisions and opting for choices. This, of course, is not without pitfalls. Part of the way we avoid some of these pitfalls is by ensuring that we follow a process. By arguing that doing research is being involved in a process, we are really stating that researchers work through a series of linked activities or steps. In sum, *research* is a dynamic process that involves rigorous application of a series of interrelated decisions.

The process is not rigid, as it is in the natural sciences, in the sense that the series of steps that one researcher takes might not be taken by another researcher in exactly the same time frame or manner. However, researchers do generally adhere to the same basic stages and confront the same methodological issues. Before we discuss the actual process, we should first clarify what we mean by undertaking research and what it actually involves.

Research allows us to answer the questions we set ourselves in a disciplined manner. This is what distinguishes research from other ways of answering questions. It is an informed way of knowing whether our suspicions are true or of finding out whether theories are correct or applicable. We might also argue that research is a way of verifiably describing what is going on and why it may be so. Thus, research requires discipline on the part of the researcher. If a researcher is disciplined and follows a process, the likelihood is that the research produced will be reliable. And, as we know, reliability is a crucial characteristic of empirical or scientific study.

Disciplined research requires the researcher to ask the "right" question, to be honest and accurate, and to keep records of what has been done. Asking the "right" question means that the researcher asks questions that are limited in scope and that can be answered through the gathering of observations. To be honest and accurate requires that the researcher attempt to be as objective as possible and there is no effort to force data to fit the researcher's personal agenda.

The research process can be viewed as a three-stage operation with steps within each stage. *Research design* is the first stage. This can be viewed as pre-analysis. The second stage is *data gathering*. This is the observation, measurement, and recording of information that will provide the basis for answering the question that has motivated the research. The third stage is *data analysis.* This is the arrangement and organization of data so that its significance can be perceived, or so that we can make generalizations and interpret what is going on. All interpretation must be *grounded,* which means it must be related to and follow logically from the evidence collected. In sum, all conclusions drawn from research must be ones supported and sustained by the data at hand. Each of these stages and the activities within each must be addressed suitably for if they are not, then the resulting research may be flawed in some way.

THE RESEARCH DESIGN STAGE

This stage involves a series of steps that can be deemed vital to the other two stages, for they set the foundation upon which any piece of research is built. The steps are set forth below.

Formulating the Question

The questions and problems that motivate political scientists initially are immense. Often they are so large that we cannot really find a focus to them and thus they cannot really be answered well. These types of questions we can call *global questions.* They represent the beginning; our task is to narrow the global question and formulate a much more focused question. This latter type of question can be called a *researchable question.*

Researchable questions are questions limited in scope. We previously referred to the "right" question—that is, the researchable question—as one that is narrow in focus and empirically testable, for example, to certain periods or places and conditions. One should view political knowledge as a jigsaw puzzle. The only way that we can put the whole puzzle together is to put each piece in place. Thus it is that by asking a series of narrow questions we can eventually answer the big political question. How does one then move from the global to the researchable question? The most useful way is through something called *unpacking*.[1] This process allows the researcher to select what they want to study through a clarification of the problem. Clarification is achieved by listing all of the issues that one sees being involved with the question. From that list, the researcher chooses an item and then starts to list questions that come to mind about it. Once this is done, the researcher then consults already established research on the problem. In other words, a *literature review* is conducted. The point of the literature review is to not only see what has already been researched but also to generate new questions or ways in which the problem may be looked at. The literature review helps to narrow the focus and places research in a proper theoretical context. Once the review has been completed, the researcher can restate the original question or problem in a much narrower way—that is, as a researchable question.

Researchable questions may take one of two forms. The first form is the *research objective*. In such a question, there is no specification of relationship between variables. The purpose of the research is to find out what is going on. Thus the stated goal is description rather than explanation. The second form a researchable question may take is a *hypothesis*, which is a statement that asserts a relationship between variables. The key feature of a hypothesis is that it is asserting that two variables are related in a specific manner. The usual form a hypothesis takes is "x causes y," or "x is related to y." We are asserting that in some way we believe these variables are related. Thus, basic to the logic of a hypothesis is the development of a statement that requires one variable to cause, affect, or influence another. Often, there is the notion of the *conditional* relationship, stated as "if . . . then." Also, hypotheses cannot be limited in scope. Thus, they must refer to a specific class. Finally, hypotheses can imply positive or negative relationships. Hypotheses and variables are further discussed in the next chapter, "There's Method to This Madness."

This whole process of unpacking is best illustrated through an example. Let us imagine that we are interested in researching AIDS. That is an enormous topic. The first thing we would do is to unpack it. Thus we would list everything that came to us about it. For example, our list of issues could look as follows:

> Who gets it?
> What is it?
> Where is it?
> What's happening research wise?
> What are governments doing about it?
> What are the treatments?
> How many have it?
> How do you get it?
> How do you prevent it?

This of course is hardly an exhaustive list; if we were really conducting this piece of research, we would create a more exhaustive list. But, from here, we would center upon one or two of the issues that interest us. In our case, let us say it is "Who gets it." The next stage is to conduct the literature review. From this search, we find that there are certain groups in which transmission is more prevalent. Thus, we are ready to restate the problem as a hypothesis. If you are male and live in an urban center, then you have a greater chance of being HIV positive. We can view this as a theoretical hypothesis that in many ways is abstract or highly general.

Operationalization

The next step in research design is to link the hypothesis to the empirical. In other words to link it to the observable. What this really means is we refine our hypothesis through a process known as *operationalization*. What this achieves is the defining of variables in specific measurable terms. Again, to best understand this, let us return to our example of AIDS. We take the statement and identify within it *variables*. A *variable* is something that varies in kind. Thus, in our example, the variables to be operationalized are male and urban center. Operationalization should be viewed as refining or moving from the general to the specific. We could refine the male variable several ways; for example, by sexual preference, age, or ethinicity. The urban center variable could be specified by size of population or geographic location. Once this has been done, we can now restate the theoretical hypothesis as an operational hypothesis. One such restatement would be as follows: if male homosexuals between the ages of 25 to 39 live in a city of one million or more, then there is a greater likelihood for them to be HIV positive than heterosexual males 25 to 39 who live in cities of one million or more. Now this allows us to go out and collect data and compare male homosexuals with heterosexual males living in cities of one million or more. It also allows us to look at different age categories for both groups.

Who Do We Study?

Once we have an operational hypothesis we must next decide who it is we wish to study. That is to say, we must choose our population. In the above-stated example, it would be both heterosexual and homosexual men living in cities of one million or more. The population is whoever the researcher wishes it to be. The crucial factor here is size. The population must be large enough that any findings are statistically significant. There are exceptions to this. For example, sometimes researchers are only interested in studying a single entity, such as an individual, or they are interested in studying a small group. However, what if the population is large? Obviously, in such instances, it is impossible to talk to everyone. One way to compensate for this is to talk to a representative *sample* of the population, that is to say, a group that accurately reflects the makeup of the population. A sample is a reflection of the whole. If the sample is not an accurate reflection of the population, then any conclusions drawn cannot be applied to the population as a whole. Thus, the crucial factor in sampling is how the actual sample is drawn.

The operational hypothesis gives the researcher the population to be studied, but the sample must be chosen by the researcher. There are two types of *sampling procedure*: *random* and *nonrandom*. The former allows the researcher to be confident that the sample is a representative one, whereas the latter really only allows us to draw conclusions about the people in the sample and not the population as a whole. Thus, if researchers truly want their research based on a sample to be an accurate capture of a population and if they want to be able to calculate the margin of error within their sample, then they should always opt for the random sample. However, there are many examples of researchers using nonrandom samples, often because they are less time consuming and less expensive to conduct. Nonrandom samples include the accidental, quota, and judgmental, whereas random samples include the simple random, systematic, stratified, and cluster. Table 11–1 compares and contrasts each of these sampling procedures.

The size of the sample is determined by the level of statistical analysis to be conducted, the homogeneity of the population, the desire for accuracy, the amount of information required, and the size of an acceptable margin of error. We will not elaborate on how one actually statistically calculates sample size, since this chapter takes a nonstatistical approach to the discussion of the research process. Those interested in the sample statistical procedures might consider the selected selections on surveys and sampling in Appendix A.

Selecting the Research Design

Once a hypothesis or a research objective has been developed, the researcher must now design the research plan to either test the hypothesis or provide the evidence for the research objective. There are commonly accepted types of research or research design that are available to political scientists. Research design basically asks a question or a combination of questions. Which research design a researcher chooses depends on (1) the kind of question or questions motivating the research; (2) the availability of resources such as time and money; and (3) the need for validity; which is to say, certain designs will be more sound than others.

The first question is, "What has been happening?" If this is the question, then the purpose of the research is descriptive. The research design best suited to this purpose is the *case study*. In such a design, a single case (an individual or a single group or one nation) is looked at for a stated period. For example,

TABLE 11-1 Types of Sample

Nonrandom (Nonprobability)	Random (Probability)
Do not specify the probability of each element of the population being included in the sample	Specify the probability of each element of the population being included in the sample
(1) Accidental Sample Select people because they are available to you, not because they are representative of some large group	**(1) Simple Random Sample** Each element of a population has an equal chance of being selected. Also, every possible combination of the specified number of elements has an equal chance of selection
(2) Quota Sample Select individuals or groups on the basis of a set criteria	**(2) Systematic Samples** Select every other case in a list of the total population
(3) Judgemental/Purposive Sample Select cases you think are typical	**(3) Stratified Random Samples** Divide population into 2 or more groups (strata), draw simple random samples from each strata, then combine them to form sample Two types exist: 1. Proportionally stratified 2. Disproportionally stratified
	(4) Cluster Samples Divide population into large number of groupings (clusters), draw a sample randomly of the clusters, then draw a sample of each cluster

we may look at school retention policies in California from 1967 to 1997. Case studies may provide the researcher with a description of what is going on in general and also what relationships exist.

The second question is, "Can we see any change over time?" This question essentially involves looking at a case study at two or more points in time. The research design in this instance would be a *longitudinal study*. The purpose is to see if there has been change and how much. An example of a longitudinal study would be if we looked at a group of student attitudes toward their studies when they were in their college freshman year and then again in their college senior year.

So far, the questions have been dealing with a single entity. However, we know that often in political science we are interested in two or more entities. Here the question that motivates the researcher is whether two or more phenomena differ from each other. Here we would use a comparative research design. The purpose of such a study would be to compare one measure of two or more groups at the same time. *Comparative studies* allow us to see similarities and differences between entities. An example would be if we compared legislative rules in the United States to those in Great Britain.

As with a longitudinal analysis of a case study, we may also compare two or more entities at two or more points in time. Thus, we are asking whether there has been any change in the entities over time. The research design to be used here would be a *longitudinal comparison*. An example would be to see whether voting behavior in the United States and Great Britain was different in the 1960s from that in the 1990s.

The last question that often motivates researchers is whether there exists a cause-and-effect relationship. The purpose is to determine the effect a change in one variable has on another. This is the most rigorous test of "Does x cause y" that is available to us. The research design in this situation would be an *experimental study*. In any such study, the researcher must have a high degree of control over the variables. In experimental studies, we are examining the effect of certain factors on others. An example of an experimental study might be an examination of the impact of adult literacy, age, and income on voting.

THE DATA-GATHERING STAGE

If the "right" question has been asked in the right manner about the "right" people and the most appropriate research design has been selected, we are ready to go out and collect the information to best answer the question or solve the problem we have set ourselves. Certain procedures must be followed while gathering data. First, always keep records of what is done, how it is done, and when it is done. Next, always be considerate with anyone you run across in your research. Third, always keep in mind a professional code of ethics. Fourth, pay attention to detail and record all data very carefully.

There are many types of data collection one can undertake and various techniques that can be utilized with each type. However, we can argue that there are two general types of data gathering. They are *primary* and *secondary data collection*.

Primary Data Collection

In this type of data collection, the researcher observes behavior, either directly or indirectly. The main methods researchers utilize in primary data collection are outlined below:

Field Research: *Field research* takes place when the researcher observes the behavior of the subject under study in the subject's own environment. For example, if we were studying legislative behavior, we might sit in on legislative committees to see what occurs. There are weaknesses with this method. For example, there are some things that cannot be observed directly. Also, researchers need to be particularly skillful in their ability to observe so that they report exactly what they see and hear. And, third, field research is incredibly time consuming. Its strength is that it provides a direct witnessing of behavior.

The Survey: A *survey* is not an actual observation of the respondent's behavior; rather, it is requesting self-identification of behavior and attitudes. Surveys have become prevalent and are extremely expedient. Surveys can be conducted directly or indirectly—that is, they can be given to a respondent orally or respondents may complete it themselves. There are several types of survey designs that can be used. All revolve around whether the researcher is interested in acquiring information about the current period or different periods of time. The main strength of the survey instrument is that researchers can collect vast amounts of standardized information about large numbers of people. The main disadvantage is that it is not only a costly procedure but it is one that requires some sophisticated skills by the researcher. These skills range from questionnaire design to sample design to statistical analysis.

Personal Interview: A *personal interview* is exactly that: a face-to-face questioning of individuals. The weaknesses of this method are that it is very time consuming and that it is hard to explain phenomena by relying on individual explanation. Its strength is it often presents interesting anecdotal information.

Secondary Data Collection

In this type of data collection, the researcher uses information that others have collected. There are many sources available to researchers, among which are data archives, published data, census data, statistical abstracts, government reports, and polls. Often researchers "make" data. In short, they take existing secondary data and quantitatively manipulate it to form new data sets. Two main methods are used to achieve this, outlined below.

Content Analysis:　*Content analysis* is the systematic reduction of published material by looking for frequency and presence of previously established characteristics. For example, let us imagine we are interested in looking at the ideological orientation of major networks' nightly newscasts. We would set a time period (let's say one month), look at the networks' newscasts, and code statements as either liberal or conservative (we would have defined what we meant by liberal and conservative). Then we would count how many of each type of statement occurred.

Indexes and Rankings:　In an *index,* a concept is operationalized and then cases are assigned scores based on a previously established scale. There is no order to the cases after they have been scored. Order is assigned in a *ranking,* usually from best to worst. Indexes and rankings are best understood through an illustration. Let us say we were interested in creating an index of democratic performance for a selected group of nations. The first step would be to operationalize democratic performance by identifying what is generally considered to be indicators of democracy. Next, we would establish the scale by totaling the indicators. Let us say we came up with eleven indicators. Thus, our scale would be zero to eleven, 0 representing the least democratic 11 representing the most democratic. We would then look at each nation, see how many indicators were present, and that would represent their score. Finally, we would list each nation alphabetically and report the scores of each. A ranking would be created when we reordered this index according to performance, from best to worst . The major weakness of indexes and rankings is subjectivity.

THE DATA ANALYSIS STAGE

In this stage, the researcher relates the information collected in the data-gathering stage to the question set in the research design stage. The researcher should also draw conclusions about the question through the interpretation of the data. Before analysis, it is sometimes beneficial to arrange collected data. Researchers do this mostly through tables and graphs. This requires that data be summarized into categories, coded, and then presented in the form of a table or graph. This allows the researcher to see whether there are any obvious patterns or relationships that need to be analyzed. The next chapter, "There's Method to This Madness," discusses the fundamentals of data analysis.

SUMMARY

In this chapter, we have looked at research as a process. Such an assumption posits that researchers must undertake a series of linked activities that have a definite beginning and end. We perceive the research process to be composed of three distinct stages: research design, data gathering, and data analysis. Each of these stages needs to be conducted carefully, for bad execution will result in the next stage being flawed in some way. Many errors made in political science research are the result of researchers failing to conduct the activities of each stage of the research process correctly.

NOTE

1. This term is coined by Gary D. Bouma and G. B. J. Atkinson, in *Social Science Research*, 2nd ed. (New York: Oxford University Press, 1995).

12

There's Method to This Madness: The Fundamentals of Applied Social Statistics

Stella Z. Theodoulou

There's an old saying, "You can't tell the forest for the trees." The study of human social interactions can be a wild and often unpredictable endeavor, and sometimes it is made more difficult by the way researchers study it. Often what we end up with is a "madness" that we do not understand. The "madness" is the quantitative methodology often utilized by many political scientists. In this chapter, we will show that there are particular reasons for the employment of certain statistical procedures and thus a "method" to the "madness" of quantification. This chapter explores how and why political scientists apply social statistics in their study of political phenomena. Often students of politics do not see the relevance of statistics. As we understand better not only what it is we are trying to do as political scientists, but also how statistics can be utilized as we struggle to analyze the social scene, it becomes obvious that to ignore this resource would be to leave ourselves without a proper method to pursue our studies. As Herbert Weisberg argues, the key step in data analysis is not the use of statistics but the decision about which statistical procedure to employ.[1]

THE METHOD BEHIND THE MADNESS

When political scientists use statistics, it is with the following intentions: (1) reducing the level of bias in the research; (2) identifying possible relationships, including cause-effect; and (3) determining the probability that what we find is applicable to other or larger settings. It is hoped that if we are clear and specific in our quantitative methodology, much of what we find is verifiable and replicable.

Primarily, political scientists describe and analyze what is going on politically or they test hypotheses that they have formulated. A *hypothesis* is a statement that posits a possible relationship existing between two or more variables. The researcher is making an educated guess about the relationship between the variables under study. A *variable* is an entity that varies in amount or kind. In short, it is possible to have more or less or different kinds of it.

Variables are the phenomena being observed. A political scientist might want to test to what extent turnout is dependent on a high political party competition rate. This is an example of a hypothesis. It is stating that there is a possible relationship between the variables of party competition and turnout. Variables may be identified as being dependent , independent, antecedent, or controlling. *Dependent variables* are those phenomena that are being affected by other variables. In the stated example, turnout is the dependent variable. *Independent variables* are used to explain the dependent variable. In other words, they have some effect on the dependent variable. Using our example, party competition is the independent variable. In our example, we hypothesize that the higher the party competition, the higher the turnout. Thus, we are positing a relationship between turnout and competition.

Antecedent variables are factors that affect the independent variable. In our example, any factor affecting how high party competition is would be the antecedent variable. Intervening variables are those factors that affect the relationship between the dependent and independent variable. In our example, an intervening variable might be the type of party or the party system.

Control variables are entities we are "controlling for," that we want to keep constant or use as the standard against which we can measure changes in other variables. If we wanted to see whether our example hypothesis varied depending on another factor, we could, for example, control for gross national product (GNP). That is to say, we could see whether the relationship between turnout and party competition changed or differed according to the level of a nation's GNP.

Often, individuals become confused about the type of variable an entity is. The reason for this confusion is that it is possible for an entity or phenomenon to be one type of variable in one hypothesis and act as another type of variable in another hypothesis. Just because the party competition rate is the independent variable in our example hypothesis, it does not mean that it will always be treated as an independent variable in other hypotheses. What type of variable an entity is depends on how the researcher frames the hypothesis and how the relationship is posited.

We construct hypotheses to see what kind of relationship exists between phenomena. We can also use hypotheses to talk about the form of the relationship between the independent and dependent variables. In essence, in political science, we are trying to determine the extent to which a relationship exists. If our independent and dependent variables are related, the most basic question we can ask about the form and nature of the relationship is whether the dependent variable increases or decreases in value as a result of changes in the value of the independent variable. This we refer to as *correlation*. One can get different types of correlation. *Direct correlation* is when both variables increase or decrease in line with each other. Thus, as the independent variable increases or decreases, so does the dependent variable in the same manner. In those cases in which one variable increases and the other decreases, we have *inverse correlation*. For example, in our example hypotheses, if party competition increased but turnout decreased, we would say there was an inverse correlation. There also may be situations in which the independent and dependent variables increase or decrease at different rates. This we call *logarithmic correlation*. It should be noted that correlation does not infer causality; rather, it confirms that there is a relationship. Hypotheses are deemed "true" if the relationship posited is found to exist. This then leads to the construction of generalizations that can be applied to similar situations and conditions. Calculations of correlation will be discussed later in the chapter.

The question now to ask is, "How are hypotheses tested?" Hypothesis testing requires that we measure how much change in one variable is accompanied by change in the other. This leads to the determination of appropriate levels of measurement. There are four levels of measurement, nominal, ordinal, interval, and ratio. With each of these measurements, specific statistical procedures must be used (see Table 12–1).

Nominal measurement is the classification of observations into a set of categories that have no direction or order to them. We cannot say that the observations in one category have more or less of the variable being measured than do the observations in a different category. Variables such as gender, ethnicity, place of birth, and religion are examples of nominal measures. *Ordinal measurement* consists of classification into a set of categories that do have direction to them. We can say that the observations in one category have more or less of the variable being measured than do observations in a different category. However, we cannot assume that the intervals between categories are equal. Examples of ordinal measures would be income categories or levels of political interest. *Interval measurement* assigns real numbers to

TABLE 12–1   Levels of Measurements and Statistical Procedures

Levels of Measurement	Statistical Procedure
Nominal and nominal	Chi square; Cramers V; Lambda; Qules Q
Nominal and ordinal	Cramers V; Lambda; Yules Q
Ordinal and ordinal	Tau; Somers D; Gamma
Interval and interval	Pearson's r

observations, and there are equal intervals of measurement. An example would be IQ scores. *Ratio measurement* assigns real numbers to observations that have equal intervals of measurement and an absolute zero point. If we placed income in dollars or education in number of years, we would have ratio measures.

Political scientists may also undertake different levels of analysis when looking at relationships. If we look at the distribution of one variable at a time, we are undertaking *univariate analysis.* If we are looking at the relationship between two variables, we are undertaking *bivariate analysis.* Finally, if we are looking at the relationship of multiple independent variables with a dependent variable, we are conducting *multivariate analysis.*

WHICH STATISTICAL PROCEDURE: THE TECHNIQUES OF APPLIED SOCIAL STATISTICS

In the following discussion, we will provide an introduction to some of the basic or fundamental statistical measures and procedures used by political scientists. For the most part, these are all easily generated by computer statistical software packages, however, we should be able to understand the logic behind each of the procedures before we sit at our computers. The kinds of questions we ask or the hypotheses we formulate and the kind of data we collect determine the analysis we undertake. Sometimes it is sufficient to display data in tables or to discuss simple percentages. But if we wish to analyze whether there are relationships and the nature of these relationships, we must conduct statistical analysis. In the following discussion, we will discuss some of the basic statistical procedures that are most utilized by political scientists.

I—Frequency Distribution

Let us say we are interested in an analysis of the heights of female students at our college. It is obviously not possible to measure the height of every female student at the college, so we take a random sample of 100 students. A *random sample* of a set, briefly, is one where each member of the set has an equal chance of inclusion. It should, therefore, be quite representative of the population as a whole. The immediate result is a list of 100 unsorted figures, recorded as we collected them. To make some sort of sense from these raw data, the first thing we do is list them in the order of size. However, after doing this, we still cannot get an overall picture because we have too much detail, but we can note the range of heights. Once we have this range, we divide the range of heights into equal groups and see how many students fall into each group. The groups we refer to as *class intervals,* and the number in each group is the *frequency,* or the number of cases pertaining to each value.

Height, when measured in centimeters, is an interval measure, but in this instance, by reporting heights in groups, height is an ordinal measure. This is also referred to as *group frequency distribution*. Frequency is more easily reported with nominal and ordinal measures. The best way to show frequency distribution is to depict it. If we are going to show the frequency distribution for nominal and ordinal measures, we would construct a histogram or bar chart. Such charts depict changes in a variable by means of bars that rise or fall on a scale that is shown on an axis. For example, if we wished to show the frequency of gender on a histogram, the horizontal axis would represent gender and the vertical axis the frequency of each group.

Interval data converted into ordinal data is best shown through the construction of line graphs, which can also be referred to as *frequency polygons*. These connect the frequencies of the variable at the mid-value of each group or class of intervals with a straight line. The values of the variable are reported on the horizontal axis and the amount or frequency on the vertical axis. In our example of the height of female students, we would label the horizontal axis "heights" and the vertical axis "number of female students." When there is cumulative frequency, *frequency curves* may be drawn. These are smooth continuous curves through the plotted points of the polygon.[2]

II—Measures of Central Tendency

It is often useful to represent the frequency distribution by a single figure, in our example, it would be the height of a "typical" female student. We call this an *average of the distribution*. Averaging is referred to as *central tendency*, or the value around which most of the data are clustered. In short, it is the center in a series of observations. There are many types of central tendency, but we shall deal with just three of them: the mode, the mean, and the median.

The Mode: This type of central tendency is used with all levels of measurement but is most useful for nominal and ordinal variables. The *mode* is the greatest density of frequency, the most commonly occurring value in a series of values. In a grouped frequency distribution, the modal class is the one that comes up highest on the histogram. If there were more Democrats than Republicans in your class, you would conclude the modal distribution of partisan identification was Democrat.

The Mean: This type of central tendency is used with interval, ratio, and, sometimes, ordinal variables. The mean is calculated by adding up all the numbers in a series together and dividing by the total frequency. For example, the mean of a group of 7 students, with heights of 172, 175, 181, 176, 174, 179, and 173 centimeters is given by

$$\bar{X} = \frac{172 + 175 + 181 + 176 + 174 + 179 + 173}{7}$$

$$= \frac{1230}{7}$$

$$= 175\frac{5}{7} \text{ cms } (5'10'')$$

Thus, the *mean* is the simple average.

The Median: This type of central tendency is used for interval or ratio variables and sometimes for ordinal measures, but it should never be used with nominal variables. The *median* is the midpoint in a series of ordered observations. To obtain the median, we must arrange the numbers in order of size (smallest to largest) and find the middle figure. The procedure for finding this middle figure is to take the number of cases, add 1, and divide by 2. So, for *n* cases, the median is

$$\frac{n+1}{2}$$

Using our example, 7 students have heights of 172, 175, 181, 176, 174, 179, and 173 cm., and we would first arrange them in order of height:

172 173 174 175 176 179 181

Second, $n = 7$, so the median for our example would be

$$\frac{7+1}{2} = 4\text{th case} = 175$$

The median, then, in our example is the height of the fourth tallest (or fourth shortest) student, or 175 cm. The student with the median height has as many students who are taller than she and as many who are shorter. In other words, there are 50 percemt of cases above it and 50 percent of cases below it.

III—Measures of Dispersion

As well as knowing the central tendency of a set of cases, we would also like to know how widely the numbers are *dispersed*; in other words, the extent to which the data are spread out from their central tendency. The simplest measure of dispersion is the *range*, which is the difference between the largest and smallest items. In our example of 7 student heights, the heights range from 172 to 181 cm. Therefore, the range is $181 - 172 = 9$ cm. The range can be reported for ordinal data, but it suffers from two defects. First, being obtained from only two of the cases (highest and lowest), it is to a certain extent unrepresentative of the distribution as a whole. And, second, since these two cases are the extremities of the distribution, the range is vulnerable to the influence of freak occurrences. In sum, the range is misleading if there are too few low or high scores. To correct for these biases, we can use the *semi-interquartile range,* which relies on the difference between the value for the 75th percentile of a distribution and the value for the 25th percentile. Another measure of dispersion is the *mean absolute deviation,* which is the mean deviation of each number from the sample mean. For instance, consider the following set of numbers: 1, 5, 6, and 8. Their mean is

$$\bar{X} = \frac{1 + 5 + 6 + 8}{4} = \frac{20}{4} = 5$$

Now consider the *deviation,* or distance, of each number from the mean. The distances are 4, 0, 1, and 3 respectively, so the mean distance is

$$\frac{4 + 0 + 1 + 3}{4} = \frac{8}{4} = 2$$

Strictly speaking, the deviation of 1 from 5 is –4, so that the mean deviation is

$$\frac{-4 + 0 + 1 + 3}{4} = 0$$

but we are taking the absolute values of the deviations, obtaining the mean absolute. To do so we must apply the following formula:

$$\frac{\left(\sum |x|\right)}{N}$$

Applying this to our example using the set of numbers 1, 5, 6, and 8, whose mean is 5, the mean absolute deviation is:

$$\frac{(1-5) + (5-5) + (6-5) + (8-5)}{4}$$
$$= \frac{(-4) + (0) + (1) + (3)}{4}$$
$$= \frac{8}{4}$$
$$= 2$$

The point of departure of applied social statistics (and its basic assumption) is that there is variation or variance in human behavior. For example, we know through simple observation that individuals vary in age, in how much money they earn, and in how they vote. There are also many types of organizations, which also vary in character and purpose. For example, trade unions vary in size of membership and in the pressure they can put on governments; corporations vary in terms of output and productivity, and nation states vary in levels of economic development, in social policy provision, in international status, and in frequency with which they go to war. Thus, irrespective of whether we look at individuals or aggregates of individuals in social groups, we find variation in behavior in virtually all areas of activity.

Whenever we refer to a *variable* in our study of politics, we acknowledge that the phenomenon or property can take on a range of different values. As an alternative to taking the absolute value through the calculation of the mean absolute deviation, we can calculate *variance* and *standard deviation* for interval measures for what we refer to as the *normal distribution*. This distribution simply indicates that a relatively small number of cases are very low in value or very high in value, and that most of the cases fall between these two extremes. Variance and standard deviation are used to measure a dispersion based on finding the variation around the mean. Variance increases as dispersion increases. In order to calculate standard deviation, we must first calculate variance, for standard deviation is the square root of variance. The formula is as follows:

$$\text{Standard deviation} = \frac{\sqrt{\sum (x_1 - \bar{x})^2}}{N}$$

Applying this to our example, where x has the values 1, 5, 6, and 8, with mean of 5, variance and standard deviation would be calculated as follows. Subtract the mean (5) from each value of x, which gives us $-4, 0, 1, 3$; then, square the deviations and add them up: $-4^2 + 0^2 + 1^2 + 3^2 = 16 + 0 + 1 + 9 = 26$. So, variance is equal to 26 divided by N. In our example, $N = 4$, because that is how many values of x there are. The example's variance is 26 divided by 4, which is equal to 6.5. Standard deviation would be the square root of variance, or 2.55.

IV—Relative Dispersion

Consider the three sets of numbers depicted below:

Set		Mean	Standard Deviation
A	1 3 5 7 9	5	2.828
B	10 30 50 70 90	50	28.28
C	101 103 105 107 109	105	2.828

Although the standard deviation of A and B vary by a factor of 10, one feels that compared with the size of the figures involved they are the same. On the other hand, although the standard deviations of A and C are the same, one feels that relatively speaking, the variation in C is smaller than that in A, since the figures are much larger. A relative measure of dispersion, or spread, about the mean that does justice to these intuitions is the *coefficient of variation*, which, expressed as a fraction, is the standard deviation divided by the mean, and, expressed as a percentage, is multiplied by 100. So, for our three sets we have

$$A = \frac{\text{standard deviation}}{\text{mean}} = \frac{2.828}{5} = .5656, \text{ or } 56.56\%$$

$$B = \frac{\text{standard deviation}}{\text{mean}} = \frac{28.28}{5} = .5656, \text{ or } 56.56\%$$

$$C = \frac{\text{standard deviation}}{\text{mean}} = \frac{2.828}{5} = .0269 \text{ or } 2.69\%, \text{ (less than twentieth that of A and B)}$$

V—Regression Analysis

Another widely used technique of applied social statistics is *regression analysis*. Its basic objective is to discover the degree of relationship between two or more variables. Regression analysis has two main strengths. First, it enables us to predict values in a dependent variable from an independent or several independent variables (if we use more than one independent variable, we talk of *multiple regression*). Second, it permits us to evaluate how well we can predict a dependent variable. This evaluation takes the form of examining how well an independent variable can "explain" the variation in a dependent variable. The second strength, therefore, is that regression analysis can be used to "explain" variance.

Let us say we are interested in looking at the relationship between turnout and political party competition in six districts (in any real life research setting, we would, of course, examine far more than six districts), and have found the following values:

Case	Turnout (T)	Party Competition (C)
1	40	1
2	50	1
3	50	2
4	60	2
5	60	3
6	70	3

We can make a simple plot, or *scattergram,* of these values. By convention, the vertical (y) axis is used for the dependent variable (voting turnout, in this case) and the horizontal (x) axis for the independent variable; in this case, party competition. For each case, we plot a point representing its values on the two variables. For example, for case 1, we go 1 along the x-axis and then up 40 on the y-axis. We then repeat this procedure for each case (see Figure 12–1).

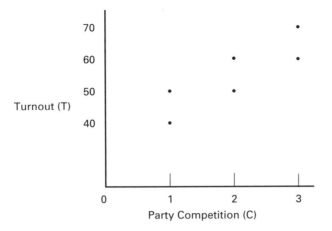

FIGURE 12–1   Scattergram plot of turnout (T) and party competition (C)

The scattergram tells us roughly three things, the first of which is whether there is a consistent pattern. (For example, if the independent variable increases in size, does the dependent variable?) Next , it reveals the slope of the pattern. This tells us how much change in one variable is associated with change in the other. Third, it helps us to see how strong the relationship is through how closely the regression line fits. It also, in this way, shows whether there are any deviant cases that would merit individual attention. From Figure 12–1, it is clear by eye that there is a positive relationship between party competition and turnout—that is, turnout increases with higher values of party competition. Now we are ready to calculate and construct the *regression line,* which is a line drawn through the scattergram. Such a line represents the best possible "fit" for predicting *y* from *x*. The regression equation takes the following form:

$$y = a + bx$$

The *y* is the dependent variable; the *a* is known as the *constant* or *intercept;* the *b* is known as the *regression coefficient;* and *x* is the independent variable. In our particular example, we first calculate the slope, then the intercept. The calculation would be as follows:

$$b = \frac{\sum(x_1 - \bar{x})(y_1 - \bar{y})}{\sum(x_1 - \bar{x})^2}$$

$$b = \frac{35}{4} = 8.75$$

$$a = \bar{y} - b\bar{x}$$

$$a = 55 - (8.75)(2)$$

$$= 37.5$$

The regression line is

$$37.5 + (8.75)(1) = 46.25$$
$$37.5 + (8.75)(2) = 55.00$$
$$37.5 + (8.75)(3) = 63.75$$

We would start the regression line at 46.25 and proceed according to the remaining values. If we now plot these predicted values on the plot of the actual values (see Figure 12–2) and join the predicted values together, we find we have a straight line (this is because our regression equation conforms to the general equation of $y = a + bx$, which is, in turn, the equation for a straight line). We should also note that our predicted values, which go from 37.5 to 46.25 to 55 to 63.75, increase in units of 8.75 (the value of b, or the regression coefficient) for every unit increase in party competition. The value of 8.75 is, in fact, the slope of the regression, and it tells us how much the dependent variable will change if the independent variable increases by one unit. Thus, turnout is responsive to party competition.

FIGURE 12–2   The regression line of the party competition (C) and turnout (T)

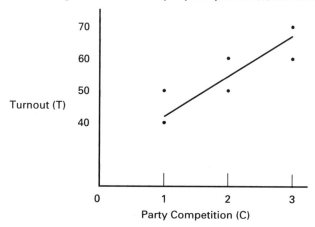

However, can we be more precise. In this instance, because we are using interval-level data we can measure the strength of relationship by computing *Pearson's correlation coefficient*, which is denoted by r. The formula is as follows:

$$r = \frac{n\sum xy - \sum x \sum y}{\sqrt{n\sum x^2 - (\sum x)^2}\sqrt{n\sum y^2 - (\sum y)^2}}$$

Pearsons r ranges from –1.0 to +1.0, +1.0 being a perfect positive correlation and –1.0 being a perfect negative correlation.

Using the previous figures on party competition and turnout, r would be calculated in the following manner:

Cases	x	x^2	y	y^2	xy
1	1	1	40	1600	40
2	1	1	50	2500	50
3	2	4	50	2500	100
4	2	4	60	3600	120
5	3	9	60	3600	180
6	3	9	70	4900	210
$n = 6$	$\Sigma x = 12$	$\Sigma x^2 = 28$	$\Sigma y = 330$	$\Sigma y^2 = 18700$	$\Sigma xy = 700$

$$r = \frac{6(700) - (12)(330)}{\sqrt{6(28) - 12^2}\sqrt{6(18700) - 330^2}}$$

$$= \frac{4200 - 3960}{\sqrt{168 - 144}\sqrt{112200 - 108900}}$$

$$= \frac{240}{\sqrt{24}\sqrt{3300}}$$

$$= \frac{240}{(4.899)(57.446)}$$

$$= \frac{240}{281.428}$$

$$= .85$$

Thus, in our example we have found a correlation that is extremely strong. We may conclude for our six cases the more competitive the party system the higher the voting turnout. To further interpret r we can square it to obtain the coefficient of determination or r^2. This is the percentage held in common of the total variation of the two variables. In other words, how much of the dependent variable can be explained by the independent variable. Here $r^2 = .7$. Thus, 70% of the variation in y can be explained by x. In this instance, party competition is very helpful in explaining turnout.

If we have nominal or ordinal measures and we wish to calculate strength of relationship, we can supplement percentage differences with a single statistic similar to r that indicates the strength of relationship by summarizing the overall pattern of the data in a table. Strength also ranges from –1.0 to +1.0. If we have nominal level data arranged as a dichotomy, we would calculate *Yules Q*. If it were nominal level data arranged in a table larger than a dichotomy, we would calculate *lambda*. For ordinal level data, we would calculate strength of relationship through the calculation of *gamma* and *tau*. We should point out that we are not concerned with explaining how each of these are calculated as they are more than adequately computed by various computer statistical software packages. Rather, the objective is to help you understand when to use each of them and how one denotes strength. You might ask why regression and Pearson's r calculations were explained. It is this author's belief that once you understand the logic behind these and the mechanics of calculating them, it is easier to comprehend what each of the other procedures mean.

We should point out that once we have calculated a statistic, we often like to see how significant our finding is. *Significance* does not refer to importance; rather, it reveals whether what we found is applicable to a larger setting—that is, that what we have found is probable or true for a larger group. If we are dealing with interval data, significance is determined by the p value. If p is greater than .5, we have a statistically significant finding. In the case of nominal level measures—and, sometimes, ordinal—for a sample statistic, we determine significance of a strength of relationship statistic by the calculation of *chi square* (χ^2). The larger the chi square, the more confident we can be that there is a relationship and the more statistically significant our results. Once again, we rely today on statistical software to calculate p and χ^2. The point is, you should be able to understand how significance is indicated.

In this chapter, we have discussed the fundamentals of data analysis. More sophisticated procedures have not been covered. Many of you will never have to calculate, without the use of a computer, the statistical procedures we have discussed. However, only by understanding how they are calculated will you truly understand what they demonstrate and when and how they can be used.

NOTES

1. Herbert Weisberg, "The Fundamentals of Data Analysis," in Asher, H. B., Weisberg, H. F., Kessel, J. H., and W. Phillips Shively, *Theory-Building and Data Analysis in the Social Sciences* (Knoxville: University of Tennessee Press, 1984).
2. There are five different types of curve that can be drawn; the normal curve, the platykurtic, the skewed, the J-Shaped, and the reversed J-shaped.

13

How to Statisticulate, *and* How to Talk Back to a Statistic

Darrell Huff

HOW TO STATISTICULATE

Misinforming people by the use of statistical material might be called statistical manipulation; in a word (though not a very good one), statisticulation.

. . . Possibly more important to keep in mind is that the distortion of statistical data and its manipulation to an end are not always the work of professional statisticians. What comes full of virtue from the statistician's desk may find itself twisted, exaggerated, over-simplified, and distorted-through-selection by salesman, public-relations expert, journalist, or advertising copywriter.

But whoever the guilty party may be in any instance, it is hard to grant him the status of blundering innocent. False charts in magazines and newspapers frequently sensationalize by exaggeration, rarely minimize anything. Those who present statistical agruments on behalf of industry are seldom found, in my experience, giving labour or the customer a better break than the facts call for, and often they give him a worse one. When has a union employed a statistical worker so incompetent that he made labour's case out weaker than it was?

As long as the errors remain one-sided, it is not easy to attribute them to bungling or accident.

One of the trickiest way to misrepresent statistical data is by means of a map. A map introduces a fine bag of variables in which facts can be concealed and relationships distorted. My favourite trophy in this field is "The Darkening Shadow." It was distributed not along ago by the First National Bank of

Boston and reproduced very widely—by so-called taxpayers groups, newspapers, and *Newsweek* magazine.

The map shows what portion of the American income is now being taken, and spent, by the federal government. It does this by shading the areas of the states west of the Mississippi (excepting only Louisiana, Arkansas, and part of Missouri) to indicate that federal spending has become equal to the total incomes of the people of those states.

The deception lies in choosing states having large areas but, because of sparse population, relatively small incomes. With equal honesty (and equal dishonesty) the map maker might have started shading in New York or New England and come out with a vastly smaller and less impressive shadow. Using the same data he would have produced quite a different impression in the mind of anyone who looked at his map. No one would have bothered to distribute that one, though. At least, I do not know of any powerful group that is interested in making public spending appear to be smaller than it is.

If the objective of the map maker had been simply to convey information he could have done so quite easily. He could have chosen a group of in-between states whose total area bears the same relation to the area of the country that their total income does to the national income.

The thing that makes this map a particularly flagrant effort to misguide is that it is not a new trick of propaganda. It is something of a classic, or chestnut. The same bank long ago published versions of this map to show federal expenditures in 1929 and 1937, and these shortly cropped up in a standard book, *Graphic Presentation,* by Willard Cope Brinton, as horrible examples. This method "distorts the fact," said Brinton plainly. But the First National goes right on drawing its maps, and *Newsweek* and other people who should know better—and possibly do—go right on reproducing them with neither warning nor apology.

If you think there's inflation now, consider this. At one time the U.S. Bureau of the Census came up in its annual way with word that the "income of the average family was $3,100." But if you read a newspaper story on "philanthropic giving" handed out by the Russell Sage Foundation you learned that, for the same year, it was a notable $5,004. Possibly you were pleased to learn that folks were doing so well, but you may also have been struck by how poorly that figure squared with your own observations. Possibly you know the wrong kind of people.

Now how in the world can Russell Sage and the Bureau of the Census be so far apart? The Bureau is talking in medians, as of course it should be, but even if the Sage people are using a mean the difference should not be quite this great. The Russell Sage Foundation, it turns out, discovered this remarkable prosperity by producing what can only be described as a phoney family. Their method, they explained (when asked for an explanation), was to divide the total personal income of the American people by 149,000,000 to get an average of $1,251 for each person. "Which," they added, "becomes $5,004 in a family of four."

This odd peice of statistical manipulation exaggerates in two ways. It used the kind of average called a mean instead of the smaller and more informative median. . . . And then it goes on to assume that the income of a family is in direct proportion to its size. Now I have four children, and I wish things were disposed in that way, but they are not. Families of four are by no means commonly twice as wealthy as families of two.

In fairness to the Russell Sage statisticians, who may be presumed innocent of desire to deceive, it should be said that they were primarily interested in making a picture of giving rather than of getting. The funny figure for family incomes was just a by-product. But it spread its deceoption no less effectively for that, and it remains a prime example of why little faith can be placed in an unqualified statement of average.

For a spurious air of precision that will lend all kinds of weight to the most disreputable statistic, consider the decimal. Ask a hundred citizens how many hours they slept last night. Come out with a total of say, 783.1. Any such data are far from precise to begin with. Most people will miss their guess by fifteen minutes or more, and there is no assurance that the errors will balance out. We all know someone who will recall five sleepless minutes as half a night of tossing insomnia. But go ahead, do your arithmetic, and announce that people sleep an average of 7.831 hours a night. You will sound as if you knew precisely what you were talking about. If you had been so foolish as to declare only that people sleep 7.8 (or "almost 8") hours a night, there would have been nothing striking about it. It would have sounded like what it was, a poor approximation and no more instructive than almost anybody's guess.

Karl Marx was not above achieving a spurious air of precision in the same fashion. In figuring the "rate of surplus-value" in a mill he began with a splendid collection of assumptions, guesses, and round numbers: "We assume the waste to be 6 per cent . . . the raw material . . . costs in round numbers £342. The 10,000 spindles . . . cost, we will assume, £1 per spindle. . . . The wear and tear we put at 10 per cent. . . . The rent of the building we suppose to be £300. . . ." He says, "the above data, which may be relied upon, were given me by a Manchester spinner."

From these approximations Marx calculates that: "The rate of surplus-value is therefore $80/52 = 153\tfrac{11}{13}$ per cent." For a ten-hour day this gives him "necessary labour = $3\tfrac{31}{33}$ hours and surplus-labour = $6\tfrac{2}{33}$."

There's a nice feeling of exactness to that two thirty-thirds of an hour, but it's all bluff.

Percentages offer a fertile field for confusion. And like the ever-impressive decimal they can lend an aura of precision to the inexact. The United States Department of Labor's *Monthly Labor Review* once stated that of the offers of part-time household employment with provisions for car fare, in Washington, D.C., during a specified month, 4.9 per cent were at $18 a week.

This percentage, it turned out, was based on precisely two cases, there having been only forty-one offers altogether. Any percentage figure based on a small number of cases is likely to be misleading. It is more informative to give the figure itself. And when the percentage is carried out to decimal places you begin to run the scale from the silly to the fraudulent.

"Buy your Christmas presents now and save 100 per cent," advises an advertisement. This sounds like an offer worthy of old Santa himself, but it turns out to be merely a confusion of base. The reduction is only fifty per cent. The saving is one hundred per cent of the reduced or new price, it is true, but that isn't what the offer says.

Likewise when the president of a flower growers' association said, in a newspaper interview, that "flowers are 100 per cent cheaper than four months ago," he didn't mean that florists were now giving them away. But that's what he said.

In her *History of the Standard Oil Company,* Ida M. Tarbell went even further. She said that "price cutting in the southwest . . . ranged from 14 to 220 per cent." That would call for seller paying buyer a considerable sum to haul the oily stuff away.

The Columbus *Dispatch* declared that a manufactured product was selling at a profit of 3,800 per cent, basing this on a cost of $1.75 and a selling price of $40. In calculating percentage of profits you have a choice of methods (and you are obligated to indicate which you are using). If figured on cost, this one comes to a profit of 2,185 percent; on selling price, 95.6 per cent. The *Dispatch* apparently used a method of its own and, as so often seems to happen, got an exaggerated figure to report.

Even the *New York Times* lost the Battle of the Shifting Base in publishing an Associated Press story from Indianapolis:

> The depression took a stiff wallop on the chin here today. Plumbers, plasterers, carpenters, painters and others affiliated with the Indianapolis Building Trades Unions were given a 5 per cent increase in wages. That gave back to the men one-fourth of the 20 per cent cut they took last winter.

Sounds reasonable on the face of it—but the decrease has been figured on one base—the pay the men were getting in the first place—while the increase uses a smaller base, the pay level after the cut.

You can check on this bit of statistical misfiguring by supposing. for simplicity. that the original wage was $1 an hour. Cut twenty per cent, it is down to 80 cents. A five per cent increase on that is 4 cents, which is not one-fourth but one-fifth of the cut. Like so many presumably honest mistakes, this one somehow managed to come out an exaggeration which made a better story.

All this illustrates why to offset a pay cut of fifty per cent you must get a raise of one hundred per cent.

It was the *Times* also that once reported that, for a fiscal year, air mail

"lost through fire was 4,863 pounds, or a percentage of but 0.00063." The story said that planes had carried 7,715,741 pounds of mail during the year. An insurance company basing its rates in that way could get into a pack of trouble. Figure the loss and you'll find that it came to 0.063 per cent or one hundred times as great as the newspaper had it.

It is the illusion of the shifting base that accounts for the trickiness of adding discounts. When a hardware jobber offers "50 per cent and 20 per cent off list," he doesn't mean a seventy per cent discount. The cut is sixty per cent since the twenty per cent is figured on the smaller base left after taking off fifty per cent.

A good deal of bumbling and chicanery have come from adding together things that don't add up but merely seem to. Children for generations have been using a form of this device to prove that they don't go to school.

You probably recall it. Starting with 365 days to the year you can subtract 122 for the one-third of the time you spend in bed and another 45 for the three hours a day used in eating. From the remaining 198 take away 90 for summer vacation and 21 for Christmas and Easter vacations. The days that remain are not even enough to provide for Saturdays and Sundays.

Too ancient and obvious a trick to use in serious business, you might say. But the United Automobile Workers insist in their monthly magazine, *Ammunition,* that it is still being used against them.

> The wide, blue yonder lie also turns up during every strike. Every time there is a strike, the Chamber of Commerce advertises that the strike is costing so many millions of dollars a day.
>
> They get the figure by adding up all the cars that would have been made if the strikers had worked full time. They add in losses to suppliers in the same way. Everything possible is added in, including street car fares and the loss to merchants in sales.

The similar and equally odd notion that percentages can be added together as freely as apples has been used against authors. See how convincing this one, from *The New York Times Book Review,* sounds.

> The gap between advancing book prices and authors' earnings, it appears, is due to substantially higher production and material costs. Item: plant and manufacturing expenses alone have risen as much as 10 to 12 per cent over the last decade, materials are up 6 to 9 per cent, selling and advertising expenses have climbed upwards of 10 per cent. Combined boosts add up to a minimum of 33 per cent (for one company) and to nearly 40 per cent for some of the smaller houses.

Actually, if each item making up the cost of publishing this book has risen around ten per cent, the total cost must have climbed by about that proportion also. The logic that permits adding those percentage rises together could lead to all sorts of flights of fancy. Buy twenty things today and find

that each has gone up five per cent over last year. That "adds up" to one hundred per cent, and the cost of living has doubled. Nonsense.

It's all a little like the tale of the roadside merchant who was asked to explain how he could sell rabbit sandwiches so cheap. "Well," he said, "I have to put in some horse meat too. But I mix 'em fifty-fifty: one horse, one rabbit."

A union publication used a cartoon to object to another variety of unwarranted adding-up. It showed the boss adding one regular hour at $1.50 to one overtime hour at $2.25 to one double-time hour at $3 for an average hourly wage of $2.25. It would be hard to find an instance of an average with less meaning.

Another fertile field for being fooled lies in the confusion between percentage and percentage points. If your profits should climb from three per cent on investment one year to six per cent the next, you can make it sound quite modest by calling it a rise of three percentage points. With equal validity, you can describe it as a one hundred per cent increase. For loose handling of this confusing pair watch particularly the public-opinion pollers.

Percentiles are deceptive too. When you are told how Johnny stands compared to his classmates in algebra or some aptitude, the figure may be a percentile. It means his rank in each one hundred students. In a class of three hundred, for instance, the top three will be at the 99 percentile, the next three at the 98, and so on. The odd thing about percentiles is that a student with a 99-percentile rating is probably quite a bit superior to one standing at 90, while those at the 40 and 60 percentiles may be of nearly equal achievement. This comes from the habit that so many characteristics have of clustering about their own average, forming the "normal" bell curve we mentioned in an early chapter.

Occasionally a battle of the statisticians develops, and even the most unsophisticated observer cannot fail to smell a rat. Honest men get a break when statisticulators fall out. The Steel Industry Board has pointed out some of the monkey business in which both steel companies and unions have indulged. To show how good business had been in the year just ended (as evidence that the companies could well afford a raise), the union compared that year's productivity with the productivity of 1939—a year of especially low volume. The companies, not to be outdone in the deception derby, insisted on making their comparisons on a basis of money received by the employees rather than average hourly earnings. The point to this was that so many workers had been on part time in the earlier year that their incomes were bound to have grown even if wage rates had not risen at all.

Time magazine, notable for the consistent excellence of its graphics, published a chart that is an amusing example of how statistics can pull out of the bag almost anything that may be wanted. Faced with a choice of methods, equally valid, one favouring the management viewpoint and the other favouring labour, *Time* simply used both. The chart was really two charts, one superimposed upon the other. They used the same data.

One showed wages and profits in billions of dollars. It was evident that although both were rising, the increase in wages in the last year was roughly twice that in profits. And that wages involved perhaps six times as many dollars as profits did. The great inflationary pressure, it appeared, came from wages.

The other part of the dual chart expressed the changes as percentages of increase. The wage line was relatively flat. The profit line shot sharply upwards. Profits, it might be inferred, were principally responsible for inflation.

You could take your choice of conclusions. Or, perhaps better, you could easily see that neither element could properly be singled out as the guilty one. It is sometimes a substantial service simply to point out that a subject in controversy is not as open-and-shut as it has been made to seem.

Index numbers are vital matters to millions of people now that wage rates are often tied to them. It is perhaps worth noting what can be done to make them dance to any man's music.

To take the simplest possible example, let's say that milk cost 10p a quart last year and bread was 10p a loaf. This year milk is down to 5p and bread is up to 20p. Now what would you like to prove? Cost of living up? Cost of living down? Or no change?

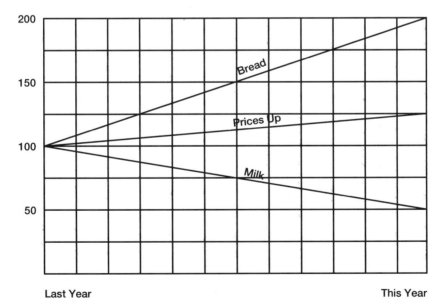

Consider last year as the base period, making the prices of that time 100 per cent. Since the price of milk has since dropped to half (50 per cent) and the price of bread has doubled (200 per cent) and the average of 50 and 200 is 125, prices have gone up 25 per cent.

Try it again, taking this year as base period. Milk used to cost 200 per cent as much as it does now and bread was selling for 50 per cent as much. Average: 125 per cent. Prices used to be 25 per cent higher than they are now.

To prove that the cost level hasn't changed at all we simply switch to the geometric average and use either period as the base. This is a little different from the arithmetic average, or mean, that we have been using but it is a perfectly legitimate kind of figure and in some cases the most useful and revealing. To get the geometric average of three numbers you multiply them together and derive the cube root. For four item, the fourth root; for two, the square root. Like that.

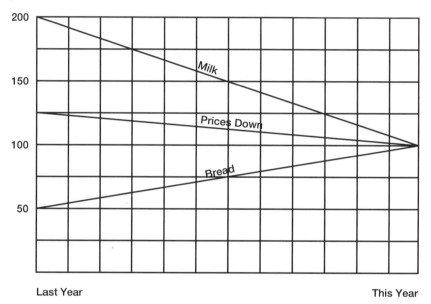

Take last year as the base and call its price level 100. Actually you multiply the 100 per cent for each item together and take the root, which is 100. For this year, milk being at 50 per cent of last year and bread at 200 per cent, multiply 50 by 200 to get 10,000. The square root, which is the geometric average, is 100. Prices have not gone up or down.

The fact is that, despite its mathematical base, statistics is as much an art as it is a science. A great many manipulations and even distortions are possible within the bounds of propriety. Often the statistician must choose among methods, a subjective process, and find the one that he will use to represent the facts. In commercial practice he is about as unlikely to select an unfavourable method as a copywriter is to call his sponsor's product flimsy and cheap when he might as well say light and economical.

Even the man in academic work may have a bias (possibly unconscious) to favour, a point to prove, an axe to grind.

This suggests giving statistical material, the facts and figures in newspapers and books, magazines and advertising, a very sharp second look before accepting any of them. Sometimes a careful squint will sharpen the focus. But arbitrarily rejecting statistical methods makes no sense either. That is like refusing to read because writers sometimes use words to hide facts and relationships rather than to reveal them. After all; a political candidate in Florida not long ago made considerable capital by accusing his opponent of "practising celibacy." A New York exhibitor of the motion picture *Quo Vadis* used huge type to quote *The New York Times* as calling it "historical pretentiousness." And the makers of Crazy Water Crystals, a proprietary medicine, have been advertising their product as providing "quick, ephemeral relief."

HOW TO TALK BACK TO A STATISTIC

Not all the statistical information that you may come upon can be tested with the sureness of chemical analysis or of what goes on in an assayer's laboratory. But you can prod the stuff with five simple questions, and by finding the answers avoid learning a remarkable lot that isn't so.

About the first thing to look for is bias—the laboratory with something to prove for the sake of a theory, a reputation. or a fee; the newspaper whose aim is a good story: labour or management with a wage level at stake.

Look for conscious bias. The method may be direct misstatement or it may be ambiguous statement that serves as well and cannot be convicted. It may be selection of favourable data and suppression of unfavourable. Units of measurement may be shifted, as with the practice of using one year for one comparison and sliding over to a more favourable year for another. An improper measure may be used: a mean where a median would be more informative (perhaps all too informative), with the trickery covered by the unqualified word "average."

Look sharply for unconscious bias. It is often more dangerous. In the charts and predictions of many statisticians and economists in 1928 it operated to produce remarkable things. The cracks in the economic structure were joyously overlooked, and all sorts of evidence were adduced and statistically supported to show that we had no more than entered the stream of prosperity.

It may take at least a second look to find out who-says-so. The who may be hidden by what Stephen Potter, the *Lifemanship* man, would probably call the "O.K. name." Anything smacking of the medical profession is an O.K. name. Scientific laboratories have O.K. names. So do universities, more especially ones eminent in technical work. The writer who proved a few chapters back that higher education jeopardizes a girl's chance to marry made good use of the O.K. name of Cornell. Please note that while the data came from Cornell, the conclusions were entirely the writer's own. But the O.K. name helps you carry away a misimpression of "Cornell University says.. . . ."

When an O.K. name is cited, make sure that the authority stands behind the information, not merely somewhere alongside it.

You may have read a proud announcement by the Chicago *Journal of Commerce.* That publication had made a survey. Of 169 corporations that replied to a poll on price gouging and hoarding, two-thirds declared that they were absorbing price increases produced by the police action, or undeclared war, in which the United States was then as usual engaged in the Far East. "The survey shows," said the *Journal* (look sharp whenever you meet those words!), "that corporations have done exactly the opposite of what the enemies of the American business system have charged." This is an obvious place to ask, "Who says so?" since the *Journal of Commerce* might be regarded as an interested party. It is also a splendid place to ask our second test question:

How Does He Know?

It turns out that the *Journal* had begun by sending its questionnaires to 1,200 large companies. Only fourteen per cent had replied. Eighty-six per cent had not cared to say anything in public on whether they were hoarding or price gouging.

The *Journal* had put a remarkably good face on things, but the fact remains that there was little to brag about. It came down to this: Of 1,200 companies polled, nine per cent said they had not raised prices, five per cent said they had, and eighty-six per cent wouldn't say. Those that had replied constituted a sample in which bias might be suspected.

Watch out for evidence of a biased sample, one that has been selected improperly or—as with this one—has selected itself. Ask the question we dealt with in an early chapter: Is the sample large enough to permit any reliable conclusion?

Similarly with a reported correlation: Is it big enough to mean anything? Are there enough cases to add up to any significance? You cannot, as a casual reader, apply tests of significance or come to exact conclusions as to the adequacy of a sample. On a good many of the things you see reported, however, you will be able to tell at a glance—a good long glance, perhaps—that there just weren't enough cases to convince any reasoning person of anything.

What's Missing?

You won't always be told how many cases. The absence of such a figure, particularly when the source is an interested one, is enough to throw suspicion on the whole thing. Similarly a correlation given without a measure of reliability (probable error, standard error) is not to be taken very seriously.

Watch out for an average, variety unspecified, in any matter where mean and median might be expected to differ substantially.

Many figures lose meaning because a comparison is missing. An article in *Look* magazine says, in connection with Mongolism, that "one study shows that in 2,800 cases, over half of the mothers were 35 or over." Getting any meaning from this depends upon your knowing something about the ages at which women in general produce babies. Few of us know things like that.

Here is a pollution note from nearly a generation ago, from *a New Yorker* magazine "Letter from London":

> The Ministry of Health's recently published figures showing that in the week of the great fog the death rate for Greater London jumped by twenty-eight hundred were a shock to the public, which is used to regarding Britain's unpleasant climatic effects as nuisances rather than as killers . . . The extraordinary lethal properties of this winter's prize visitation. . . .

But how lethal *was* the visitation? Was it exceptional for the death rate to be that much higher than usual in a week? All such things do vary. And what about ensuing weeks? Did the death rate drop below average, indicating that if the fog killed people they were largely those who would have died shortly anyway? The figure sounds impressive, but the absence of other figures takes away most of its meaning.

Sometimes it is percentages that are given and raw figures that are missing, and this can be deceptive too. Long ago, when Johns Hopkins University had just begun to admit women students, someone not particularly enamoured of co-education reported a real shocker: Thirty-three and one-third per cent of the women at Hopkins had married faculty members! The raw figures gave a clearer picture. There were three women enrolled at the time, and one of them had married a faculty man.

Some years ago the Boston Chamber of Commerce chose its American Women of Achievement. Of the sixteen among them who were also in *Who's Who,* it was announced that they had "sixty academic degrees and eighteen children." That sounds like an informative picture of the group until you discover that among the women were Dean Virginia Gildersleeve and Mrs. Ullian M. Gilbreth. Those two had a full third of the degrees between them. And Mrs. Gilbreth, about whose offspring *Cheaper by the Dozen* was written, supplied two-thirds of the children.

A corporation was able to announce that its stock was held by 3,003 persons. who had an average of 660 shares each. This was true. It was also true that of the two million shares of stock in the corporation three men held three-quarters and three thousand persons held the other one-fourth among them.

If you are handed an index, you may ask what's missing there. It may be the base, a base chosen to give a distorted picture. A national labour organization once showed that indexes of profits and production had risen much more rapidly after the depression than an index of wages had. As an argument for wage increases this demonstration lost its potency when someone dug out the missing figures. It could be seen then that profits had been almost bound to rise more rapidly in percentage than wages simply because profits had reached a lower point, giving a smaller base.

Sometimes what is missing is the factor that caused a change to occur. This omission leaves the implication that some other, more desired, factor is responsible. Figures published one year attempted to show that business was on the upgrade by pointing out that April retail sales were greater than in the year before. What was missing was the fact that Easter had come in March in the earlier year and in April in the later year.

A report of a great increase in deaths from cancer in the last quarter-century is misleading unless you know how much of it is a product of such extraneous factors as these: Cancer is often listed now where "causes unknown" was formerly used; autopsies are more frequent, giving surer diagnoses; reporting and compiling of medical statistics are more complete; and people more frequently reach the most susceptible ages now. And if you are looking at total deaths rather than the death rate, don't neglect the fact that there are more people now than there used to be.

Did Somebody Change the Subject?

When assaying a statistic, watch out for a switch somewhere between the raw figure and the conclusion. One thing is all too often reported as another.

As just indicated, more reported cases of a disease are not always the same thing as more cases of the disease. A straw-vote victory for a candidate is not always negotiable at the polls. An expressed preference by a "cross-section" of a magazine's readers for articles on world affairs is no final proof that they would read the articles if they were published.

A year came when encephalitis cases reported in the central valley of California were triple the figure for the worst previous year. Many alarmed residents shipped their children away. But when the reckoning was in, there had been no great increase in deaths from sleeping sickness. What had happened was that state and federal health people had come in in great numbers to tackle a long-time problem; as a result of their efforts a great many low-grade cases were recorded that in other years would have been overlooked, possibly not even recognized.

It is all reminiscent of the way that Lincoln Steffens and Jacob A. Riis, as New York newspapermen, once created a crime wave. Crime cases in the papers reached such proportions, both in numbers and in space and big type given to them, that the public demanded action. Theodore Roosevelt, as president of the reform Police Board, was seriously embarrassed. He put an end to the crime wave simply by asking Steffens and Riis to lay off. It had all come about simply because the reporters, led by those two, had got into competition as to who could dig up the most burglaries and whatnot. The official police record showed no increase at all.

"The British male over 5 years of age soaks himself in a hot tub on an average of 1.7 times a week in the winter and 2.1 times in the summer," says a newspaper story. "British women average 1.5 baths a week in the winter and 2.0 in the summer." The source is a Ministry of Works hot-water survey of "6,000 representative British homes." The sample was representative, it says, and seems quite adequate in size to justify the conclusion in *The San Francisco Chronicle's* amusing headline: BRITISH HE'S BATHE MORE THAN SHE'S.

The figures would be more informative if there were some indication of whether they are means or medians. However, the major weakness is that the subject has been changed. What the Ministry really found out is how often these people said they bathed, not how often they did so. When a subject is as intimate as this one is, with the British bath-taking tradition involved, saying and doing may not be the same thing at all. British he's may or may not bathe oftener than she's; all that can safely be concluded is that they say they do.

Here are some more varieties of change-of-subject to watch out for.

A back-to-the-farm movement was discerned when a census showed half a million more farms in the U.S. than five years earlier. But the two counts were not talking about the same thing. The definition of farm used by the Bureau of the Census had been changed; it took in at least 300,000 farms that would not have been so listed under the earlier definition.

Strange things crop up when figures are based on what people say— even about things that seem to be objective facts. Census reports have shown more people at thirty-five years of age, for instance, than at either thirty-four or thirty-six. The false picture comes from one family member's reporting the ages of the others and, not being sure of the exact ages, tending to round them off to a familiar multiple of five. One way to get around this: ask for birth dates instead.

The "population" of a large area in China was 28 million. Five years later it was 105 million. Very little of that increase was real; the great difference could be explained only by taking into account the purposes of the two enumerations and the way people would be inclined to feel about being counted in each instance. The first census was for tax and military purposes. the second for famine relief.

Something of the same sort has happened in the United States. A decennial census found more people in the sixty-five-to-seventy age group than there were in the fifty-five-to-sixty group ten years before. The difference could not be accounted for by immigration. Most of it could be a product of large-scale falsifying of ages by people eager to collect social security. Also possible is that some of the earlier ages were understated out of vanity.

Another kind of change-of-subject is represented by U.S. Senator William Langer's cry, back in days when San Francisco's notorious island was a boarding house for hard cases and hotels charged less than they do now, that "we could take a prisoner from Alcatraz and board him at the Waldorf-Astoria cheaper . . ." The North Dakotan was referring to earlier statements that it cost eight dollars a day to maintain a prisoner at Alcatraz, "the cost of a room at a good San Francisco hotel." The subject has been changed from total maintenance cost (Alcatraz) to hotel-room rent alone.

The *post hoc* variety of pretentious nonsense is another way of changing the subject without seeming to. The change of something *with* something else is presented as *because of.* The magazine *Electrical World* once offered a composite chart in an editorial on "What Electricity Means to America." You could see from it that as "electrical horsepower in factories" climbed, *so* did "average wages per hour." At the same time "average hours per week" dropped. All these things are long-time trends, of course, and there is no evidence at all that any one of them has produced any other.

And then there are the firsters. Almost anybody can claim to be first in *something* if he is not too particular what it is. At the end of 1952 two New York newspapers were each insisting on first rank in grocery advertising. Both were right too, in a way. The *World-Telegram* went on to explain that it was first in full-run advertising, the kind that appears in all copies, which is the only kind it runs. The *Journal-American* insisted that total linage was what counted and that it was first in that. This is the kind of reaching for a superlative that leads the weather reporter on the radio to label a quite normal day "the hottest June second since 1967."

Change-of-subject makes it difficult to compare cost when you contemplate borrowing money either directly or in the form of instalment buying. Six per cent sounds like six per cent—but it may not be at all.

If you borrow £100 from a bank at six per cent interest and pay it back in equal monthly instalments for a year, the price you pay for the use of the money is about £3. But another six per cent loan, on the basis sometimes called £6 on the £100, will cost you twice as much. That's the way most automobile loans are figured. It is very tricky.

The point is that you don't have the £100 for a year. By the end of six months you have paid back half of it. If you are charged at £6 on the £100, or six per cent of the amount, you really pay interest at nearly twelve per cent.

Even worse was what happened to some careless purchasers of freezer-food plans in America. They were quoted a figure of anywhere from six to twelve per cent. It sounded like interest, but it was not. It was an on-the-dollar figure and, worst of all, the time was often six months rather than a year. Now £12 on the £100 for money to be paid back regularly over half a year works out to something like forty-eight per cent real interest. It is no wonder that so many customers defaulted and so many food plans blew up.

Sometimes the semantic approach will be used to change the subject. Here is an item from *Business Week* magazine.

> Accountants have decided that "surplus" is a nasty word. They propose eliminating it from corporate balance sheets. The Committee on Accounting Procedure of the American Institute of Accountants says: . . . Use such descriptive terms as "retained earnings" or "appreciation of fixed assets."

This one is from a newspaper story reporting Standard Oil's record-breaking revenue and net profit of a million dollars a day.

> Possibly the directors may be thinking some time of splitting the stock for there may be an advantage . . . if the profits per share do not look so large. . . .

Does It Make Sense?

"Does it make sense?" will often cut a statistic down to size when the whole rigmarole is based on an unproved assumption. You may be familiar with the Rudolf Flesch readability formula. It purports to measure how easy a piece of prose is to read, by such simple and objective items as length of words and sentences. Like all devices for reducing the imponderable to a number and substituting arithmetic for judgement, it is an appealing idea. At least it has appealed to people who employ writers, such as newspaper publishers, even if not to many writers themselves. The assumption in the formula is that such things as word length determine readability. This, to be ornery about it, remains to be proved.

A man named Robert A. Dufour put the Flesch formula to trial on some literature that he found handy. It showed "The Legend of Sleepy Hollow" to be half again as hard to read as Plato's *Republic*. The Sinclair Lewis novel *Cass Timberlane* was rated more difficult than an essay by Jacques Maritain, "The Spiritual Value of Art." A likely story.

Many a statistic is false on its face. It gets by only because the magic of numbers brings about a suspension of common sense. Leonard Engel, in a *Harper's* article, has listed a few of the medical variety.

> An example is the calculation of a well-known urologist that there are eight million cases of cancer of the prostate gland in the United States—which would be enough to provide 1.1 carcinomatous prostate glands for every male in the susceptible age group! Another is a prominent neurologist's estimate that one American in twelve suffers from migraine; since migraine is responsible for a third of chronic headache cases, this would mean that a quarter of us must suffer from disabling headaches. Still another is the figure of 250,000 often given for the number of multiple sclerosis cases: death data indicate that there can be, happily, no more than thirty to forty thousand cases of this paralytic disease in the country.

Hearings on amendments to the Social Security Act have been haunted by various forms of a statement that makes sense only when not looked at closely. It is an argument that goes like this: Since life expectancy is only about sixty-three years, it is a sham and a fraud to set up a social-security plan with a retirement age of sixty-five, because virtually everybody dies before that.

You can rebut that one by looking around at people you know. The basic fallacy, however, is that the figure refers to expectancy at birth, and so about half the babies born can expect to live longer than that. The figure, incidentally, came from the 1939–41 period and remained in use long after it was out of date. Presumably the current figure, calculated a generation later, of 69.7 will produce a new and equally silly argument to the effect that practically everybody now lives to be sixty-five.

Product planning at a big electrical-appliance company was going great guns some years ago on the basis of a declining birth rate, something that had been taken for granted for a long time. Plans called for emphasis on small-capacity appliances, apartment-size refrigerators. Then one of the planners had an attack of common sense: He came out of his graphs and charts long enough to notice that he and his co-workers and his friends and his neighbours and his former classmates with few exceptions either had three or four children or planned to. This led to some open-minded investigating and charting—and the company shortly turned its emphasis most profitably to big-family models. It is to be hoped that the planners will respond more quickly to the present turnaround.

The impressively precise figure is something else that contradicts common sense. A study reported in New York City newspapers announced that a working woman living with her family needed a weekly pay cheque of $40.13 for adequate support. Anyone who has not suspended all logical processes while reading his paper will realize that the cost of keeping body and soul together cannot be calculated to the last cent. But there is a dreadful temptation; "$40.13" sounds so much more knowing than "about $40."

You are entitled to look with the same suspicion on the report, some years ago, by the American Petroleum Industries Committee that the average yearly tax bill for automobiles is $51.13.

Extrapolations are useful, particularly in that form of soothsaying called forecasting trends. But in looking at the figures or the charts made from them, it is necessary to remember one thing constantly: The trend-to-now may be a fact, but the future trend represents no more than an educated guess. Implicit in it is "everything else being equal" and "present trends continuing." And somehow everything else refuses to remain equal, else life would be dull indeed.

For a sample of the nonsense inherent in uncontrolled extrapolation, consider the trend of television. The number of sets in American homes increased around 10,000 per cent in one five-year period early in the game. Project this for the next five years and you'd have found that there were about to be a couple of thousand million of the things. Heaven forfend, or forty sets to the family. If you want to be sillier yet, begin with a base year even earlier in the telly scheme of things and you can just as well "prove" that each family will soon have not forty but forty thousand sets.

What Harry Truman did to Tom Dewey, in a U.S. Presidential-election upset unparalleled before or since, is nothing to what Truman did to the poll people. A Government research man, Morris Hansen, has called that Gallup election forecast "the most publicized statistical error in human history."

It was a paragon of accuracy, however, compared to some of our most widely used estimates of future population, which have earned a nationwide horselaugh. As late as 1938 a Presidential commission loaded with experts doubted that the population of the United States would ever reach 140 million; it was 12 million more than that just twelve years later. Yet college textbooks published so recently that they were still in use at that time predicted a peak population of not more than 150 million and figured it would take until about 1980 to reach it. These fearful underestimates came from assuming that a trend would continue without change. A similar assumption a century ago did as badly in the opposite direction because it assumed continuation of population-increase rate of 1790 to 1860. In his second message to Congress, Abraham Lincoln predicted the U.S. population would reach 251,689,914 in 1930.

Not long after that, in 1874, Mark Twain summed up the nonsense side of extrapolation in *Life on the Mississippi:*

> In the space of one hundred and seventy-six years the Lower Mississippi has shortened itself two hundred and forty-two miles. That is an average of a trifle over one mile and a third per year. Therefore, any calm person, who is not blind or idiotic, can see that in the Old Oölitic Silurian period, just a million years ago next November, the Lower Mississippi River was upward of one million three hundred thousand miles long, and stuck out over the Gulf of Mexico like a fishing-rod. And by the same token any person can see that seven hundred and forty-two years from now the Lower Mississippi will be only a mile and three-quarters long, and Cairo and New Orleans will have joined their streets together, and be plodding comfortably along under a single mayor and a mutual board of aldermen. There is something fascinating about science. One gets such wholesale returns of conjecture out of such a trifling investment of fact.

14

Surfing Bytes: Utilizing the Internet and Your Computer for Social Science Research

Stella Z. Theodoulou, Paula Lackie, and Matthew Alan Cahn

Many political science students fear statistics, computers, or anything they perceive has something to do with numbers! This leads to a dislike and distrust of statistical analysis. However, the reader should realize the computer is a useful tool in the research process. How can the computer be utilized by political scientists? First, it is an obvious tool in the writing process. Many of you may have already come to understand the utility of word processing. Next, it is a tool for statistical analysis, for example, through crunching numbers in a spread sheet or statistical software program. These first two uses are things at which personal computers have excelled at since the early 1980s. A third way in which computers can be utilized by political scientists became apparent by the early 1990s. At that time, the Internet hit the scene and a whole new world of easily accessible information and communication suddenly opened through computers. Through computer use, there is a capability and tremendous potential of a vast array of resources that are available to political scientists. More information is available today than at any time in history—and, increasingly, it is available online.

Since our research is increasingly interconnected to resources and data that are available through the Internet, it is appropriate that—as a methodology text—we introduce the major uses and utilities of Internet-related resources. This chapter will introduce the reader to the variety of resources available on the Internet. We start first with an overview of the use of the computer as a tool in statistical analysis. Then we move to a general discussion of the Internet. Next, we explore the issues of connectivity (connecting to the network) and Internet protocols. And, finally, we introduce the reader to the tools that bring the Internet alive.

USING THE COMPUTER

Using computers allows us to conduct research in a time-efficient manner. Computers process words and numbers thousands of times faster than any individual can manually, even with the use of a calculator or a typewriter. We can accomplish with a computer in only a short time what would take hours and hours manually. This is especially true of projects that are extremely large. In statistical analysis, what is time consuming is data entry. However, the mathematical accuracy that computer analysis brings us is worth the time spent preparing and entering data.

We can utilize the computer in each of the stages of the research process. On-line data searching is now a basic step in the conduct of the literature review. PC-based data storage allows the importation of large data sets, such as the General Social Survey, for secondary analysis. Statistical software programs such as SPSS-WIN allow us to analyze data statistically with relative ease and minimal training. Statistical analysis using the computer allows political scientists to take data they have gathered and analyze it systematically. Finally, word processing allows us to draft and revise written work in such a way that the final written product is far superior to anything that can be produced on a typewriter. In the upcoming section, we will concentrate on the methods for analyzing data rather than discussing the utility of word processing.

It is important that from the very beginning the student realize that the computer is a tool that can be used in understanding the conceptual development of the research process. That it is to say, the computer will help expediate every step that must be carried out in any study. Computers today do not really need any special aptitude. The personal computer and the software developed for it through Windows™ applications allow relatively inexperienced students to carry out sophisticated statistical procedures with relative ease. What is important is that any student, before undertaking analysis on the computer, first understand the logic and methodology behind the statistical procedure. The only way we can make sense of what the computer produces—that is, the numbers, is to know what is being done with the numbers. That requires that we understand how to analyze data by hand with a calculator, in other words, that we familiarize ourselves with the fundamentals of applied social statistics.

There are a number of microcomputer packages that can be used for quantification and qualitative data analysis. Some of the most popular are SPSS-PC, SPSS-WIN, Excel, Statview, Mystat, Wingz, Full Impact, MacCalc, and Systat. The package choice should take into account the following requirements. First, the package should be as comprehensive as possible. It should generate both descriptive and inferential statistics. With respect to inferential statistics, both parametric and nonparametric tools should be an option. Second, consider whether you will need to import data. Some packages have limitations on data imports, requiring the creation of new sets by hand. Any data available on tape can be defined and edited to fit on a standard 3.5-inch floppy, which easily imports into programs such as SPSS-PC or SPSS-WIN. Next, consider that the package should be relatively easy to run. SPSS-WIN adopts the Windows™ spreadsheet environment common to easier packages such as Excel. Fourth, the package should be flexible so it can be applied to a variety of analytic situations. Fifth, it should be able to generate visual perspectives so that data can be displayed in a useful manner. That is to say, the package should have a graphics component. Sixth, the package should have spreadsheet capacity. Spreadsheets allow individuals to be up and running on the computer within a short time. They also provide a useful approach to learning basic statistical analysis and organizing a simple data set. For example, SPSS-WIN allows for manipulation of numbers—including basic data analysis techniques, storing, retrieving, and displaying data through the graphics component. Grafton and Permaloff review several windows based statistical packages and provide an excellent overview of the options available.[1]

There are some weaknesses that apply to computer-generated statistical analysis. First, because computers are very efficient at performing complicated calculations, there is a temptation to employ statistical techniques that are otherwise not really understood. Thus, there is insufficient understanding of the substantive implications of the results. The point here is that techniques should be used with sufficient understanding. Next, there is a tendency to let the computer grind out every possible coefficient. That is to "go fishing" in the hope of finding something. This negates the conduct of a well-planned study and research design. A final weakness is to take everything the computer produces as truth. Remember, computers only process the data that is given to them. People do make mistakes. Computers only guarantee the mathematical accuracy of what they compute. They cannot guarantee on empirical validity.

THE INTERNET: AN OVERVIEW

The Internet is an international network of computer networks whose managers have agreed on a set of computer protocols. In general, computer networks connect two or more computers together, which allows computers and people to exchange information. The Internet is a way to connect these existing networks that greatly extends the reach of each participating system in a vast global highway of networks.

The Internet first came into existence as the *Arpanet* in 1969. It was a project funded by the U.S. Defense Department during the height of the Cold War in the 1960s. The object was to develop a computer network that could allow U.S. authorities to keep in contact with each other in the aftermath of a nuclear attack. The basic design was to enable the network to divert traffic via other links when a link or a city was in some way cut off from the rest.

With the fish-net design, computers (and the people behind them) at other locations could continue to communicate among themselves because of the alternate routes. Years later, this design inspired an initial connection between four universities around the U.S. From this tiny beginning sprang the Net. Now multimillions of connections strong, it covers the entire globe with links between more than 4.8 million computers, in over 80 countries, with more than 43,000 subsidiary networks and 36 million people—and the numbers continue to grow daily.

THE ROAD TO THE INTERNET

It's tough to participate in society and not have some sense that the Internet is having an impact on human communications. This sense has come with a fair amount of folklore and a lot of jargon. It is important to get past the fluff and hype of the Internet so you can quickly maximize your access to and use of Internet resources. The key word is *resources.* As political scientists, we study the importance of resource allocation. The Internet is perhaps best examined as a collection of resources—a very complex collection of resources where those who *have* are in a wide range of access levels and those who *have not* are literally out of the loop.

How you access the Internet depends on several layers of technical and political hierarchies. Your connection to the Internet can only be as good as the weakest link in the chain of computers and wiring between you and the rest of the networks. The basic layers start with the computer at which you sit, how that computer connects to the local network, how that network connects to the next, and so on until you electronically connect to the computer that has the information in which you are interested. The analogy of the Internet as an information superhighway can be useful in our breakdown of the levels of access to information through the Internet.

WHAT ARE YOU DRIVING? (YOUR DESKTOP ENVIRONMENT)

Computers come in a mind-boggling array of configurations reflecting different architecture, operating systems, options, and add-ons—all of which can have a significant impact on your Internet capabilities. Because we are living in a dynamic computing environment, it is best that you familiarize yourself with the strengths and limitations of the computer(s) you are using. Learning to navigate on the Internet is an ongoing process—the Internet and the tools that utilize it are constantly changing. Efficiency on the Internet involves combining basic library skills with basic computing skills—and a dash of luck. Add tenacity and focus to your task and you've got a winning combination for research success!

WHAT IS THE CONDITION OF YOUR DRIVEWAY?

Data transmission is a two-way process. Unlike an actual highway, where the links between your car and your ultimate destination are fairly independent, on the virtual superhighway, the links between you and your destination are all quite interdependent. How quickly these messages can be sent back and forth through the various wires and various computers to and from your desktop will dictate how quickly you are able to access the information you are after. There are generally two categories of information transmission from the desktop level. Serial connections require data to move in one direction at a time. Direct Ethernet connections and PPP/SLIP connections (that emulate Ethernet) allow simultaneous data transmission both to and from the server. Most servers now provide PPP/SLIP connections, though some campuses are still limiting access to serial (e.g., one-way) connections. Determine the category of your connectivity because it can dictate what level of Internet access you have.

Category I

Serial, standard modem, micom line (coax), terminal or terminal emulation style. This is the basic connection. Whatever tools you can access here are available to those in Category II (PPP or direct Ethernet connection). With a Category I connection, you will only see text in a monochrome interface and just about everything you do would involve key-commands that more or less approximate English. In this style of connection, you are a taking a bus to a central location which then may have an address on the Internet. Once there, you are free to travel about the Internet but every interaction you have must be funneled through the one-way serial connection between you and your centrally located computer.

Category II

With SLIP/PPP, or Ethernet-style, connection you should have access to desktop software that enables Internet access in a more user-friendly fashion. You can cruise directly from your local computer to any part of the Internet you desire because your desktop computer can already be directly on the Internet. You can, for instance, receive your e-mail to your desktop through programs like Eudora or Popmail, access and take full advantage of the World Wide Web through browsers such as that by Netscape Communications. The convenience of this type of connection is ease of use and ease of access. The disadvantage is that because these utilities are run on your local desktop they require substantially more local power (CPU speed, RAM, and disk space).

The Server

Whichever category of connectivity you have, you still need a server to which to connect. The server is the computer network that you plug into—either directly through an ether-net or dial into with your modem. If you are connecting through your campus network, that network is your server. If you subscribe through an independent Internet Service Provider (ISP) such as Microsoft Network, Earthlink, or America Online, that service provider is your server. If your desktop computer is your vehicle, and your connectivity your driveway, your server is essentially your on-ramp to the highway.

YOU'RE ON THE SUPERHIGHWAY NOW!

This is where the Internet really begins. The basic design of the Internet is based on a protocol, a set of standards and agreements known as the Internet Protocol (IP), which allows all types of computers to understand and communicate with each other. Every computer on the Internet has an IP address—just like a postal address—it gives the exact location of the computer on the Internet. IP addresses take the form of numbers separated by periods. Fortunately, most sites and servers also follow the domain name system (DNS), which is designed to help humans remember the addresses. For instance, *whitehouse.gov* is an example of a domain name. To tell the applications who is who, there are the Domain Name Servers. The idea here is that the Internet is an astonishing collection of Internet Service Providers (ISPs) who work more or less together to keep their local part of the Internet up and running. They maintain the special cable connections to the next collection of Internet links.

WHAT CAN YOU *DO* WITH THE INTERNET?

So now you're there, and you need to know what that means in more practical terms. It used to be that the tools available for use on the Internet were a bit arcane. It was an environment that attracted computer wizards and other technically inclined folk. But new technology has made the tools quite simple to use, especially if you have a stable and fast connection. The rate of change on the Internet is more reliably measured in weeks so it would be unreasonable for anyone publishing a book to claim to definitively describe all the tools and information available on the Internet. What we can do is suggest some strategies for using some of the tools available as of the publication date and encourage you to look for these tools on the Internet while you learn more about what is current when you are out surfing.

INTERNET TOOLS

Electronic Mail (e-mail)

- Electronic mail is the most widely used Internet service. Using programs such as Eudora or Pine, e-mail allows users to send immediate electronic notes to any other Internet user on the planet, as well as to non-Internet networks via e-mail gateways.
- The widely used protocol has been incorporated into dozens of specific e-mail programs allowing for greater user convenience.
- E-mail provides a medium for e-mail discussion groups or mailing lists on a multitude of topics, allowing for interested participants to contribute to text-based discussion.

Usenet News

- Usenet Newsgroups are discussion forums which behave something like a bulletin board. Contributors post their message for all to see; readers can post responses; other readers can post responses to the responses. It is essentially an electronic public forum that is broken into thousands of subject classifications (currently over 30,000).
- Newsgroups allow for uploading and downloading any type of digital information, so in addition to text-based discussions many newsgroups share public domain software, photographs (from the Space Shuttle to weather maps to puppies), and even audio and video files.

Telnet

- Telneting allows users to log on to other computers on the Internet and use them as though they were directly connected to them. This is often done to access electronic library card catalogues without having to actually visit the library. Since most libraries are now online, it is possible for anyone to check the stacks electronically at their favorite university, overcoming the traditional constraints of time and space. To this end, many libraries have instituted interlibrary loan programs, which allow an exchange of books and journal articles.

File Transfer Protocol (FTP)

- FTP provides a common way to safely retrieve files across the Internet. Anonymous FTP allows a user to log on to public hosts using the log-in name *anonymous* and his or her e-mail address as a password.
- FTP access has increasingly been incorporated into more user-friendly Internet environments, such as the World Wide Web.

Archie

- Archie is a software tool for finding files stored on anonymous FTP sites. You need to know the exact file name or a substring of it to find available files.

Gopher

- Gopher is a hierarchical Internet information browser. It predates the World Wide Web but still links many types of information located all around the Internet. There are still a number of governmental resources using this service. Gopher resources can also be accessed using a Web browser.

Veronica

- Veronica is used to search Gopherspace. It is available from within Gopher, but can be replaced by most Word Wide Web search engines.

Internet Relay Chat (IRC)

- IRC allows you to communicate with another person or in chat rooms with many other computer users. Conversations are in real time and only limited by your typing skills and the rules of the room. The room operator can disconnect users who step out of line. Most chat rooms have a particular discussion topic (which you are expected to discuss), so it could be analogous to a class meeting.
- Chatting on the Internet can take place via Web pages at places known as chat rooms or on other IRC channels (Users use Telnet to connect to specific Internet locations set up for IRC use). Either way, when participating in a chat discussion, your messages are instantaneously relayed to other members and their messages. Look for guides to chat rooms and upcoming events on the Web. (You might try looking for the page: *http://www.globalchat.com/schedule.html*).

The World Wide Web

- The World Wide Web is a nonhierarchical, hypermedia-based Internet information system. It is the Internet utility that brought the network out of the university and onto the streets. Its success is in its simplicity. Web browsers such as Mosaic, Netscape, Navigator, or Internet Explorer allow a user to easily browse and retrieve Internet information using a friendly point-and-click interface.
- The Web links together various types of Internet information, including

files, images, video, databases, and miniature software programs. The Web often acts as a front-end to many other Internet services, such as the Internet Gopher and FTP.

As with much of what we come across relating to Internet applications, the jargon is thick, precise, and ever-changing. The list above is just the tip of the iceberg.

IF THE WEB DOES IT ALL, WHO CARES ABOUT THE REST?

While the Web is the most impressive Internet service developed so far, it is not necessarily the only tool you'll want to use when you need to get your research done. As mentioned above, the other tools that you are most likely to encounter from within the Web are e-mail, Telnet, news, FTP, and Gopher. For instance, there are a number of libraries that are more quickly accessed if you simply Telnet directly to their library catalog server and use their search tools as though you were standing right in their lobby. Speak with your local librarian for advice and guidance. Telneting to other libraries and resources can be tricky but it is often a very fruitful use of your time.

One of the most common problems with accessing data through the Web is that the Web browser software sometimes can't handle extra-large file sizes very well. With FTP, you can bypass the Web and go directly to the file you need. This program gives you more control over where you place the file when it is retrieved and in what form that file is transferred. If you have never done this before, we suggest that you read the help or tips section of your FTP program before you begin. Still, the vast majority of your research work on the Internet will be via the World Wide Web.

SURFING THE INTERNET: THE WORLD WIDE WEB

Given the explosive growth in the use of the World Wide Web for publishing, electronic commerce, lifelong learning, and the delivery of government services, it is vital that the Web be accessible to everyone. The Web Accessibility Initiative will develop the tools, technology, and guidelines to make it possible to display information in ways that are available to all users.

—President Bill Clinton

The World Wide Web is the most widely publicized aspect of the Internet today. What makes it so special is the relative ease with which individuals can both access and provide access to all types of Internet information, including files, images, video, databases, and a gateway to use other Internet tools. The Web is, literally, an electronic web of files connected by hypertext links.

Hypertext links are connections (or gateways) that let you move from one file to another with a keystroke or a click on your mouse through a local browser. *Browsers* allow you to wander, or "surf," the Web, browsing information on computers, or "sites," all around the world. The actual location is irrelevant to your computer but very important to you. For instance, you might wonder about the authenticity of a site that claims to be the *official governmental source for Iraq*, yet the site appears to be hosted by a company based in Utah. It is especially important to adopt a healthy amount of skepticism when browsing the Web because the authors of posted documents may or may not honestly make themselves known. It is up to you to decide what information to trust.

SOME HISTORY AND TECHNICAL BACKGROUND

The Web was developed at the Conseil European pour la Recherche Nuclarie (known as CERN) in Switzerland and put into use on the Internet in 1990. It is offically described as a wide-area hypermedia information retrieval initiative aiming to give universal access to a large universe of documents. The rapid expansion of the Internet in the 1990s was driven by the immense success of the Web.

In 1995, a virtual explosion occurred when the graphical interface to the Web was introduced. With this easily accessible tool, people all over the world started using the Web with little to no prior training. This is largely why many people have come to assume that the Internet and the Web are one in the same. However, the Web is a subset of computers that use the Internet as its transport mechanism based on a continuously developing set of standard computer codes. Your browser translates these codes into a display format. This set of codes is the transport mechanism known as *hypertext*. Information on the Web is organized on hypertext pages.

Hypertext allows you to navigate among pages onscreen by clicking on *hyperlinks* with your mouse. Hypertext links show up as colored, underlined, or highlighted phrases and words in text. When you click on the link, your Web browser directly connects with the computer which it refers to and retrieves the specifically addressed file to which it is linked—which may be another page containing hyperlinks. Transitions to other resource providers are not always obvious. It is up to you to pay attention to where the page is located and to figure out who is responsible for the content on it.

GET TO KNOW YOUR BROWSER

You may need to take some time just getting to know the *browser* (or client software) program you are using. Most programs will have an easily accessible link having something to do with *Help*. Don't be shy about spending some time with this section of the browser. Learning the simple ins and outs of the program, as well as learning your immediate computing environment, will make a difference in your success rate on the Web.

What Is a URL?

One of the planned advances for web use is to eliminate the need for people to understand the *URL* (Uniform Resource Locator). However, these addresses will continue to be important, if less obvious, to the user, so it is necessary to understand what they are all about. The URL describes the location and access method of a resource on the Internet. For example, the URL *http://www. whitehouse.gov* describes the type of access method being used (http) and the server location that hosts the Web site (*www.whitehouse.gov*). All Web sites have URLs. Although Web-site URLs are sometimes long and hard to read, let alone remember, most browsers have a bookmark or hotlink feature that gives you the opportunity to save the location (URL) of Web sites for future reference.

Searching the Web—Surfing Smarter for Better Results

The Web is a mainstream publishing medium. Because it is cheaper to publish on the Web than it is to publish on paper or in other electronic media, a wide range of interests are represented there. This is limited only by the fact that the population of the Internet is not yet as diverse as the population of the real world. Fortunately, that is changing as Web access becomes more and more readily available. Still, it is very important to remind yourself that if you don't find what you are looking for on the Web, that does not mean it doesn't exist. Don't forget to also go to your library and do some traditional project research as well!

We are faced with an increasingly dizzying amount of Web-based resources—some exceptionally useful and some exceptionally bad—to sort through to help us with our various research tasks. There are a number of alternatives to aimlessly clicking through the Web with the hope of chancing upon a useful item. Your Web includes a button or a drop-down menu choice for information on searching the Web. This is a good place to start.

Search Engines (Boolean, Field, Meta, Phrase, Proximity, Subject Catalogs)

There are many companies that specialize in searching the web and produce tools for this task. These tools are called *search engines*. Every search engine produces a slightly different collection of Web pages even when asked to search for the exact same material. It is a good idea to do a little homework on the available engines (you should read any sections on their sites, which give

Web-searching tips or tricks for their engine) and to try several search engines when starting to research a project.

More about That URL

Once you are familiar with the various search engines and have focused your search to minimize the number of erroneous *"hits"* (pages the search engine found for you), you must then begin to sift through what is available and determine what is useful. Luckily, there are some tricks you can use to speed this along. For one, there is a pattern for URLs that you may find useful. For instance, as we have said, the U.S. White House Web address is: *http://www.whitehouse.gov.* Compare this with the e-mail address of the First Lady: *first-lady@whitehouse.gov.* Notice the similarity? What do you think the URL for the Web server is at the House of Representatives? The Senate? The FBI? In many cases you can guess at the correct URL for a site without having to use a search engine at all.

What if you need the text from the most recent Supreme Court ruling? If your browser returns 700,000 hits, you surely don't want to sort through them all to find the most recent ruling! Notice that the URL is usually listed—from this you can get an idea of where that page is located. As you look through these, try and find the ones that have a domain name that seem legitimate. For instance, you wouldn't want to waste your time reading through a Web page that describes a rock band called "The Supreme Court" when the next link leads you to the domain: *www.uscourts.gov* or the *www.fjc.gov* (Federal Judicial Center). Recognizing a URL as legitimate isn't always a cut-and-dried situation. It is very important that as a researcher you maintain a healthy skepticism about the authenticity of a resource. Legitimate sources will include alternative (non-Internet based) contact information somewhere on a page within the domain name of the page you are trying to verify. Hunt around for it. If you find the information puzzling, ask your professor or a librarian for assistance.

NOTE

1. Carl Grafton and Anne Permaloff, "Windows Statistics Packages," *PS: Political Science and Politics* (December 1993) 87: 789–795.

15

Formal Models in Political Science

Morris P. Fiorina

WHEN ARE FORMAL MODELS MOST USEFUL?

As with any other technique, the construction or application of a formal model is sometimes more appropriate for a given research area and other times less so. In this section I will offer some opinions about research areas ripe for modeling. First, consider the descriptive or explanatory use of models.

If our purpose is to explain observable political behavior in a given context, then it seems to me that models can be used most advantageously where there exists a body of accepted empirical findings about political behavior in that context. After all, how does one go about choosing concepts, defining them precisely, and making appropriate assumptions in a substantive vacuum? Consider for a moment the empirical process of constructing explanatory models, a process Arthur Goldberg (1968) terms "retroduction."

Given some empirical findings(s), X, one poses the question, "How might the world be structured such that X holds, occurs, or is true?" The answers to this question are models, all of which have in common that they assume or imply X. To be worthy of consideration a model must have at least this one tie (X) to the empirical world. For example, Downs appears to have had several "facts" in mind when he formulated his theory—that parties in a two-party system are alike but in a multiparty system distinct; that many citizens are ill-informed and vote on the basis of shortcuts such as party ID and ideology; that democratic governments do "too little;" and no doubt several others. A second example is John Ferejohn's (1974, ch. 7) model of the congressional conference committee bargaining process. Ferejohn requires that his model be consistent with two seemingly inconsistent findings: (1) that interview evidence suggests that the House has a stronger position in the conference than the Senate; (2) that examination of conference outcomes suggests that the Senate is more successful in conference. Another example is Shepsle's (1974) model of the House committee assignment process. Rather than construct a highly abstract general model of how party leaders and the Committee on Committees distribute committee posts, Shepsle incorporates in the model the detailed rules currently prevailing in the House (e.g., only one assignment if to an exclusive committee, no more than one assignment to a semiexclusive committee, etc.), as well as other empirical findings about the committee assignment process. In each of these examples empirical facts establish constraints on the models constructed; one requires a priori that the model be consistent with these facts.

The value of "retroduction" is self-evident. Innumerable models are conceivable; far fewer are interesting. The size of the interesting class will partially be determined by what we know in a given area. Many, many models will imply X; somewhat fewer will imply both X and Y; fewer still will imply all of X, Y, and Z; and so forth. The more we know, the more restrictions we can place on our models, and the less likely will our models be serious misrepresentations of the empirical world.

With the preceding comments in mind, I will suggest various areas ripe for the application of formal models. As one would expect, the first is where some modeling has already occurred—the electoral process. We have great quantities of data, mostly American, but increasingly foreign as well. Numerous capable researchers are mining these data, and some generalizations are beginning to emerge. Such a situation is close to ideal.

Consider what has already occurred. Building on traditional wisdom and early voting studies, Downs presented a model of party competition in a democratic system. Authors such as Garvey (1966), Davis, Hinich, and Ordeshook (1970), Shepsle (1972), and McKelvey (1972) refined various aspects of the Downsian model. These efforts directly influenced some empirical research (Shapiro, 1969; Rabinowitz, 1973; Page and Brody, 1972) and perhaps indirectly provided some of the impetus for the upsurge of research on issue voting (see Kessel, 1972, for citations). Aranson and Ordeshook (1972), Coleman (1971), and Black (1975) extended the earlier simple models to take into account empirical research on party activists. Inconsistencies between the Downsian voter model and empirical turnout levels motivated Riker and Ordeshook (1968) and Ferejohn and Fiorina (1974a) to try new theoretical avenues, which in turn led to new hypotheses to be tested (1974b). And in a related area of research, findings about the correlates of political participation led to additional theorizing about the nature of the participation decision (Tollison and Willett, 1973). In the area of voting behavior and electoral process I believe it fair to conclude that there has been considerable interchange between empirical research and formal models, and that both have profited from it.

A second area in which formal models almost certainly will prove valuable is the legislative process. Again, there exist numerous informative empirical studies ranging from detailed interview materials to highly quantitative roll call studies. Aspects of the legislative process that have been modeled thus far include coalition formation (Koehler, 1974), roll call voting (Fiorina, 1974, 1975; Gilbert, 1973) conference committee decisionmaking (Ferejohn, 1974), and committee assignments (Shepsle, 1974). This first generation of models has not as yet had much impact on empirical research, however.

The study of the judicial process presents virtually the same picture as that of the legislative process. Again, there are numerous high quality empirical studies in which to ground formal models. Already Rohde (1972a, b) has applied Riker's (1962) and Axelrod's (1970, ch. 8) theories of coalition formation to the study of opinion coalitions on the Supreme Court. In the future I expect that formal models will appear quite frequently in studies of the legislative and judicial processes.

By implication, formal models are not so usefully applied where little is know about the behavior of interest. I will not be so foolish as to name any areas of the discipline which fit that category, but certainly in some subfields there is little agreement even on what should be studied and how, let alone on what is known. Possibly, by adopting the categories and approach of one of the contending sides, a researcher could build a model which would bring order out of chaos, but I would not be optimistic about the possibility.

Thus far I have discussed the use of models to explain political behavior, and the conditions under which that use is most appropriate. But there exists another type of research question for which formal models are quite appropriate. That question involves the abstract properties of alternative institutional arrangements. Formal analysis of political institutions and "rules of the game" are very revealing.

With no more than simple arithmetic Duncan Black (1958) suggested effects and properties of various voting schemes, e.g., pairwise voting (exhaustive and not), rank-order voting, and extraordinary majorities. He also clarified and carried forward the analysis of single-member district, multimember district, plurality winner, and proportional representation systems. Many political scientists are familiar with the interesting institutional analyses in Buchanan and Tullock's *The Calculus of Consent* (1962). But scores of other studies can be cited. May (1954), Murikami (1968), Rae (1969), Plott (1967), and numerous others have examined majority rule. Ferejohn and Grether (1974) have probed into the rule of extraordinary majorities. Fishburn (1971), Murikami, and Fine (1972) have attempted to formalize and analyze what it means to have a representative system. Institutional analysis virtually demands a formalized study; the effects of rules and procedures can be extremely subtle. Formal analyses reveal possibilities that verbal discussions anticipate only vaguely, if at all (Fishburn, 1974).

From institutional analysis it is but a short step to political philosophy. Why should majority rule be adopted? Which institutions are the fairest or most just? Ironically, here, where formal models have had little impact, is where they profitably could be applied. Broadly construed, the abstract analyses in modern social choice theory focus on the same questions (albeit more narrowly) as does classical political theory (Shepsle, 1974b; Plott, 1972). I find it very interesting that John Rawls' (1971) prize-winning book, *A Theory of Justice*, contains ample documentation of the influence of various individual and social choice models; moreover the book recently has been critiqued by formalizing its argument and examining its consequences (Plott, 1974). In 1968 Riker and Shapley pointed to the relevance of formal models for normative analysis. I would reemphasize their observation here. Perhaps an unforeseen byproduct of the development of formal models will be a renewed interest in the study of institutional and normative political science, areas which have fallen into relative neglect during the behavioral era.

As the preceding pages make evident, I have no simple answer to the question which leads off this section. When are formal models most useful? If I were allowed only one sentence in which to provide an answer, I would probably focus less on the inappropriateness of a given subject than on the inappropriateness of given models. Tailor the model to the research question, not vice versa. Models become inappropriate when they cease to be tools and become ends. Just as there are a few individuals who see the political world only as an arena for the application of some cherished statistical method, so there are people who see the world as something to be twisted and bent to fit some particular model. We can only hope that their tribe does not increase.

KINDS OF MODELS

Existing formal models can be classified in various ways, but before suggesting several possible categorizations I will argue against one which rears its head far too often: normative vs. positive, or normative vs. empirical.[1] In my opinion this distinction serves no useful purpose. It has wasted far too much scholarly time and energy in the past, and unfortunately it shows a recent tendency to become the last refuge of formal modelers reluctant to confront the real world.

Theories are theories. The structure of a normative theory looks no different from that of a positive theory. Sometimes it is claimed that the premises of a normative theory contain imperatives, whereas the premises of a positive theory contain only declaratives. But I suggest that such distinctions do not lie in the theory or model itself, but rather in the mind of the theorist, in his attitude towards the theory. Let me elaborate.

The "normative theorist" regards certain axioms of his theory as true, as nonfalsifiable, whether this status stems from revelation, intuition, natural law, or whatnot. Given this attitude it is clear that the implications of these axioms are similarly nonfalsifiable; they are prescriptions, not hypotheses. If the real world does not conform to these prescriptions, the response of the theorist is to censure the behavior, to recommend that the world should change.

In contrast, the positive theorist regards the axioms of his theory as approximations to behavioral laws and characteristics of the situation being modeled. Given this attitude, the implications of the axioms are propositions subject to falsification, hypotheses about what is present in the real world. If the world does not conform to the hypotheses, the hypotheses must give way. The theorist goes back to the drawing board to revise or abandon some of the axioms.

For the positive theorist the model must accommodate the world. For the normative theorist the world must conform to the model. To see that the distinction is purely one of attitude, consider how the same model can be used in both ways.

Take some economic model which posits that atomized individuals interact under perfectly competitive conditions. Such a model can illuminate some spheres of economic activity even today—it has some exploratory power. Yet note that libertarians take that same model as a norm. If the model does not describe behavior in some sectors of the economy (because of statist or do-gooder interference with the market), the libertarian does not switch to a new model (monopoly, oligopoly, central planning, etc.). Rather, he condemns the conditions which prevent the model from being descriptive.

A second example is perhaps more compelling. Take the theory of subjective expected utility (Savage, 1954). Howard Raiffa (1968) and his associates at the Harvard Business School teach this theory to their students, but they teach it as a "normative" theory. Through proof, paradox, and case study, Raiffa attempts to convince decisionmakers that to act in their own best interests, they *should* act so as to maximize subjective expected utility. But note that if a student learns well and uses the theory in making decisions, the theory will predict, explain, and describe his decisions. The same theory is normative to Raiffa, positive to the scholar studying the decisions of Raiffa's students, and *both* to those making the decisions. Enough said.

Turning to the constructive side, I will suggest three somewhat useful classifications of existing formal models. These are not meant to be mutually exclusive or exhaustive. They simply convey some general information about the model under consideration.

One way of classifying models is according to the general theory (paradigm?) of human behavior which underlies them. That is, models used in political science are examples or applications of more general models. These general models in turn reflect certain basic beliefs about the nature of human behavior.

Most formal models in political science are examples of rational-choice models, a class of models which dominates economics. Such models reflect a view of man as a purposive being: individual behavior is seen as an attempt to maximize individually held goals. Decision theoretic models, game theoretic models, spatial models—all are examples of this basic class of models. Several attempts to analyze the individual voting decision (Riker and Ordeshook, 1968; Ferejohn and Fiorina, 1974a) illustrate very clearly the basic elements of a rational-choice model.

Other models of individual behavior have been developed in psychology and sociology. These models generally emphasize the responsive side of man rather than his purposive side. There are various mathematical learning models (Estes, 1964) which grew out of the basic stimulus-response-reward paradigm. But to the best of my knowledge there are as yet no literal political applications of such models. The leading model in sociology—the role model—similarly reflects a view of human behavior as primarily responsive.[2] Behavior is seen as a response to internalized norms and the expectations of significant others. Obviously, political science has been strongly influenced by the sociological paradigm (e.g., social determinist model of voting behavior, political socialization studies, legislative role studies). But there are not many formal models which reflect the sociological paradigm.[3] One exception occurs in the work of Wayne Francis (1965). Also, in McPhee and Glaser (1962) there are a number of interesting political applications of models set within the sociological tradition.

A second dimension along which to array models is micro-macro. Are individuals the basic unit of analysis, or are groups, classes, nations, etc. the basic analytic unit? Those who employ individualistic models frequently hold the view that macro phenomena should be completely explainable in micro terms. For example, in macroeconomics the aggregate supply and demand relationships should be built up from individual demand and supply curves (easier to believe than to demonstrate, incidentally). Or in political science, some analysts maintain that an election is no more than the sum of numerous citizen, activist, and candidate decisions. Others, however, would dispute this position. Some argue that modeling macro events is simply much easier if individual behavior is not considered explicitly. Others (Przeworski, 1973) argue that individual behavior is affected by contextual influences that individualistic models do not capture. At any rate, one can find examples of models which cut into the micro-macro continuum at various points. Whether one chooses to analyze the behavior of unified collective actors (Richardson, 1960), atomized individuals, or something in between depends mostly on what one wishes to explain, how soon one wishes the answer, and what one wishes to do with it. Depending on the answers, either individualistic or macromodels might be more appropriate.

Finally, one might differentiate among models according to their static or dynamic nature.[4] Our present applications of decision and game theoretic models are static. One seeks to find an optimal choice or equilibrium outcome, given an unchanged set of initial parameters (e.g., the strategy set, payoff functions, etc.). In contrast there are models whose basic concern is representing change. The collection of articles in McPhee and Glaser's *Public Opinion and Congressional Elections* (1962) contains several such models. Models have been constructed to predict attitude change (Kreweras, 1966), the spread of rumors, arms races, and other dynamic phenomena (Boulding, 1962, chs. 2, 6, 7; Rapoport, 1960, part 1). Again, the type of model which is appropriate depends on the questions one is asking. A priori there is no reason to prefer micro or macro, static or dynamic, purposive or responsive. The important question is what model best answers the questions of concern.

CRITICAL JUDGMENT OF MODELS

When reading about the construction of a new model or the application of an old one, what should one look for? What are some criteria of judgment that one might apply?

If the model is intended as an explanation of some political phenomenon, then the critical question is just what is the model intended to explain? Banal? Not at all. Identification of the primary research question(s) enables one to bring to bear one's critical acumen (and personal biases) on several major questions: should the model be micro or macro? Static or dynamic? Rational choice or sociological? Identification of the primary research question enables one to make an initial judgment about the appropriateness of the model. For example, early spatial models (Davis, Hinich, and Ordeshook, 1970) are static, micro, rational choice models.[5] If one views the electoral process as quintessentially a dynamic, macro process, one might simply reject out of hand spatial models of the electoral process.

Turning to more specific matters, one should carefully study the assumptions of the model. Are they reasonable attempts to approximate aspects of the situation under study, or are they made in the spirit of "This assumption is crazy, but I can't get any results without it"? If the latter, beware. All modeling involves a trade-off between simplicity and realism. But one must take care not to trade away the problem in order to get enough simplicity to analyze it. Consider the model proposed by Robert Barro (1973) to analyze the electorate's control of their representatives. Barro whets our interest when he writes (1973, p. 19):

> The model focuses on the division of interest between the public and its political representatives. The division of interest arises because the public officeholder is assumed to act to advance his own interests, and these interests do not coincide automatically with those of his constituents. The electoral process and some elements of the political structure are then analyzed as mechanisms which can be

used to move the officeholder toward a position where the advancement of self-interest approximates the advancement of the interests of his constituents.

But upon reading further we learn that:

> *In order to facilitate the analysis* of political control, the theoretical model incorporates an extremely simplified version of the underlying "public interest." In section *I an assumption of common tastes on private goods versus the single type of public good insures unanimous agreement among individuals on the ideal aggregate level of governmental activity.* Given this unanimity, the model abstracts from differences of opinion among the public and focuses on the problem of the public's control over its political representatives. (Emphasis mine.)

Barro remarks that his model complements other work which allows divergent tastes, but I remain skeptical.

Given that the assumptions of a model capture the essential aspects of the situation under study, one should ask an additional question. Are some assumptions so specific that the model lacks robustness? If certain variables are assumed to follow particular probability distributions, or if variables are assumed to be related via specific functional forms, then hard questions should be asked. Do we have evidence (either empirical or as the conclusions of other accepted models) that the specific distributions of functional forms are justified? If not, we should be skeptical of the conclusions of the model, for they may be totally dependent on the distributions or functional forms assumed. Slight perturbations of the assumptions could alter the conclusions drastically.

For example, the Brams-Davis (1974) model of campaign resource allocation depends critically on the assumption that candidates expend exactly the same amount of resources in each state. The Gilbert (1973) model of roll call voting assumes that representatives strive for 50% + 1 votes. If some recalcitrant representative wishes 55% of the vote, the conclusions of the model may not hold for him. In my book (Fiorina, 1974) I assume that a roll call vote against a constituency group always hurts a representative more than a vote for them helps.

I hasten to emphasize that such specific assumptions by no means make a model useless. After all, they may be exactly correct. Highly specific assumptions simply raise a caution flag. The implications of the model may result directly from the specificity assumed, so examine it carefully.

Even if the model is not intended as explanatory, one still must pay careful attention to the assumptions. In analyses of institutional arrangements, one will come across abstract axioms labeled "anonymity," "positive responsiveness," "liberalism," "nondictatorship," etc. Do such axioms capture the essence of such concepts? If not, there is uncertainty about the meaning of the model's implications. An example is an impossibility theorem proved by Sen (1970). Loosely speaking, Sen shows that under certain general conditions an additional condition he calls liberalism is incompatible with the existence of a collective choice rule which designates a best alternative from every subset of alternatives. The essence of Sen's "liberalism" is that for every individual there is at least one pair of alternatives for which his preference alone determines the social choice (e.g., pink walls in his bedroom rather than white walls). As Sen recognizes, however, liberalism can be defined in various ways. An alternative formulation might be to designate some subset of alternatives as simply outside the domain of feasible alternatives ("Congress shall make no law. . . .").

The essence of the preceding discussion is simple. Do not skip over the technical portion of a formal model and go directly to the conclusions. Rather, examine carefully the definitions and assumptions of the model. The model's conclusions are implicit in the definitions and assumptions. Scrutinize the latter as well as the former.

Finally, examine the correspondence between the conclusions of a formal model and the researcher's interpretations of them. Theorems sometimes may be terribly abstract. And (down deep) many formal modelers are just as concerned over the relevance of their work as are more empirically oriented researchers. Thus, a little wishful thinking sometimes can creep in between theorem and interpretation. The consumer of such work should be aware of the possibility.

Otherwise, judge work involving models as one would judge any other work. Is it careful, insightful, and does it advance our understanding? In the end every study must be judged against those standards.

NOTES

1. Sometimes one sees a trichotomous classification of theories into normative-positive-descriptive, or normative-positive-empirical. In my own usage I do not differentiate between a positive and a descriptive theory; a positive theory is intended to explain and describe behavior. A poll of my colleagues in the field of economics elicited the same point of view. Thus, I consider only the proposed dichotomy referred to in the text.

2. Ralf Dahrendorf (1968, pp. 90–91) writes:
   > With the existence of these few categories (e.g., expectations, social role, sanctions—M. F.) . . . we may formulate the proposition that implicitly or explicitly underlies all research and theoretical work in modern sociology. *Man behaves in accordance with his roles.* Thus man basically figures in sociological analyses only to the extent that he complies with all the expectations associated with his social positions. This abstraction, the scientific unit of sociology, may be called *homo sociologicus.*

3. William Mitchell (1969) remarks that political sociologists are particularly reluctant to sacrifice realism for analytical simplicity. Such an attitude obviously is not conducive to formal modeling. Of course, the "to hell with realism" attitude shown by some political economists is not conducive to *useful* formal modeling.

4. Here is an appropriate spot to make an observation about simulation models (which are not automatically dynamic as is sometimes believed—see Pool, Abel-

son, and Popkin, 1964, for example). In the natural sciences, if one's model contains so many variables and relationships that a paper and pencil analysis is impractical, one turns it loose on the computer. In political science, however, even very simple models sometimes get put on the computer because they are used to manipulate large amounts of data (Pool, Abelson, and Popkin, 1964; Matthews and Stimson, 1974). At any rate, simulation models should be evaluated in the same fashion as other formal models, with the exception that repeated runs and sensitivity testing typically will replace logical proofs.

5. Later developments of the model (McKelvey, 1972) relax the rational choice part by representing citizen behavior by aggregate "support functions" rather than individually rational decision rules.

REFERENCES

Aranson, Peter, and Ordeshook, Peter. 1972. "Spatial Strategies for Sequential Elections," in Richard Niemi and Herbert Weisberg, eds., *Probability Modeling in Political Science.* Columbus: Merrill.

Ashby, W. Ross. 1970. "Analysis of the System to be Modeled," in Ralph Stogdill, ed., *The Process of Model-Building in the Behavioral Sciences.* New York: Norton, pp. 94–114.

Axelrod, Robert. 1970. *Conflict of Interest.* Chicago: Markham.

Barro, Robert. 1973. "The Control of Politicians: An Economic Model," *Public Choice,* Spring 1973, pp. 19–42.

Black, Duncan. 1948. "On the Rationale of Group Decision Making," *Journal of Political Economy,* February 1948, pp. 23–34.

———. 1958. *The Theory of Committees and Elections.* Cambridge: Cambridge University Press.

Black, Gordon. 1975. *Parties and Elections.* San Francisco: Freeman.

Boulding, Kenneth. 1962. *Conflict and Defense.* New York: Harper.

Brams, Steven, and Davis, Morton. 1974. "The 3/2's Rule in Presidential Campaigning," *American Political Science Review,* March 1974, pp. 113–134.

Brodbeck, May. 1959. "Models, Meaning, and Theories," in Llewellyn Gross, ed., *Symposium on Sociological Theory.* New York: Harper.

Buchanan, James, and Tullock, Gordon. 1962. *The Calculus of Consent.* Ann Arbor; University of Michigan Press.

Cherryholmes, C., and Shapiro, M. 1968. *Representatives and Roll-Calls: A Computer Simulation of Voting in the Eighty-Eighth Congress.* Indianapolis: Bobbs-Merrill.

Coleman, James. 1971. "Internal Processes Governing Party Positions in Elections," *Public Choice,* Fall 1971, pp. 35–60.

Dahrendorf, Ralf. 1968. "Sociology and Human Nature," *in Essays in the Theory of Society.* Stanford: Stanford University Press, pp. 88–106.

Davis, O.; Hinich, M.; and Ordeshook, P. 1970. "An Expository Development of a Mathematical Model of the Electoral Process," *American Political Science Review,* June 1970, pp. 426–448.

Downs, Anthony. 1957. *An Economic Theory of Democracy.* New York: Harper and Row.

———. 1959. "Dr. Rogers' Methodological Difficulties—A Reply to His Critical Note," *American Political Science Review,* December 1959, pp. 1094–1097.

Estes, William. 1964. "Probability Learning," in A. W. Melton, ed., *Categories of Human Learning*. New York: Academic Press.

Fenno, Richard. 1973. *Congressmen in Committees*. Boston: Little, Brown.

Ferejohn, John. 1974. *Pork Barrel Politics*. Stanford: Stanford University Press.

Ferejohn, John, and Fiorina, Morris. 1974a "The Paradox of Not Voting: A Decision Theoretic Analysis," *American Political Science Review*, June 1974, pp. 525–536.

———. 1974b. "To p or Not to p," Caltech Social Science Working Paper No. 53, Pasadena, California, September 1974.

Ferejohn, John, and Grether, David. 1974. "On a Class of Rational Social Decision Procedures," *Journal of Economic Theory*, in press.

Fine, Kit. 1972. "Some Necessary and Sufficient Conditions for Representative Decision on Two Alternatives," *Econometrica*, November 1972, pp. 1083–1090.

Fiorina, Morris, 1974. *Representatives, Roll Calls and Constituencies*. Lexington, Mass. Heath.

———. 1975. "Constituency Influence: A Generalized Model and Implications for Quantitative Studies of Roll Call Behavior," *Political Methodology*, forthcoming.

Fishburn, Peter. 1971. "The Theory of Representative Majority Decision," *Econometrica*, March 1971, pp. 273–284.

———. 1974. "Paradoxes of Voting," *American Political Science Review*, June 1974, pp. 537–546.

Francis, Wayne L. 1965. "The Role Concept in Legislatures: A Probability Model and a Note on Cognitive Structures," *Journal of Politics*, August 1965, pp. 567–585.

Friedman, Milton. 1953. "The Methodology of Positive Economics," in *Essays in Positive Economics*. Chicago: University of Chicago Press, pp. 3–43.

Garvey, Gerald. 1966. "The Theory of Party Equilibrium," *American Political Science Review*, March 1966, pp. 29–38.

Gilbert, Jane. 1973. "Constituent Preferences and Roll Call Behavior" (unpublished paper).

Goldberg, Arthur. 1968. "Political Science as Science," in Robert Dahl and Deane Neubauer, eds., *Readings in Modern Political Analysis*. Englewood Cliffs, N.J.: Prentice Hall, pp. 15–30.

Hinich, Melvin; Ledyard, John; and Ordeshook, Peter. 1973. "A Theory of Electoral Equilibrium: A Spatial Analysis Based on the Theory of Games," *Journal of Politics*, February 1973, pp. 154–193.

Kessel, John. 1972. "The Issues in Issue Voting," *American Political Science Review*, June 1972, pp. 459–465.

Koehler, David. 1974. "A Theory of Legislative Coalition Formation," a paper presented at the MSSB Workshop on Mathematical Models of Congress, Aspen, Colorado, June 1974.

Kreweras, Germain. 1968. "A Model for Opinion Change During Repeated Ballotting," in Paul Lazarsfeld and Neil Henry, eds., *Readings in Mathematical Social Science*. Cambridge: M.I.T. Press, pp. 174–191.

Lipset, S. M., ed. 1969. *Politics and the Social Sciences*. New York: Oxford University Press.

Matthews, Donald, and Stimson, James. 1974. *Yeas and Nays: Normal Decision Making in the House of Representatives*. New York: Wiley.

May, K. O. 1954. "Transitivity, Utility and Aggregation in Preference Patterns," *Econometrica*, January 1974, pp. 1–13.

McKelvey, Richard. 1972. "Policy Related Voting and its Effects on Electoral Equilibrium," a paper presented at the American Political Science Association Meeting, Washington, D.C., September 1972.

McPhee, William, and Glazer, William. 1962. *Public Opinion and Congressional Elections.* New York: Free Press.

Mitchell, William. 1969. "The Shape of Political Theory to Come: From Political Sociology to Political Economy," in S. M. Lipset, ed., *Politics and the Social Sciences.* New York: Oxford University Press, pp. 101–136.

Murakami, Y. 1968. *Logic and Social Choice.* New York: Dover.

Niemi, Richard, and Weisberg, Herbert, eds. 1972. *Probability Models in Political Science.* Columbus: Merrill.

Page, Benjamin, and Brody, Richard. 1972. "Policy Voting and the Electoral Process: The Vietnam War Issue," *American Political Science Review,* September 1972, pp. 979–995.

Plott, Charles. 1967. "A Notion of Equilibrium and its Possibility under Majority Rule," *American Economic Review,* September 1967, pp. 788–806.

———. 1972. "Ethics, Social Choice theory, and the Theory of Economic Policy," *Journal of Mathematical Sociology,* July 1972, pp. 181–208.

———. 1974. "Rawls' Theory of Justice: An Impossibility Result," Caltech Social Science Working Paper No. 49, Pasadena, California, August 1974.

Polsby, Nelson, and Riker, William. 1974. "New Math," *American Political Science Review,* June 1974, pp. 733–734.

Pool, Ithiel; Abelson, Robert; and Popkin, Samuel. 1964. *Candidates, Issues and Strategies.* Cambridge, Mass.: M.I.T. Press.

Przeworski, Adam. 1974. "Contextual Models of Political Behavior," *Political Methodology,* Winter 1974, pp. 27–61.

Rabinowitz, George. 1973. "Spatial Models of Electoral Choice: An Empirical Analysis." Institute for Research in Social Science Working Paper in Methodology No. 7, Chapel Hill, North Carolina.

Rae, Douglas. 1969. "Decision Rules and Individual Values in Constitutional Choice," *American Political Science Review,* March 1969, pp. 40–56.

Raiffa, Howard. 1968. *Decision Analysis.* Reading, Mass.: Addison-Wesley.

Rapoport, Anatol. 1960. *Fights, Games, and Debates.* Ann Arbor: University of Michigan Press.

Rawls, John. 1971. *A Theory of Justice.* Cambridge: Harvard University Press.

Richardson, L. F. 1939. "Generalized Foreign Policy," *British Journal of Psychology Monographs Supplements.*

———. 1960. *Arms and Insecurity.* Chicago: Quadrangle.

Riker, William. 1962. *The Theory of Political Coalitions.* New Haven: Yale University Press.

Riker, William, and Ordeshook, Peter. 1968. "A Theory of the Calculus of Voting," *American Political Science Review,* March 1968, pp. 25–42.

———. 1972. *An Introduction to Positive Political Theory.* Englewood Cliffs, N.J.: Prentice Hall.

Riker, William, and Shapley, Lloyd. 1968. "Weighted Voting: A Mathematical Analysis for Instrumental Judgments," in Roland Pennock and John Chapman, eds., *Nomos X: Representation.* New York: Atherton, pp. 199–216.

Rogers, W. Hayward. 1959. "Some Methodological Difficulties in Anthony Downs' *An*

Economic Theory of Democracy," American Political Science Review, June 1959, pp. 483–485.

Rohde, David. 1972a. "A Theory of the Formation of Opinion Coalitions in the United States Supreme Court," in Richard Niemi and Herbert Weisberg, eds., *Probability Models of Collective Decision Making.* Columbus: Merrill.

———. 1972b. "Policy Goals and Opinion Coalitions in the Supreme Court," *Midwest Journal of Political Science,* May 1972, pp. 208–224.

Savage, Leonard. 1954. The Foundations of Statistics. New York: Wiley.

Sen, Amartya. 1970. "The Impossibility of a Paretian Liberal," *Journal of Political Economy,* January–February 1970, pp. 152–157.

Shapiro, Michael. 1969. "Rational Political Man: A Synthesis of Economic and Social-Psychological Perspectives," *American Political Science Review,* December 1969, pp. 1106–1119.

Shapley, L. S., and Shubik, M. 1954. "A Method for Evaluating the Distribution of Power in a Committee System," *American Political Science Review,* September 1954, pp. 787–792.

Shepsle, Kenneth. 1972. "The Strategy of Ambiguity: Uncertainty and Electoral Competition," *American Political Science Review,* June 1974, pp. 555–568.

———. 1974a. "A Model of the Congressional Committee Assignment Process: Constrained Maximization in an Institutional setting," *Public Choice,* in press.

———. 1974b. "Theories of Collective Choice," in Cornelius Cotter et al., eds., *Political Science Annual V: Collective Decision Making.* Indianapolis: Bobbs-Merrill, pp. 1–87.

Simon, Herbert, and Samuelson, Paul. 1963. "Problems of Methodology—Discussion," *American Economic Review* (supplement), May 1963, pp. 229–236.

Stokes, Donald E. 1963. "Spatial Models of Party Competition," *American Political Science Review,* June 1963, pp. 368–377.

Stokes, Donald E., and Miller, Warren. 1962. "Party Government and the Saliency of Congress," *Public Opinion Quarterly,* Winter 1962, pp. 531–546.

Tollison, R. D. and Willett, T. D. 1973. "Some Simple Economics of Voting and Not Voting," *Public Choice,* Fall 1973, pp. 59–71.

Weisberg, Herbert. 1974. "Dimensionland: An Excursion into Spaces," *American Journal of Political Science,* November 1974, pp. 743–776.

Wilson, Robert. 1972. "The Game-Theoretic Structure of Arrow's General Possibility Theorem," *Journal of Economic Theory,* August 1972, pp. 14–20.

Additional Articles Illustrating
the Political Research Process

The following citations are (1) illustrations of kinds of political science research and (2) general texts that introduce specific methodological techniques and tools. Although they vary with respect to their level of difficulty, they are all easily accessible. They are listed here according to the chapter in *Understanding Political Science* to which they pertain.

GENERAL METHODS AND STATISTICAL PROCEDURES

Babbie, E., *The Practice of Social Research*, 7th ed. Belmont, Calif.: Wadsworth, 1995.
Bernstein, R. A., and J. A. Dyer, *An Introduction to Political Science Methods*, Englewood Cliffs, N.J.: Prentice Hall, 1984.
Champney, L., *Introduction to Quantitative Political Science*, New York: HarperCollins,1995.
Cole, R. L., *Introduction to Political Science & Policy Research*, New York: St. Martin's, 1996.
Ethridge, M. E., *The Political Research Experience*, Guildford, Conn.: Dushkin, 1994.
Hessler, R. M. *Social Research Methods*, St. Paul, Minn.: West Publishing, 1992.
Kay, S. A., *Introduction to the Analysis of Political Data*, Englewood Cliffs, N.J.: Prentice Hall,1991.
King, G., R. O. Keohane, and S. Verba, *Designing Social Inquiry*, Princeton, N.J.: Princeton University Press, 1994.

MckAgnew, N. & S. W. Pike, *The Science Game,* 6th ed. Englewood Cliffs, N.J.: Prentice Hall, 1994.

Manheim, J. B., and R. C. Rich, *Empirical Political Analysis,* 3rd ed. New York: Longman, 1995.

Mantzopoulos, V. L., *Statistics for the Social Sciences,* Englewood Cliffs, N.J.: Prentice Hall, 1995.

Mechan, E. J., *Social Inquiry,* Chatham, N.J.: Chatham House, 1994.

Nachmias, D., and C. Nachmias, *Research Methods in the Social Sciences,* 3rd ed. New York: St. Martin's Press, 1987.

Shively, W. Phillips, *The Craft of Political Research,* Englewood Cliffs, N.J.: Prentice Hall, 1980.

Salkind, N. J., *Exploring Research,* New York: Macmillan, 1991.

Singleton, R. A,. Jr., B. C. Straits, and M. Miller Straits, *Approaches to Social Research,* 2nd ed. New York: Oxford University Press, 1993.

White, L. G., *Political Analysis,* 3rd ed. Belmont, Calif.: Wadsworth, 1994.

PART ONE, CHAPTERS 1 AND 4

Reinharz, S., *Feminist Methods in Social Research,* New York: Oxford University Press, 1992.

Sommer, B. B., and R. Sommer, *A Practical Guide to Behavioral Research: Tools and Techniques,* 4th ed. New York: Oxford University Press, 1997.

Susser, B., *Approaches to the Study of Politics,* New York: Macmillan, 1991

PART TWO, POLITICAL THEORY

Avineri, Shlomo, *The Social and Political Thought of Karl Marx,* Cambridge, Mass.: Cambridge University Press, 1968.

Bluhm, William T., *Theories of the Political System: Classics of Political Thought and Modern Political Analysis,* 3rd ed. Englewood Cliffs, N.J.:Prentice Hall, 1978.

Gubrium, J. F., and J. A. Holstein, *The New Language of Qualitative Method,* New York: Oxford University Press, 1997.

Portis, Edward Bryan, *Reconstructing the Classics: Political Theory from Plato to Marx,* Chatham, N.J.: Chatham House, 1994.

Russell, Bertrand, *A History of Western Philosophy,* New York: Simon & Schuster,1972.

Sabine, George H., *A History of Political Theory,* New York: Holt, Rinehart and Winston, 1961.

Spragens, Thomas A. Jr., *Understanding Political Theory,* New York: St. Martin's Press, 1976.

Strauss, Leo, and Joseph Cropsey, *History of Political Philosophy,* 3rd ed. Chicago, Ill.: The University of Chicago Press, 1987.

Tinder, Glenn, *Political Thinking: The Perennial Questions,* 2nd ed. Boston, Mass.: Little, Brown, 1974.

Tucker, Robert C., ed., *The Marx-Engels Reader,* 2nd ed. New York: W. W. Norton, 1978.
Wolff, Robert Paul, ed., *Political Man and Social Man: Readings in Political Philosophy,* New York: Random House, 1966.

PART THREE, CHAPTERS 12 AND 13

Case Study

Tate, C. Neal, "Personal Attribute Models of Voting Behavior of U.S. Supreme Court Justices: Liberalism in Civil Liberties and Economics Decisions, 1946–1978," *American Political Science Review* (1981) 75: 355–367.
Theodoulou, S. Z. *The Louisiana Republican Party 1948–1984: The Building of a State Political Party,* New Orleans, La.: Tulane University, 1986.

Content Analysis

Kelly, R. M., L. M. Williams, and K. Fisher, "Women and Politics: An Assessment of Its Role within the Discipline of Political Science," *Women & Politics* (1994) 14: 3–18.
Larson, D. Welch, "Problems of Content Analysis in Foreign-Policy Research: Notes from the Study of the Origins of the Cold War Belief Systems," *International Studies Quarterly,* (June 1988) 32: 241–255.
Martz, J. D., "Political Science and Latin American Studies: Patterns and Asymmetries of Research and Publication," *Latin American Research Review* (1990) 25: 67–86.
Miller, A. H., and L. Erbring, "Type-Set Politics: Impact of Newspapers on Public Confidence," *American Political Science Review* (1979) 73: 67–84
Nicolay, J., "A Content Analysis from South Africa: Nontraditional Literature in the Teaching of Minority Politics," *PS,* (June 1995) 25: 228–230.
Theodoulou, S. Z., G. Y. Guevara, and H. Minnassians, "Myths and Illusions: The Media and AIDS Policy," in Stella Z. Theodoulou, *AIDS: The Politics and Policy of Disease,* Upper Saddle River, N.J.: Prentice Hall, 1996.

Comparative Study

Banasak, L. A,. and E. Plutzer, "Contextual Determinants of Feminist Attitudes: National and Subnational Influences in Western Europe." *American Political Science Review* 87 (March 1993): 147–157.
De Mesquita, B. Bueno, R. M. Siverson, and G. Woller, "War and the Fate of Regimes: A Comparative Analysis." *American Political Science Review* (September 1992) 86: 638–646.
Powell, G. Bingham, Jr., "American Voter Turnout in Comparative Perspective," *American Political Science Review* (March 1986) 80: 25.

Theodoulou, S. Z. "Responding to AIDS: Governmental Policy Responses," in S. Z. Theodoulou, *AIDS: The Politics and Policy of Disease*, Upper Saddle River, N.J.: Prentice Hall, 1996.

Experiments

Campbell, D., and J. Stanley, *Experimental and Quasi Experimental Designs of Research*, Chicago, Ill.: Rand-McNally, 1966.

Rapaport, R. B., K. L. Metcalf, and J. A. Hartman, "Candidate Traits and Voter Inferences: An Experimental Study," *Journal of Politics* (1989) 51: 917–932.

Shocket, P. A., N. R. Heighberger, and C. Brown, "The Effect of Voting Technology on Voting Behavior in a Stimulated Multi-Candidate City Council Election: A Political Experiment of Ballot Transparency." *Western Political Quarterly* (1992) 45: 521–537.

Indexes and Rankings

Shaffer, W. R., "Rating the Performance of the ADA in the U.S. Congress." *Western Political Quarterly* (1989) 42: 33–52.

Wright, G. C., Jr., R. S. Erikson, and J. P. McIver, "Public Opinion and Policy Liberalism in the American States." *American Journal of Political Science* (1987) 31: 980–1001.

Longitudinal & Longitudinal Comparative Studies

Haynes, S. E., "Macroeconomics, Economic Stratification, and Partisanship: A Longitudinal Analysis of Contingent Shifts in Political Identification," *American Journal of Sociology* (July 1994) 100: 70–103.

Gibson, J. L., C. P. Cotter, and J. F. Bibby, "Whither the Local Parties? A Cross-sectional and Longitudinal Analysis of the Strength of Party Organizations," *American Journal of Political Science* (February 1985) 29: 139–160.

Schneider, S. K., and P. Ingraham, "The Impact of Political Participation on Social Policy Adoption and Expansion: A Cross-national, Longitudinal Analysis," *Comparative Politics* (October 1984) 17: 107–122.

Shaffer, S. D., "A Multivariate Explanation of Decreasing Voter Turnout in Presidential Elections, 1960–1976," *American Journal of Political Science* (February 1981) 25: 68–95.

Theodoulou, S. Z., et al., "Myths and Illusions: The Media and AIDS Policy," in Stella Z. Theodoulou, *AIDS: The Politics and Policy of Disease*, Upper Saddle River, N.J.: Prentice Hall, 1996.

Operationalization

Bernstein, R. A., "Determinants of Differences in Feelings toward Senators Representing the Same State." *Western Political Quarterly* (1992) 45: 701–726.

Jackman, R. W., "The Predictability of Coups d'État: A Model with African Data." *American Political Science Review* (1978) 72: 1262–1275.

Jones, B. D., "Public Policies and Economic Growth in the American States." *Journal of Politics* (1990) 52: 219–233.

Hill, K. Q., and Jan E. Leighley, "The Policy Consequences of Class Bias in State Electorates," *American Journal of Political Science* (May 1992) 36: 351–365.

Personal Interviews

DeGregoio, C., "Leadership Approaches in Congressional Committee Hearings." *Western Political Quarterly* (1992) 45: 971–983.

Kessel, J. H., "The Structures of the Carter White House." *American Journal of Political Science* (August 1983) 27: 431–463.

Theodoulou, S. Z., *The Louisiana Republican Party: The Building of a State Political Party, 1948–1984*, New Orleans, La.: Tulane University, 1986.

Regression Analysis and Correlational Analysis

Brunk, G. G., and T. G. Minehart, "How Important Is Elite Turnover to Policy Change?" *American Journal of Political Science* (August 1984) 28: 559–569.

Chatterjee, S., and F. Wiseman, "Use of Regression Diagnostics in Political Science Research," *American Journal of Political Science* (August 1983) 27: 601–613.

Enelow, J. M., N. R. Mendell, and S. Ramesh, "A Comparison of Two Distance Metrics through Regression Diagnostics of a Model of Relative Candidate Evaluation," *The Journal of Politics* (November 1988) 50: 1057–1071.

King, G., "Variance Specification in Event Count Models," *American Journal of Political Science* (August 1989) 33: 762–784.

Land, K. C., "Are Contributions Rational? Untangling Strategies of Political Action Committees," *Journal of Political Economy* (June 1992) 100: 647–664.

Overby, L. M., B. M. Henschen, J. Strauss, and M. H. Walsh, "Courting Constituents? An Analysis of the Senate Confirmation Vote on Clarence Thomas," *American Political Science Review* (December 1992) 86: 997–1003.

Uhlaner, C. J., and K. Lehman Schlozman, "Candidate Gender and Congressional Campaign Receipts," *Journal of Politics* (February 1986) 48: 30–50.

Surveys and Samples

Bennett, V,. *Sample Survey Principles and Methods,* Sevoaks: Arnold, 1991.

Fine, A., and J. Kosecoft, *How to Conduct Surveys: A Step by Step Approach,* London: Sage, 1985.

Hurwitz, J., and M. Peffley, "Public Images of the Soviet Union: The Impact on Foreign Policy Attitudes." *Journal of Politics* (1990) 52: 3–28.

Mosher, C., and G. Kalton, *Survey Methods in Social Investigation*, Aldershot: Gower, 1985.

Verba, S., K. Lehman Schlozman, H. Brady, and N. H. Nie, "Citizen Activity: Who Participates? What Do They Say?" *American Political Science Review* (June 1993) 87:303–318.

B

Resources for Research

What follows is a listing of various resources available to the student in the area of political science. This appendix has been organized to help the researcher in his or her pursuit of knowledge. This list, then, is actually three separate lists, grouped to show the student some of the resources for conducting the literature review. The lists are

- Journals in Political Science
- Indexes and Other Sources
- World Wide Web Sites

JOURNALS IN POLITICAL SCIENCE

This is an introduction to the journals most regularly cited, and, thus, is not exhaustive. The references given here include (1) the name of the journal, (2) the beginning year of publication, and, where appropriate, (3) a brief description of the journal.

> *American Political Science Review.* (1906–   ) This publication is the official journal of the American Political Science Association.
> *American Politics Quarterly.* (1973–   ) Focuses on American political behavior.

Annals (American Academy of Political and Social Sciences). (1899–   )

Comparative Politics. (1968) Covers the field of comparative politics.

Congress and the Presidency. (1972–   ) As its name implies, this journal focuses on these two branches of government.

Foreign Affairs. (1922–   ) Deals with important current issues and trends in U.S. foreign policy through articles by official of the government, academics and others.

Foreign Policy. (1970–   ) Covers the range of foreign affairs, again, with a focus on American foreign policy.

International Affairs. (1922–   )

International Political Science Review. (1980–   ) The official publication of the International Political Science Association.

Journal of Development Studies. (1964–   ) This interdisciplinary journal includes articles on economic and social development in less developed countries.

Journal of Politics. (1939–   ) Includes articles on American government and politics.

Parliamentary Affairs. (1947–   ) This quarterly journal focuses on the British legislature. Published by Oxford University Press in association with the Hansard Society for Parliamentary Government.

Policy Studies Journal. (1972–   ) This journal contains articles that address important public policy problems.

Political Science Quarterly. (1886–   ) Contains articles on American politics, comparative politics, and foreign affairs.

Political Theory. (1973–   ) Emphasis on political theory and philosophy.

Polity. (1968–   ) Includes articles pertaining to American politics, comparative politics, international relations, and political theory.

Presidential Studies Quarterly. (1972–   )

Public Administration Review. (1940–   ) Focuses on management issues on the level of state, local, and federal governments.

Public Opinion Quarterly. (1937–   ) Considers all aspects of public opinion and polling.

Public Policy. (1953–   ) The emphasis of this journal is on articles dealing with public policy formulation and implementation.

Resources for Feminist Research. (1971–   ) An international journal that provides not only research articles, but also other research information.

Social Sciences Quarterly. (1920–   ) Covers a wide range of topics in the social sciences.

Urban Affairs Quarterly. (1965–   ) This journal contains interdisciplinary articles on urban affairs.

Western Political Quarterly. (1948–   ) Covers both political science and public administration.

Women & Politics. (1980–   ) Focuses on the impact women have had on politics as well as the impact politics has on women.

INDEXES AND OTHER SOURCES

In addition to the most important indexes in the social sciences, we have also included information here about various bibliographies and collections of abstracts.

Newspaper Indexes

The following major newspapers in the country have their own indexes.

> *The Christian Science Monitor*
> *New York Times*
> *Wall Street Journal*
> *Washington Post*

CD-ROM Databases

Most college and university libraries will be equipped with computer databases such as the following:

> *ABC Political Science*—This index references hundreds of journals across the fields of political science, economics, sociology and law.
> *Public Affairs Information Service Bulletin* (PAIS)—One of the best known indexes in political science, PAIS covers journals, periodicals, books and government documents. Also includes the PAIS *Foreign Language Index*.
> *Sociofile*—Updated many times per year, this database includes not only publications related to sociology, but also conference papers presented at professional sociology meetings.

Hard-Copy or Text-Based Indexes

If you are unsure as to where these are located in the library or how to use them effectively, be sure to contact a reference librarian.

> *ABC Political Science*
> *Current Contents/Social and Behavioral Science*
> *Current Law Index*
> *Environment Abstracts Annual*
> *Feminist Periodicals*
> *Index to U.S. Government Periodicals*
> *International Political Science Abstracts*
> *Public Affairs Information Service Bulletin* (PAIS)
> *Readers' Guide to Periodical Literature*
> *Social Sciences Index*
> *Sociological Abstracts*
> *Women's Studies Index*

WORLD WIDE WEB SITES

Here are some current sites that we think are worth investigating. Be aware that the World Wide Web is constantly undergoing changes and updates. When using the Internet to conduct research, it is always fruitful to use a search engine (such as *Lycos* or *Webcrawler*) to make sure that you are able to source the most recent information possible.

http://www.whitehouse.gov/   If there is one best way to start an inquiry into questions that have to do with the federal government, this is the place to begin. Not only is this site a prime resource for information about the presidency and the executive branch, *www.whitehouse.gov* also includes numerous links (instant connections with other sites) relevant to U.S. politics. As an extra bonus, you can easily find out how to e-mail the president, vice president, or any other members of the executive branch.

http://www.fedworld.gov/   Here's an easy way to gain access to information concerning the federal government, including the FAA and the IRS.

http://congress.org/   This site allows you access not only to individual members of Congress (after you've e-mailed the president, how about e-mailing *your* representative?), but also to a tremendous amount of information about specific pieces of legislation. Check out *Thomas*, the House of Representatives' online service for learning about and tracking pending bills.

http://www.politicsnow.com/   This site is supported by various news agencies including: *The Los Angeles Times, ABC News, Newsweek,* and *The Washington Post.* In addition to links connecting the site with *The Buzz*, a political gossip column, *www.politicsnow.com* contains information about representatives and their districts as well as lists contacts within the federal government.

http://www.c-span.org/   This is the C-Span cable network's Web site, which offers objective coverage of Congress.

http://www.npr.org/   This is the Web site for National Public Radio, one of the nation's most important news services. Check here for up to the minute news items that deal with a variety of issues including politics and politicians.

http://www.rnc.org/   The site of the Republican National Committee offers the latest GOP information including press releases and audio/video clips.

http://www.democrats.org/   The site of the Democratic National Committee provides links to various other liberal organizations.

http://www.census.gov/   A perfect place to get information about national and international population figures. Updated on a regular basis *www.census.gov* allows you to track world population trends.

http://www.brillig.com/debt_clock/   Lift your spirits anytime of the day or night by finding out precisely how large our national debt has become. The national debt clock will provide you with great information to take to a party or family gathering.

http://www.keele.ac.uk/depts/po/psr.htm/   Comprehensive list of political science resources by subfields on the web.

http://www.nttc.edu/gov_res.html/   Over eight hundred excellent government links.

http://www.lib.umich.edu/libhome/Documents.center/govweb.html/   Major federal government document center.

http://spirit.lib.uconn.edu/Pol.Sci/polisici.html/   Comprehensive list of political science departments on the web.

http://www.lib.Isu/edu/weblio.html/   Major jump-site with links to political resources.

http://www.lib.Isu.edu/gov/fedgov.html/   Comprehensive listing of U.S. federal government agencies with links.

http://www.wcs-online.com/usfovdoc/   Provides a search engine for federal government resources.

http://www.piperinfo.com/~piper/state/states.html/   Links to all state governments on the web.

http://www.access.gpo.gov/su_docs/aces/aaces004.html/   Comprehensive list of Federal Depository Libraries, with links.

C

Putting It All Together: The Research Paper

Here's a step-by-step guide to putting together your project for your class in political analysis. This appendix will provide a practical outline for writing the political science research paper. Follow each of these steps roughly in this order.

1. RESEARCH QUESTION

First, decide on the question that you would like to answer. This can be based on observations, readings you have already encountered, or research on your topic. (For instance, if you are interested in voting behavior, you might start the process by getting a book from the library on voting.) The idea is to raise a question about some political phenomena, factor, or event.

We sometimes want to try to answer a question about political phenomena that has interested us for a long time. Other times, it is difficult to think of an appropriate idea. It is often helpful to "brainstorm" when trying to come up with research questions. You can easily do this by writing down whatever thoughts you have about politics. What interests you most about the political "scene"? Is there anything that bothers you? Start by getting down on paper all of your ideas and questions about politics and political interactions.

If your project is going to involve conducting original survey research, think in terms of questions that might be answered by asking a group of people their opinions or ideas. In other words, your research question itself should have something to do with the way people think about a particular issue if you plan to use "public opinion" as a component.

It is important that early in the research process you *define your purpose*. In order to do this, think of what it is you are trying to accomplish with your project. See how the function of your social science research project might fit into one these categories.

1. **Definitional.** Does your research question ask what something is? Does it define some political phenomena or notion? If so, you are probably engaged in a *definitional* pursuit.
2. **Classification.** This type of work typically tries to make sense of some pattern in society, or to *classify* institutions, groups, or political ideas.
3. **Compare and Contrast.** Your project may seek to highlight the differences between variables by comparing and/or contrasting some aspect of the social or political world.
4. **Analysis.** Is your research project oriented toward the relationship between different aspects of social or political phenomena? If your concern is over how variables relate to one another, then your project will ultimately include an overview, or *analysis,* of social interaction.

Also, be sure to *assess your audience* as you begin to do research. Decide to whom you are writing. In most cases, you will be writing for an audience of one—your instructor! But you can still think of terms of the audience you would ideally target. You will develop more confidence in your own research abilities if you will allow yourself to become immersed, to some extent, in the discipline itself.

2. THEORETICAL FRAMEWORK

Next, tie your research question to a theory. Here's where the library research work really begins. You next need to discover how academics have dealt with the sort of question you are raising. Start by defining the area into which your question falls (in other words, define the subject area in which you are interested—for example, voting behavior or welfare reform). Then, use the various library resources at your disposal to find examples of professional journal articles and books that relate to your topic (see Appendix B).

Next, you must complete two tasks. First, identify the theory (or theories) that are behind the research others have done on your subject. What sort of theoretical framework do professional researchers in your field use to create their hypotheses? Second, answer the question, "How do others attempt to explain the phenomena in this subject area?"

As you begin your library research, be sure to do the following:

1. **Develop a working schedule for research and stick to it!** Unfortunately, the research process is often tedious and time consuming. Don't expect to complete all of your library research in just one or two sessions. You will probably find that the more time you spend in library research at the beginning of your project, the easier it will be for you at the end of the semester.
2. **Don't waste resources.** Try to use as many of the resources you discover that pertain to your topic as possible. Keep notes on the bibliographic entries you encounter in the literature. Make sure you know where to return later on, in case you need a source you discovered earlier.
3. **Ask for help.** Librarians are there to help you get through the research process, and the more questions you ask, the better your project will turn out in the end.

3. HYPOTHESIS

Once you discover a theory that pertains to your topic, you will be ready to think about the various elements that you'll be studying. Begin by being as specific as you possibly can be. Part of your job is to figure out how you can measure the different things or phenomena you are looking at. The things themselves that we measure are referred to as *variables,* and the process of figuring out how to measure them is called *operationalization.* The *hypothesis* is a provisional explanation for the research question you started with. This should be a "testable" statement about how one variable *effects* or is *affected by* another variable. Your *dependent* and *independent variables* should be identified here, as well as the relationship between them.

This is, in most instances, the most difficult task for students that we have covered thus far. Turning your research question into a hypotheses is an unusual experience, especially the first time. But, once you have taken your idea and formalized it into this sort of statement, the rest of the process becomes much easier.

4. ABSTRACT

Open your paper with a brief abstract (these are generally single-spaced and written as one long paragraph) giving an overview of your entire project. The abstract quickly lets the reader know what your project is all about. If you are unsure as to how an abstract looks or what its function is, look at almost any article included in a profession political science journal. You will find that the article begins with a brief statement that allows you to get an idea of what the article is all about! This is particularly helpful to the researcher who is attempting to review a wide range of contributions to the literature. Without even reading through an article you are able to at least get a general idea about approach, focus, and type of research of its author.

5. INTRODUCTION

In the introductory part of your paper, discuss your topic in greater detail, presenting information with regard to your central theory, the hypothetical relationship between variables, and the sort of research project you have undertaken.

6. LITERATURE REVIEW

As you review the literature relevant to your topic, you will be writing about

- what other commentators have had to say on this topic
- the research that has been done in your area
- whether there are consistent findings in the literature

Your literature review should be used to develop the argument behind your provisional explanation for the research question. Remember: it is more important what *you* say about an article than what the author of the study has to say about his or her research project. Review and critique the literature by analyzing both the study and the findings of the author. You may include the following in your literature review:

- the subject of the article
- the author's purpose for writing
- the author's main points
- the relevance of the article to the field of study, and/or any practical or policy implications.

You can paraphrase and use short quotations from important articles..
    Use the research materials you have gathered to tie together the different aspects of your hypothesis. Try to show the direct relationship between your problem and the literature. You want to paraphrase the literature as much as possible, not re-create it. In other words, you do not need to recount all aspects of an article or book in your literature review. The ideal is to put what the researcher has said "into your own words."

7. DATA COLLECTION AND ANALYSIS

In this section, you will discuss in detail the particulars of your research project. Be sure to include information on:

- the survey you developed
- other forms of data you utilized (databases, etc.)
- the unit of analysis for your study
- the population you were looking at
- the sample that you chose and how you chose it
- sample size and type, as well as the method of selection

Then, fully report both your application of statistics and your analysis. If you utilized a computer statistics package (such as SPSS), be sure to indicate how you developed your database and what options you had for comparing variables.

8. CONCLUSION

In your conclusion, integrate the material you discovered in the professional literature on your topic with your findings in your project. Further elaborate on your analysis of the data, if appropriate. Discuss your findings in the light of prior research and indicate how what you have found supports or refutes the current literature on the topic.

9. REFERENCES

Be sure to follow proper form for bibliographic entries. Check a style manual such as: Kate L.Tarabian, *A Manual for Writers of Term Papers, Theses and Dissertations,* 5th ed. (Chicago: University of Chicago Press, 1987), or William Strunk, Jr., and E. B. White, *The Elements of Style,* 3rd ed. (New York: Macmillan, 1979), to ensure that you prepare your list of references properly. The *bibliography* (which is a list of all sources used in the development of a project), or list of *references* (which includes only those works directly cited in your paper) can be one of the most important parts of a social science research design or report. The reader of your work is able to get a very good idea about the sort of research you have undertaken just by looking at the references on which you have relied.